Effective schools for disaffected students

Disaffected pupils respond well in circumstances where they feel secure, where they have a sense of being valued and respected, and where they perceive there to be opportunities for them to succeed. This book offers some insights into how these outcomes might be achieved in both mainstream and segregated settings.

Paul Cooper grounds his investigation in the views expressed by a group of pupils who have been excluded from mainstream schools and placed in residential schools for pupils with emotional and behavioural difficulties. The book charts the perceptions these pupils have of their current and former experience of schooling, as well as their views on the nature and causes of their difficulties. Connecting the insights gained from these pupils to work that has been done in the area of school effectiveness, he offers some guidelines on ways in which teachers and managers can work towards reducing disaffection in schools. The book's practical research base emphasises the need to find solutions to educational problems within the real-life contexts in which they occur. It will be of interest to all those whose concerns are with the everyday realities of schooling, such as teachers, teacher-managers, educational psychologists and INSET providers, as well as researchers and academics.

Paul Cooper is Research Officer in the Department of Educational Studies, University of Oxford.

To Rosanne, Catherine and Emily

Effective schools for disaffected students

Integration *and* segregation

Paul Cooper

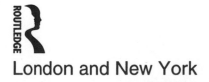

London and New York

First published 1993
by Routledge
11 New Fetter Lane, London EC4P 4EE

Simultaneously published in the USA and Canada
by Routledge
29 West 35th Street, New York, NY 10001

© 1993 Paul Cooper

Typeset in Baskerville by LaserScript Limited, Mitcham, Surrey
Printed in Great Britain by
Biddles Ltd, Guildford and King's Lynn

British Library Cataloguing in Publication Data
A catalogue record for this book is available from the British Library.

ISBN 0–415–06483–x
    0–415–06484–8 (Pbk)

Library of Congress Cataloging in Publication Data has been applied for.

ISBN 0-415-06483-X
    0-415-06484-8 (Pbk)

Contents

Acknowledgements

This, like any book, is the product of many influences. The ideas here began to develop quite early on in my teaching career, and owe a great deal to my experience of teaching in mainstream comprehensive schools, a residential school for pupils with emotional and behavioural problems, an off-site unit for pupils with adjustment difficulties, and a mainstream primary school. Thank you, to all those teachers and pupils who have made my teaching career so rewarding, to date. I must also thank those people who have helped me to develop my own (thoroughly imperfect) grasp of theoretical aspects of this work. An important formative influence here was Dr David Hartley (Dundee University). More recently I have had the privilege of studying and working with Mr Colin Smith (Birmingham University) and Professor Graham Upton (Birmingham University), both of whom are eminent in the field of behavioural problems in schools and special education in general; this has been an invaluable experience. I would also like to thank the many BPhil and MEd students I worked with during my time as Research Fellow in Behaviour Problems in Schools at Birmingham University: I'm sure I learned far more from trying to teach them, than they learned from me! Then of course there are the teachers and pupils who allowed me into their schools and classrooms, and gave so generously of their time in interviews. I know many of the pupils will be disappointed that their real names do not appear in the book. Their contribution was invaluable. I only hope I've done justice to their trust in me. Finally, I must thank my family: Rosanne, Catherine and Emily for all their patience, support and encouragement. I owe an immense debt to all of these people (and many more); my only hope is that this book is worthy of their approval.

Preface

Disaffection continues to be a major problem in our schools, and one that seems to be getting worse rather than better, in the wake of recent policy changes. In this book the author attempts to develop a perspective on this problem which draws on knowledge of the interpersonal and institutional correlates of disaffection. An important aim of the book is to show that the problem of disaffection needs to be met at both the institutional level, in terms of school policy, as well as at the individual level, in terms of the interpersonal relationships that staff develop with pupils, and staff attitudes. It is argued that no school can be effective without an appropriate pattern of organisation, and that no pattern of organisation can operate effectively without people with the right ideas and attitudes. This book shows some of the ways these different factors relate to one another through an examination of real schools in action. An underlying theme of the book is a commitment to the development of context-specific solutions to disruption. Central to this idea is the need to take very seriously the perceptions of the people who are closest to these problems, namely, pupils and their teachers. A particular concern of the author is to raise the profile of pupils' perceptions of their situations, and to use these as a basis for understanding and developing responses to disaffection. Another important message of the book is that integrated and segregated settings both have something of value to offer, in meeting the needs of pupils who become disaffected, and that we can learn important lessons from the study of both settings. It is hoped, therefore, that this book will be of interest to a wide range of people concerned with the problem of disaffection in schools. This audience will include: mainstream and support teachers, SEN coordinators, teachers in special schools and off-site units, teacher-managers, INSET organisers, INSET participants, educational psychologists, lecturers and students of education, and social workers. It is also hoped that school governors and some parents might find the book of interest.

Chapter 1

Introduction

When two young ladies I know, called Catherine (aged 7) and Emily (aged 5), role-play 'schools', it usually goes something like this:

Catherine: Right! I'm the teacher. You're the little girl, Emily.
Emily: Oh. All right.
Catherine: Sit down. Sit down. You've got to do as I say, 'cos I'm the teacher. Sit down.
[Emily eventually sits down]
Catherine: Right we're going to do sums. You like sums don't you, Emily?
Emily: I want to be the teacher.
Catherine: *I'm* the teacher. What's one and one?
Emily: Two. One and one is two. That's easy-peasy.
Catherine: Yes, Emily, that's very good. Well done. Now what's twelve and twelve?
Emily: I don't know. That's too hard for me.
Catherine: Come on now, Emily . . .
Emily: Hundred.
Catherine: Now let's just work it out, shall we?
Emily: I don't want to play this. [Gets up, starts to leave the room]
Catherine: SIT DOWN!
Emily: NO!
Catherine: You're going to have to stand by the wall.
[Emily has gone]
Catherine: [Tearfully] Mummy! Emily's not playing properly! It's not fair!

Sadly, nearly all of Catherine's lessons seem to end with outbreaks of problem behaviour. Though it has to be said: some don't. Those lessons where the class is composed of Barbie dolls, teddies and assorted toy furry animals, often seem to go off quite well. Sometimes too well. Catherine is the one who gets bored in these sessions. But just try introducing one other human being into the lesson and there are problems. Emily, even when she starts willingly, soon becomes bored with her supporting role, and after challenging Catherine's assumptions of control (sometimes more forcefully than others) she usually opts out, leaving Catherine disappointed and frustrated.

I know how Catherine feels. Most teachers do. You start off with what seems a good idea. You're going to make it interesting. You're going to be really positive, by being cheerful and giving out praise. You're all going to get along fine. But it's sometimes hard to sustain this type of optimism in the face of a group of children, some of whom have far less optimistic expectations of the oncoming lesson. At first, it is surprising when your obviously positive intentions are met with apathy, are ignored or, worse (?) openly resisted and disrupted. It is hard to accept this situation as part and parcel of the job of teaching. When these problems recur, we may also feel humiliated, threatened, angry and ashamed. We may feel that as adults we should not really accept this kind of behaviour from children – whether they are 6 or 16.

The problem is, of course, that all teachers experience these problems at some time. Many teachers face these problems regularly, sometimes daily, in one form or another (DES, 1989a). Why does it happen and what can we do about it? It is hoped that the ideas discussed in the following pages will shed at least some light on these questions.

THE ARGUMENT OF THIS BOOK

Schools are not always places fit for some of the people who use them. The problem is that regardless of their 'fitness', pupils are compelled to attend schools when they are in their most vulnerable and formative stages. The remarkable thing about human beings, of course, is that they can learn how to survive in the most inhospitable conditions. This book argues that student disaffection and problem behaviour in schools can often be usefully viewed, in part at least, as a response to the 'unfitness' of some schools. An understanding of the mechanisms which operate in schools to create and exacerbate problem behaviour and disaffection can lead us to means of solving and preventing such problems.

Throughout this book the terms 'disaffection', 'problem behaviour', 'emotional and/or behavioural difficulties' and 'deviance' are used. These terms will be familiar to people working in social/educational settings, and each can be seen to have a specific and distinctive meaning. However, this book is concerned with the common ground covered by these terms. What is being emphasised here is that these are all labels applied to certain individuals in schools and other social institutions. These labels describe behaviour that is perceived to be in some sense deviant and problematic to the smooth running of the organisation in which they are applied. The argument presented here is that the label itself is less important than the influences which produce the label and the experiences which pupils have as a consequence of bearing the label.

This argument is developed from a study of the experience of a group of boys attending two residential special schools for students with emotional and behavioural difficulties. The study set out to identify the effects of the residential experience on a group of boys whose behaviour was considered to be such that they could no longer be educated in mainstream or day special schools. The main focus of the study was the school experience as perceived by the students themselves. In the course of interviews with the students, it became clear that the importance and meaning of residential experience in the lives of these young people could not be properly understood without reference to events and situations, external to the residential setting, which they experienced prior to and during their residential placements. The students constantly compared their residential experience with their experience at home with their families, and with their experience of other schools and institutions.

The main outcomes of the study were that the overwhelming majority of the seventy-seven boys (aged 11–18) in these two schools found their residential experience rewarding and personally enriching, and there was strong evidence to suggest that, during their period of residence at the schools, many of the pupils had experienced improvements in their levels of self-esteem, as well as an improved sense of control over areas of their lives which had appeared before to be out of their control. The basis for these outcomes were found to be:

1 the RESPITE the residential schools offered the students from distressing situations which many had previously encountered in their family situations and at school;
2 the high quality of the RELATIONSHIPS the students shared with staff in the residential schools;
3 the OPPORTUNITIES provided by the residential schools for the pupils to develop an enhanced self-image through the experience of being an individually valued, participating member of a community, and the experience of personal achievement.

These findings were encouraging, and led to important, sometimes surprising conclusions.

The first major conclusion was that for this group of pupils the residential schools provided them with positive and necessary experiences which were denied to them in their home environments. The enrichment they experienced depended, for them, on their removal and segregation from the 'mainstream'. The second major conclusion was that this segregation was made necessary largely by deficiencies which existed in the home, and the school environment, and that the measures which were taken by the residential schools offered clear messages as to what mainstream and other schools could do to prevent and mitigate some of their worst effects. In short, these institutions offered insights into school effectiveness, in relation to pupils' disaffection, which, it is believed, have strong implications for the mainstream schools which provide their intake.

This book, therefore, offers expert evidence in the debate surrounding the integration of students with special educational needs into mainstream schools. The experts are the students themselves. What we conclude from their evidence is that integration is an important and desirable goal, which may well be possible to achieve in some existing mainstream schools. However, the experience of these experts would suggest that some schools are not yet able to cope with the integration of students with behaviour problems. On the contrary, these students and their former schools are often in a state of mutual estrangement which can be traced to factors that appear to be deeply embedded in the individual school system. For these students the residential experience is vital and enriching. By studying the residential setting, and its effect on these students, we can begin to identify some of the deficiencies in their mainstream experience and to offer solutions which may pave the way to genuine and successful integration of such students.

Central to the argument of this book is the idea that schools must provide opportunities to all of their students to be identified, both by themselves and others, in terms of their positive qualities and their potentialities for making a constructive personal contribution to their communities. It will be argued throughout this book that this provision of opportunity forms the core of the successful work of these residential schools. It is also argued that measures schools and teachers take to prevent and respond to problems of disaffection and behaviour difficulties in schools must be underpinned by this deceptively simple principle.

Of major importance here is the need for whole schools to be responsive to the needs of the people they contain: staff and pupils. There are two preconditions for such responsiveness. First, school staff need to appreciate the importance of such responsiveness. Second, there need to be adequate opportunities and recognised channels for students and staff to express their perceptions, concerns and interests, built into the organisational structure of schools. We must see behaviour difficulties as problems facing all sections of the school community. Teachers and pupils are not enemies of one another, rather they should be seen as allies against forces which may create conflict and difficulties between them. The emphasis should be less on 'survival' and 'control', and more on 'cooperation' and 'consultation'. The present book, through its heavy reliance on student perceptions, seeks to contribute to the development of an active dialogue between students and their educators. For, it is argued, only when such dialogue is an accepted commonplace in all schools and classrooms will school communities be able to meet the needs of all their members.

Before going any further, two disclaimers are necessary. First, it is not the author's intention to suggest that *all* residential schools for pupils with emotional and behavioural problems are successful in the ways outlined above, neither is it intended to suggest that all mainstream schools fail in these respects. It *is* the author's intention to draw attention to examples of conspicuous good practice in a neglected, often misrepresented and maligned field. Second, this book does not propose a simple, single-factor solution to disaffection from school. The process of making schools fit for all their students has implications for our education service at many levels, from the interpersonal relationships in the classroom, through staffroom relationships and family involvement, to the institutional level of school and local authority policy and organisation. Underpinning what follows, however, is the conviction that schools and teachers, given the right tools, can be effective in reducing disaffection. This book is intended as an aid to this process.

OUTLINE OF THIS BOOK

Chapters 2 and 3 deal with background issues, covering school and other social influences on student disaffection, research on school effectiveness, the role of the individual and individuality in education, and the ways in which perspectives on disaffection from school have changed and developed over recent years.

Chapter 4 introduces the students whose perceptions form the basis of this study, and describes their backgrounds, their perceptions of their previous school experience, and their perceptions of the reasons behind their referral to residential schools.

Chapters 5 and 6 focus on the residential experience, particularly the pupils' perceptions of the nature and personal effects of the schools.

Chapter 7 considers conclusions drawn from the study of the two residential schools in the light of school effectiveness research.

Chapter 8 considers the current state of education in England and Wales in the wake of the Education Reform Act (1988). It then goes on to look in detail at one comprehensive school's attempt to address the problem of pupil disaffection, within the contemporary context.

Chapter 9 is the concluding chapter, in which some of the key implications of the book are spelt out.

Part I

Background issues

This book is concerned with school disaffection and some of the ways in which schools can overcome this problem. It will be shown that certain residential schools have a powerful and positive influence on a particular group of students who have been disaffected from their mainstream and other schools. It will then be argued that many of the successful practices observed in these residential schools can be transposed to the mainstream situation to similar effect. Before we can begin to develop this argument it is necessary to explore certain important background issues.

Because this book is concerned with social and institutional influences on behaviour, the following two chapters will deal briefly with current thinking on these issues in education. Chapter 2 will discuss the effects of social institutions on behaviour. In Chapter 3 the discussion will move from the social to the individual level, and the role of the individual in education will then be considered. In the second half of Chapter 3 these social and individual factors will be discussed in relation to perspectives on the treatment and care of students with emotional and behavioural difficulties.

Chapter 2

Institutions and disaffection

FAMILIES, SCHOOLS, PEERS AND DISAFFECTION

School disaffection and problem behaviour are by definition social phenomena. It is impossible to communicate what makes a particular act an example of problem behaviour or a sign of disaffection without making some reference to the social context in which it occurs. This is not the same as saying that behaviour is *caused* in any simplistic way by the environment. What is being said here is that context has an *influence* on behaviour, and any behaviour which is performed within a given situation is the product of an *interaction* between contextual factors and aspects which the individual brings to the situation. These aspects are in turn the product of the individual's personal dispositions and experience of other situations. In the same way, an individual's judgement of whether another's behaviour is 'problematic' is also dependent upon the same interactional process.

FAMILIES

Clearly, the family is a major source of experience for most people. It would seem that children who come to be defined as 'deviant' have a greater tendency to have experience of adverse family circumstances than their non-deviant peers. Such adverse circumstances include:

- economic and material deprivation;
- severe emotional tension and discord between family members (particularly parents);
- delinquent activities of parents;
- unsatisfactory child-rearing practices.

These assertions are supported by a wide range of sources, including West and Farrington's (1973) study of 400 delinquent 8-year-olds, Reid's (1985) research into school truancy, Rutter's (1975) account of children with behavioural disorders, Feldhusen's research with children who misbehave in American schools (Tattum, 1982), Millham *et al.*'s studies of delinquent adolescents in approved schools (1975) and secure units (1978), and Hoghughi's (1978) study of 'extreme' children in a secure unit.

The precise relationship between adverse family circumstances and deviance is not easily defined. It seems reasonable to ask: 'why should a child misbehave in school or commit delinquent acts as a result of family circumstances?' It must also be noted that all children who experience adverse family circumstances do not behave in a deviant manner or become delinquent – in fact, most don't.

One view which may be important in accounting for people's different responses to outwardly similar circumstances, is that provided by personal construct theorists (Bannister and Fransella, 1980). This view suggests that each individual experiences events uniquely, in accordance with a personal set of assumptions and expectations about the world. Thus, whether a particular event is experienced as a threat to be challenged or a hardship to be tolerated, depends on the individual's view of the event. Pupil A may accept the teacher's unjust rebuke as an irritating but non-malicious and understandable error, whilst pupil B may, in a similar situation, retaliate, seeing the injustice alone as evidence of personal malice. What is important for the purposes of the present discussion is that (1) there is a cultural dimension to this theory, in that there is often seen to be a commonality in the constructs of communities of people, and (2) personal constructs can be influenced and altered by experiences which challenge individuals' assumptions.

A reasonable generalisation would seem to be that the experience of adverse family circumstances may make conforming to certain social norms particularly difficult. Such experience may even lead to the development of means of coping which are seen by others as acts of deviance. This can be illustrated by the ways in which perceptions of wealth and poverty may differ. Rutter and Giller (1983), in their study of juvenile delinquency, suggest that absolute measures of wealth are less important than the individual's perceptions and expectations. One person's necessity is another's luxury. Problems arise when something which is perceived to be a necessity is outside the range of existing available resources. Such a situation inevitably results in personal and social stress. Ironically, it can be the very desire of an individual to conform to social norms which can lead to deviance, as in the case of the child who demands of his parents an item of clothing or a toy which they cannot afford. The child is perhaps driven to make these demands by advertising and the belief that 'everyone else has one'. The parents themselves may sympathise with their child, and may take their inability to provide for their child as a sign of their failure to conform to their perception of what makes adequate parents. Such a scenario is by no means doomed to end in delinquency but the potential for family stress, inherent in this example, is clear.

More extreme levels of poverty often confront families in the guise of 'impossible choices' of a type which people who are better off never have to face (Reid, 1987). Families, through lack of funds, may be forced into substandard living accommodation, which leads to further problems of overcrowding and ill-health. It is an extremely difficult task for a parent in such circumstances to bring a child to an understanding and acceptance of this situation. The parent(s) are not only faced with the daily problems of simple physical survival, but they will also be constantly reminded of their deficiencies in relation to others, as Reid (1987) puts it:

> [children of poor families] . . . are less likely to have access to things which others take for granted and which they, themselves, see as important: a reasonable choice of toys, clothes [etc.] . . . Children can be acutely aware of these deficits in their lives and of the embarrassing situations and restrictions which they face as a result.

> (Reid, 1987, p.195)

The tension which this can produce between the parents and between parents and children may lead to further problems. Parental responses to the stress of perceived deprivation with its humiliating overtones of personal inadequacy may well cause the situation to worsen. The social pathologies among parents, which are shown by research (see above) to be associated with childhood deviance, such as delinquency, substance abuse, marital discord, violent behaviour and mental illness, can be seen as, albeit disastrous, attempts to cope with stressful situations, by denying their existence or attempting to negate them (Stott, 1982).

The direct consequences for the children of such families can be dire. Reid (1987) suggests that the experience of poverty leads some parents not only to lower their material and economic expectations, but also to 'adopt child-rearing practices of which they themselves do not approve' (ibid., p. 196). Research reported by writers already mentioned indicates that delinquent and behaviourally disturbed children have a greater tendency to experience:

- a lack of parental interest in their schooling (Reid, 1985);
- inconsistent and ineffective parental discipline (Rutter, 1975);
- a relative lack of overtly displayed parental affection (ibid.);
- parental indifference or hostility (Feldhusen, in Tattum, 1982);
- violent displays of temper by parents (ibid.);
- parental use of corporal punishment (ibid.);
- parental cruelty and neglect (Millham *et al.*, 1978);
- frequent parental absences (ibid.);
- rejecting and violent parents (Hoghughi, 1978).

It is perhaps easy to see how the frustrations arising out of deprivation, coupled with even more damaging 'coping strategies' will leave few resources for the gentle art of effective child-rearing. In such circumstances failures and frustrations seem only to lead to more of the same: apparent solutions merely produce further and greater problems. Parents who are struggling against their own sense of failure and inadequacy may find it difficult to summon interest in their children's schooling, seeing their own immediate problems as more pressing, and this may well appear to be a sign of parental indifference. Inconsistency in discipline and violent mood-swings may also be seen in terms of the parents' confusion and inability to cope.

It is difficult for anyone to provide a child with a sense of warmth and security when they themselves feel deprived of these comforts. The problem is, of course, that the failure to provide a child with such support can create further problems, which in turn become a source of family stress. Children who are not brought up in stable and caring situations are likely to be anxious and insecure. The ways in which they cope with such anxiety and insecurity may differ widely, but within the range of perceived coping strategies are the very types of behaviour which they witnessed in their parents. Furthermore, children who do not experience love and a sense of security in their relationships with their parents are unlikely to provide their own children with these experiences, which are necessary for healthy psychological development (Pringle, 1980).

The family, then, can be seen as a kind of melting-pot, in which potentially lethal ingredients, such as material deprivation and misguided parental strategies for dealing with stress, are mixed. This poisonous concoction is then imbibed by children, in the form of models of behaviour and experiences of emotional deprivation. The child then becomes a further ingredient in the mixture, adding his/her own needs and coping strategies to the already chaotic situation. And so the chances are increased that the cycle will be repeated in the next generation, when the child becomes a parent and acts out patterns of behaviour learned in his/her own childhood (see Clegg and Megson, 1968; Pringle, 1980; Stott, 1982). Furthermore, the constancy of the experience of poverty and relative deprivation in some communities is seen, by some researchers, to influence the development of a particular 'cultural' response to these difficulties, which is transmitted from generation to generation. In this culture the ability to endure discomfort, and to display the determination, autonomy and toughness engendered by this unsheltered way of life, become themselves valued traits, which may conflict with the roles required of children in some schools. Children, in these circumstances, will often model their own behaviour on that of adults who they admire within their home communities (Willis, 1978). Schooling is understandably an irrelevance to pupils who seek to emulate adults whose achievements owe little or nothing to success in school, even when those adults peddle the 'you don't want to turn out like me' line. The fact is that children often want nothing more than to turn out exactly like dominant adult models. That this negative cycle does repeat itself is then unsurprising; what is remarkable is the fact that people sometimes do manage to break out of it.

SCHOOLS

Accounts of children's disaffection and misbehaviour in schools which focus attention exclusively on family background factors are not uncommon. Such accounts may have the effect of distancing those outside the family from the problems, and have the appeal of absolving such outsiders from any sense of responsibility in these matters. This is not to say that politicians, teachers, psychologists, social workers, and other professionals who subscribe to such views, are in any sense uncaring or uninterested in the plight of such children. What is being suggested is that those who over-emphasise family and individual pathology explanations can be blind to the influence which they and their institutions can have on these problems. In particular, they can be unaware of the extent to which the very possession of such views can interact with the problem situation and so exacerbate and, in some cases, create further difficulties.

There is a key problem here which goes right to the heart of the education process, and it is as much to do with the way we, as teachers, attempt to facilitate learning, as it is to do with how we approach problematic behaviour. The problem is that, as teachers, we are constantly (and increasingly) called upon to be accountable for and make judgements about our students' knowledge and experience. We are expected to speak with authority about our students' levels of interest and motivation, their degree of mastery and understanding of multiplication, sentence structure, the principles of photosynthesis. We constantly work on the assumption that we *can* answer these questions. There is seldom enough time, however, to answer other vital questions, such as 'how far can we ever truly know what is going on inside our students' heads?' (though we sometimes act as if we know exactly what they're thinking) and 'how reliable are the judgements we make?' Instead we concentrate on the business of *making* judgements, and become oblivious of the flaws in the judging process.

Reid (1987) asserts that when school pupils become problematic, teachers and social workers often seek explanations in the home environment. Whilst these professionals often recognise poverty as a contributory factor in pupils' difficulties, they more often place a heavier emphasis on what they perceive to be the personal qualities of the parents. This can be interpreted in terms of what psychologists term attribution theory (e.g. Aronson, 1980), which states that when we interpret the behaviour of others, we tend to seek explanations which avoid challenges to our self-image. When we view what we determine to be problematic behaviour, we are more likely to attribute it to failings in the individual performing the behaviour, rather than to external factors which we might influence. We are also inclined to attribute our own problem behaviour (e.g. anger, fear, carelessness) to external factors outside our control. This process, on the one hand, performs a valuable defensive function, in protecting the individual from the debilitating consequences of constant self-doubt. On the other hand, it can lead to an avoidance of constructive self-criticism as well as facilitating the possible development of entrenched conflict between persons.

There is a compelling body of school-based research which can be seen to relate to various aspects of attribution theory. A number of important studies have shown that the particular identity that comes to be held by a school pupil can owe a great deal to the preconceptions and assumptions that teachers have about their pupils. Hargreaves *et al.* (1975) show that teachers can develop highly detailed images of individual pupils on the basis of scant knowledge of the individual. Teachers observed in this study were more inclined to define pupils as deviant, regardless of the pupil's actual behaviour, if the child was so defined by other staff, or if the child had 'deviant' siblings. Sharp and Green (1975) showed that staff in an infant school tended to make judgements about pupils' ability level, degree of social adjustment and motivational level which were largely based on social deficit theories. In this study the teachers justified the low expectations they had for many of their working-class pupils in terms of their belief in the negative effects of social deprivation. Keddie (1971) showed how teachers developed assumptions about the intellectual competence and motivation of students, on the basis of their stream placement. Because of these assumptions the teachers limited the nature of the material they presented to pupils in the lower streams, and dealt with pupils differently. Thus when a 'C' stream pupil asked 'why are we studying this?' the teacher took this as a sign of low motivation and dismissed the question, whilst when the same question was asked by an 'A' stream pupil it was treated as a serious and intelligent inquiry.

Of course, the process of attribution is only half the story; the other half involves the active participation of the person who is the object of the attribution process. What seems to have been regularly demonstrated over the last thirty years (e.g. Hargreaves, 1967; Willis, 1978; Cronk, 1987) is that school pupils are often keen to embrace the identities which schools and teachers ascribe to them. The attribution process sets in motion the self-fulfilling prophecy, whereby behaviour (by teacher and pupil) begins to conform to the initial attribution. Teacher and pupil together come to define particular behaviours as more characteristic than others, and soon, through the experience of constant reinforcement, the pupil begins to act in accordance with an identity which is borne out of possibly groundless attributions. Thus the pupils for whom teachers and schools provide opportunities for achievement and the experience of success are likely to have positive self-images and be highly motivated toward school, whilst those who experience failure and rejection internalise these experiences as indications of their inadequacy and inability to succeed in the school system, and so, in turn, reject and subvert the institution which so demeans them.

If we look at the same problem from a slightly different perspective, we can see that a major problem of schools is their tendency to neglect to display sufficient and obvious regard for their pupils' individuality (Schostak, 1982; 1983). Schools and classrooms are all too often places where children and young people go to be processed in various ways. Like products in a factory, they are often seen as 'raw material' which has to be fashioned into a particular product, 'examined' and finally dispatched to an appropriate destination. Whilst this has always been an aspect of mass schooling (Neill, 1916; Silberman, 1970; Illich, 1971; Postman, 1973), it is only in the 1980s that this view of schooling has gained primacy, to the extent that a school's physical survival may in future depend on its performance on crude output measures, such as the range of examination grades attained by its pupils and its truancy rates (re The Education Reform Act, 1988). This growing pressure on schools to perform in ways that fit crudely defined instrumental outcome measures is a cause for concern among those who consider the plight of pupils with adjustment difficulties (Cooper and Upton, 1991).

Intentionally or otherwise, this focus on the pupil as a measurable, objectifiable entity diminishes the amount of attention given to other non-quantifiable, but important, pupil characteristics. This is clearly demonstrated by studies which have sought the perceptions of pupils, particularly those who are defined as 'disaffected' and 'disruptive'. When looked at from the pupils' viewpoint, schools are often portrayed as dehumanising places, and so-called 'disruptive' behaviour comes to be seen as a rational response to intolerable circumstances. This is shown in the work of Tattum (1982), who found that disruptive pupils, when they described their motivations for misbehaviour, included reference to their teachers' failure to organise lessons effectively, their teachers' disrespect for pupils as persons, their unfairness in the enforcement of rules, and their lack of a sense of humour. Rosser and Harré (1976) found that misbehaviour in the classroom was often described by pupils as 'retribution' for teacher misdemeanours of the type described later by Tattum. Similarly, studies by Coard (1971), Driver (1981) and Wright (1986) account for the over-representation of Afro-Caribbean boys in special educational provision and suspension statistics in terms of their, often white teachers' failure to understand their black students' culture. Driver, for example, shows how teachers often misinterpret the meaning of black students' body language, perceiving sometimes innocent behaviour as oppositional, and mistaking gestures of respect for signs of disrespect.

It should be clear from the discussion so far that for some pupils it is very difficult to avoid being labelled as deviant, in one form or another, and then developing, and behaving in accordance with a deviant identity. Schostak (1983) and Silberman (1970) describe national school systems (in Britain and America, respectively) which seem to make such outcomes as these inevitable. For both these writers, mass state schooling is characterised by organisational patterns which outlaw pupil individuality and make ideals of the traits of docility and unquestioning conformity. Teachers and pupils are straitjacketed by the drive for uniformity and conformity (see Denscombe, 1985). In the maelstrom of demands in which schools are caught – from government, pupils, parents, professional associations, the public and media – the central importance of the individual is lost.

The most vulnerable – those who experience humiliation, fear or anxiety for no obvious return – are the very people in the school system who are likely to be given least opportunity to voice their concerns. These casualties will include those pupils who find it difficult to conform to a system which uses a language and culture which is, to them, alien, such as children from working-class and ethnic-minority backgrounds, and children from disrupted and disturbed family situations, where patterns of behaviour are learned which are deemed inappropriate in school. By and large, teachers are unlikely to have had similar negative experiences in their own schooling. By definition, teachers have received certain rewards from the education system in which they now serve. This makes the task of empathising with the disaffected child particularly difficult, and without empathy there is no effective communication. It is for these reasons perhaps, that when teacher–pupil relationships break down and pupils are removed to schools and units for pupils with emotional and behavioural problems, that these pupils often come from backgrounds that are alien to their teachers' experience, such as those marked by social deprivation and particular ethnic origins (see Ford *et al.* 1982; Cooper *et al.* 1991).

In short there is often a gulf across which communication between pupils and teachers takes place only with great difficulty. Pupils in our schools sometimes see themselves as belonging to an oppressed minority (Schostak, 1982, 1983), as yet without access to channels through which to voice their particular view of the world. Pupils in our schools have no monopoly on the truth about schools, but then neither do teachers, LEA advisers, educationalists and politicians.

There is a close parallel here between the disaffection and low morale of the teaching profession, which has been a constant topic of interest to educational journalists in recent years (e.g. *The Times Educational Supplement*, 1989–91), and the plight of the disaffected school pupil. The disaffection felt by some pupils can be compared with that of teachers who feel disillusioned and undervalued in the face of changes and impositions in their working lives, over which they have no control, and the loss of their pay negotiation rights. *Both* groups are in need of new negotiation rights. Pupils have a right to be heard, and one of their greatest complaints about schooling is that they are denied this right. Too often do we attribute motives to pupils on the basis of observing their behaviour (Barrett, 1989), or simply ignore their perspectives. This was recently a conspicuous feature of the Elton Report on discipline in schools (DES, 1989a), which took evidence from a wide range of sources in its quest for an understanding of the nature and causes of indiscipline in schools, but took no account of evidence from pupil perspectives. The report also contained a number of recommendations which suggest a repressive response to 'indiscipline', in the form of legal backing for teacher authority over pupils and the placing of civil liabilities on parents of such children. These recommendations would seem to be at odds with the report's other recommendations concerning the need for greater pupil involvement in school communities (see Cooper and Upton, 1990a). In the face of such contradictory messages, the task of bringing about positive changes in the quality of pupil experience in the schools where such a change is most needed, is complex and daunting.

PEERS

The peer group plays an important role in personal development, and no discussion of school disaffection would be complete without reference to this area of experience. Like the family and the school, the peer group provides the individual with a terrain to be explored. The outcome of such exploration is a representation of the self. In the family, at school and among our peers, we develop impressions of ourselves as others see us, and, to a large extent, our sense of our own identity emanates from these sources. The peer group is unique, however, as a formative influence in the lives of children and adolescents, because it involves the individual in forms of decision-making and personal expression which are not often available in the family and school situations. The peer group provides the developing individual with opportunities to establish a personal identity. This is achieved through the discovery and validation of personal beliefs and values as a result of mixing with like-minded individuals who share similar concerns, needs and interests (Coleman and Hendry, 1990).

As in all other areas of social and personal development, the concept of 'choice' requires qualification. Those other children with whom the individual child forms associations and friendships can only be drawn from the restricted pool of accessible persons. Thus the accessible peer group is likely to be composed of persons from similar socio-economic and cultural backgrounds, and they are also likely to share similar educational experiences. Individuals will also carry with them something of the values and norms which they have learned in their families, and which may make children more or less predisposed to accept the values and norms of the school.

Much has been made of the conflict and turmoil which accompanies adolescent development. Such disruption is often characterised in terms of the adolescent's rejection of adult values as part of the search for an individual identity. In reviewing the evidence for this view of adolescence, Coleman and Hendry (1990) suggest that it is often overstated. It would seem that, by and large, the vast majority of adolescents manage the transition from childhood without major upset or rebellion, and keep on good terms with their parents and other adults throughout this time. This is not, however, the case with many of those young people who come to be seen as 'deviant', as we have already noted.

The lives of the 'deviant' and disaffected are often marked with conflict and deprivation at home, and failure and rejection at school. For these individuals, the peer group becomes the chief source of emotional security, autonomy, stimulation, acceptance and success (Willmott, 1966). Acts of deviance and disruption can become, for such groups, an expression of the group's opposition to institutions which systematically devalue and denigrate its members (Hargreaves, 1967; Willis, 1978; Rutter *et al.*, 1979). In this way, the deviant peer group can be seen as a problem-solving mechanism (Hughes *et al.*, 1971). The problem, in this instance, is the need for individuals to maintain an adequate level of self-esteem, in the face of circumstances (e.g. family discord, school failure, low socio-economic status) which threaten to undermine their self-esteem. The communal response to this situation is to provide individuals' esteem needs and a simultaneous rejection of these undermining influences.

Research, referred to in the previous section, by Hargreaves (1967), Rosser and Harré (1976), Tattum (1982) and Schostack (1982; 1983) can be called upon to illustrate ways in which classroom disruption and school disaffection can be seen in terms of the norms and values of the pupil peer group. This is true both when the disruption is directed at undermining teacher authority and other pupils. In both situations pupils performing disruptive behaviour can be seen to be challenging the official norms and values of the school and classroom, and performing for the approval of their like-minded peers. This concept of performance has been exemplified by Woods (1976) in his study of the import- ance of laughter in pupil culture, and its use as a tool of subversion in the classroom.

The view being put forward here is that the peer group provides a framework and impetus for pupil resistance to the threatening institutional influences experienced by some children in schools. Words like 'rebellion' and 'rejection' appear often in discussions of the subject of pupil disaffection and disruptive behaviour, and they remind us of the extent to which schooling is *imposed* on our young people. It has been shown that common themes in pupil resistance are the rejection of the failure and low status that schools impose on some pupils. To this extent schools can be seen to contribute to the construction of the disaffected pupil peer group (see Hargreaves, 1967; Schostak, 1983).

Furthermore, a culture of conflict can be found in certain approaches to handling pupils. This culture of conflict has already been hinted at in the previous section, with reference to authoritarian responses to behaviour problems in some schools. In the classroom this conflict is exemplified in the teacher's efforts to *impose* order on the pupil group through coercive means, and the teacher's reliance on poorly grounded assumptions regarding pupils' attitudes and motivational levels. It is suggested that these, often taken for granted, practices provide both a model and a spur to pupil resistance. Askew (1989) shows how the stereotypical aggressive masculinity of pupils guilty of bullying other pupils, can be seen to mirror the behaviour of certain authoritarian teachers in their execution of discipline. In such a climate pupils are encouraged to dominate the weak (pupils and teachers) and fear the strong. The school, in such circumstances, can develop into a battleground.

This section has dealt with the importance of the peer group in sustaining the positive self-image of the pupil in the face of forces which seem to threaten the individual's self-esteem. Clearly, the individual who is insecure in his or her home environment and failing in an unsupportive school is going to be in particular need of the type of support that the peer group can offer, and may, therefore, be especially vulnerable to the risk of becoming disaffected from school, and/or performing delinquent-disruptive acts. In other words, the more problems that the individual faces in the search for a positive self-image, the more vulnerable he or she becomes to taking a deviant course through active resistance to the conventionally approved sources of personal achievement (e.g. school). It is perhaps for this reason that initiatives which have offered support to at-risk groups, in the form of community provision of clubs and advice centres, in a non-authoritarian manner, have had a positive influence on delinquency rates in some areas (Holman, 1981). What we must conclude from this is that the peer group, particularly in the adolescent stage, can be either a formidable opponent or a powerful ally. Where the peer group is isolated and threatened it is fiercely protective of its members and highly efficient in the arts of subversion and guerrilla warfare. Where the peer group is integrated with other supporting structures, such as a loving family, a caring community/school, it can work to reinforce and strengthen the values of these other structures.

EFFECTIVE SCHOOLS

Many of the issues so far dealt with in this chapter can be closely related to work which has been done, over the past fifteen years or so, in the area of 'school effectiveness' research. The importance of this research lies in what it tells us about the differences that can exist between apparently similar schools, and the ways in which schools can be organised in order to maximise positive outcomes for their pupils. Such research acts as a counterweight to those who might argue that the difficulties faced by some schools in securing the cooperation and involvement of some of their pupils are the inevitable consequence of social factors (such as low socio-economic background, family pathology) or individual factors (such as psychological disturbance, mental pathology) beyond the control of schools. School effectiveness research does not deny the existence of such influences, but rather indicates the degree to which such factors can *interact* with school influences in order to encourage or discourage positive pupil outcomes in the school process.

Deciding what actually constitutes an effective school is not as easy a task as it might first appear. Different people can have very different views on this subject. There are many examples, to be found in the literature, of schools which were considered highly effective by some, but completely ineffective by others, such as Risinghill Comprehensive (Berg, 1968), Braehead Secondary School (MacKenzie, 1970), William Tyndale Primary School (Ellis *et al.* 1976) – to name but a few (see Fletcher *et al.*, 1985). If we suspend our consideration of the political conflict which has sometimes surrounded this issue, it is possible to identify a set of factors on which there is a fair degree of consensus.

The concept of school effectiveness, as it is generally understood within the British context, owes a great deal to the detailed study of twelve inner London comprehensive schools carried out by Rutter *et al.* (1979), a study of eight comprehensive schools in south Wales, reported by Reynolds (1976, 1984), and Reynolds and Sullivan (1979, 1981), and a study of fifty junior schools carried out by Mortimore *et al.* (1988). In addition, an important study of the effects of schooling on pupils from ethnic minorities was carried out by Smith and Tomlinson (1989) in twenty urban comprehensive schools from four different areas of England. All of these studies found differences between the schools in their samples, in terms of levels of pupil achievement, pupil behaviour and attendance, which could not be attributed simply to intake variables, such as pupils' measured ability level on entry, or social factors relating to the socio-economic status of pupils' families and other catchment area factors. Levels of resourcing and quality of buildings also appeared to be unrelated to these outcomes. Behaviour, attendance and achievement, however, did appear to be related, in that where schools performed relatively well on one of these variables, they tended to perform well on the other two, the converse was also true. The common conclusion drawn from these studies is that factors within the schools themselves were responsible for the variations in pupil outcomes.

A useful and comprehensive summary of the key factors identified by researchers, such as those referred to above, as being important influences on pupil outcomes (particularly in relation to behaviour) is provided by Charlton and David (1990). These factors are:

1 methods of leadership by senior management which involve consultation with colleagues and take account of the opinions of parents and pupils;

2 a common school-wide policy which establishes clear academic and behavioural expectations that are realistic and meaningful to pupils, and which are consistently and humanely enforced;

3 a curriculum which is matched to pupils' present and future needs;

4 high, but not unreasonable, academic expectations;

5 a positive approach to pupil behaviour which emphasises the use of rewards for good behaviour rather than the imposition of punishments for bad behaviour;

6 care and vigilance by staff in efficient planning and setting, and prompt marking of pupil work; adherence to starting and ending times of lessons;

7 teachers who employ skills to arouse pupil interest and motivate them to work well;

8 approaches to classroom management which emphasise the anticipation and prevention of behaviour problems, rather than reacting to them when they arise;

9 supportive and respectful relationships amongst teachers, between teachers and pupils, amongst pupils, between the school and parents, and between the school and outside agencies;
10 opportunities for pupils to become involved in, and share responsibilities for, the running of the school;
11 an effective system of pastoral care.

(based on Charlton and David, 1990, p. 23)

The precise ways in which these factors operate to influence the behaviour and motivation of pupils are not wholly understood. It is important, for instance, to recognise that the same teacher act performed in two different schools with apparently similar pupil intakes, sometimes produces entirely different pupil behaviour, so that a teacher's leaving a class during lesson time in one school produces mayhem, whilst in another pupils continue to work diligently (Rutter *et al.*, 1979). An explanation for this is provided through the concept of 'ethos', which describes the values and ideas that underpin the social organisation of the school. Ethos is experienced as the general tone, climate and atmosphere of a school, and the in-school factors listed above are important for the extent to which they contribute to and reflect this (Rutter *et al.*, 1979).

Simply adopting a series of strategies in a piecemeal way, without the framework of a guiding ethos, is unlikely to be effective, since such an absence of a framework may lead to the adoption of contradictory and counterproductive approaches. The effects of consistency are demonstrated by Reynolds and Sullivan (1979; 1981), in their study of eight comprehensive schools in south Wales. They found the more effective schools (in terms of pupil behaviour and attendance) to be epitomised by an ethos of 'incorporation', whilst the least effective schools displayed an ethos of 'coercion'. The modes of social organisation observed in these two school types were seen as reflections of fundamental assumptions that were held by school staff. Thus staff of the 'coercive' schools viewed their pupils in negative ways, seeing them as being in need of containment, control and character training, and employing deficiency and deprivation theories to account for learning and behaviour difficulties. Teaching and management strategies that followed from this view were characterised by a punitive, confrontational stance, on the part of the teachers, and impersonal staff–pupil relationships. The 'incorporative' ethos, however, was characterised by a positive view of pupils and their parents, a recognition of the essential worth and individuality of each child, and the importance of eliciting the voluntary involvement of pupils and their parents. Teaching and management strategies following from the 'incorporative' ethos aimed to encourage pupil participation in lessons. This participation was further enacted through the involvement of pupils (and their parents) in organisational aspects of school life. Staff–pupil relationships in incorporative schools stressed positive interpersonal contact, mutual respect and partnership. Learning and behaviour problems were dealt with in therapeutic and supportive ways.

As will be clear from previous sections, patterns of causation are rarely unidirectional and lineal, but are recursive and interactional. Thus, it is easy to see how the use of coercive strategies may itself produce the type of pupil reaction which appears to justify the coercive ethos (see above); the same principle can be applied to the incorporative approach. However, since the unifying feature of what may be termed the effective school seems to be a set of fairly straightforward principles from which an almost infinite range of strategies will develop, it appears appropriate to establish these principles at a fairly early stage in the development of a school ethos. An important point to note here is the self-perpetuating nature of 'ethos', by which new staff and pupils coming into a school become socialised into the prevailing ethos (Denscombe, 1985). This demonstrates the need for schools to become aware of their prevailing ethos and the way this is reflected in interpersonal relationships and institutional practices.

Finally, it would seem that we can draw some important conclusions from this brief discussion of school effectiveness, which have important implications for the rest of this book. It is important to recognise that school effectiveness research does not deny that factors in pupils' out-of-school experience have an important influence on pupils' development. We have already seen, in earlier sections, the extent to which pupil identity can be related to such out-of-school factors. What has been stressed so far throughout this chapter has been the consequences of the *interaction* which takes place between pupils and the various influences in their lives. It is argued in this book that the effective school is one where this interactional process is recognised and acted upon. If we refer back to Charlton and David's list (see above) we find three (1, 2 and 7) of the characteristics of effective schools identified making

cont......

direct reference to the importance of pupils' perceptions of situations, relating to organisational, disciplinary and academic areas of the curriculum. These factors in addition to those referring to the importance of placing pupil needs in the forefront of curriculum design (item 3), high academic expectations (4), the emphasis on rewards for good behaviour and work (5), mutually supportive and respectful interpersonal relationships between staff and pupils (9), pupil involvement in and responsibility for aspects of the running of an effective school (10), and an effective pastoral system (11), all point to the central importance of the pupil as an individual, to be consulted about and respected for his/her needs and opinions, as well as being acknowledged for his/her strengths and achievements. It is suggested that effective schools elicit the active participation of pupils, through the use of interactional strategies. These strategies derive from an ethos which recognises the essential worth of each individual, and that individual's need for care, consideration and personal attention.

As has been noted in earlier sections of this chapter, pupils who become disaffected from school often cite the belief that they are devalued, humiliated and mistreated by their schools, as a justification for their disruptive behaviour, truancy and other manifestations of disaffection (e.g. Rosser and Harré, 1976; Tattum, 1982; Reid, 1985). As Furlong (1985) points out, 'one of the most consistent findings in studies of the relationship between indiscipline and school factors is that deviant pupils do not like school' (p. 52).

Furthermore, these same views have also been shown to be held by pupils who are not overtly disaffected, but who, to all intents and purposes, perform the role of the ideal pupil. The difference between these pupils and those who become deviant, seems to reside in the fact that non-deviant pupils accept the indignities and humiliations they experience in their schools in return for the benefits they receive, in terms of academic success, and social rewards. The deviant pupils seldom perceive themselves to have anything to gain from such acceptance (See Schostak, 1983; Reid, 1985; 1986). Effective schools recognise that they have the power to influence *all* their pupils' sense of satisfaction with schooling, and consciously seek to provide pupils with experiences which engender willing participation and enthusiasm instead of grudging cooperation, dislike and disaffection. Later sections of this book will attempt to demonstrate in greater detail the ways in which this process works.

Chapter 3

Individuality, education and approaches to disruption

This chapter is concerned with the importance of the individual in education. This is dealt with first in relation to education as a whole, and second in relation to educational policy on disruptive pupil behaviour. It will be argued that certain approaches to promoting effective learning have much in common with approaches designed to promote positive social behaviour, in that both share a common regard for the importance of individual differences between people. It will also be shown, however, that converting this perception into a workable policy is a complex and problematic task.

THE INDIVIDUAL IN EDUCATION

Problems of disaffection and deviance in education inevitably lead us to ask questions about the relationship between individuality and education. To what extent should teachers consider themselves responsible for helping to form pupils' sense of individual and social identity? To what extent should teachers cater for the individual needs of their pupils? What limits, if any, should teachers attempt to impose on pupils' scope for self-expression? Where does freedom of expression end and deviance begin? These areas of consideration turn out to be of great practical significance to educators, and others responsible for the care and nurture of young people.

Of course, there is nothing new about these questions. One of Plato's central concerns was the relationship between education and citizenship: the individual and the state. For the Ancient Greeks the highest form of service was service to the state, and education was seen as providing a vital preparation for this (Castle,

1961). Plato believed the individual was subordinate to the collective citizenship. He held that it was only through collective effort that mankind could achieve its highest purposes and so create a society for the benefit of all its members. Education aided the democratic process by helping to develop each individual's capacity for critical and creative thought. Plato recognised that the process of creating an effective citizen is an essentially personal process requiring the gradual adjustment of each developing person to the environment in which he/she lives. For this adjustment to be successful, individuals need to be given the opportunity to understand their environment in their own terms; to learn at first hand, that knowledge of the world comes from within the self and cannot be imposed. This is why Plato placed such a strong emphasis on the development of reason in children.

Later philosophers interested in education, such as Locke, Rousseau, Dewey, Whitehead and Russell, grappled with this issue of individuality and education, agreeing that the purpose of education should be to empower individuals to create and control knowledge, rather than to gain power over the pupil. If we take this view, the greatest threat to intellectual and moral growth is seen to be authoritarian impulses in education (see Whitehead, 1932; Cahn, 1970; Rubinstein and Stoneman, 1970; Chamberlin, 1989). It was Postman and Weingartner (1971) who coined the phrase 'teaching as a subversive activity', and in so doing epitomised the notion of education for the empowerment of the individual. They suggest that education should help cultivate an 'anthropological perspective' in young people, whereby:

> One views the activities of his group as would an anthropologist, observing its tribal rituals, its fears, its ethnocentrism. In this way one is able to recognise when reality begins to drift too far away from the grasp of the tribe.
>
> (Postman and Weingartner, 1971, p.17)

Central to this perspective are qualities of sensitivity, motivation and courage, which allow persons to be flexible and responsive to a world which changes at a bewildering rate. It is essential in such a world that people are free and competent to challenge the assumptions of previous generations, first in the classroom and later in the adult world. Such a perspective has perhaps never been more relevant than it is now, to a world which appears to be on the brink of ecological disaster. We must ask ourselves whether people

in our society – and throughout the developed world – have had or
are having the kind of education which prepares them for the kind of
judgements and choices that are being urged from some quarters.

Looking at the question of individuality from a more narrowly
defined educational standpoint, it becomes clear that approaches
to education which do not make central the concern for the
individual's interpretations and purposes in the world as he/she
perceives it, are not worthy of the term 'education' at all. Douglas
Barnes (1976) draws a useful distinction between 'school knowledge' and 'action knowledge'. 'School knowledge' is that which
pupils obtain only for the purpose of fulfilling school requirements, in order to complete an assignment or pass an exam. Such
knowledge is taken in and reproduced in a form predefined by
teacher and syllabus. Such knowledge ceases to have any meaning
for the pupil once its purpose has been fulfilled (i.e. the exam
passed, the essay written), and is forgotten. 'Action knowledge' on
the other hand, is knowledge which the pupil has acquired in
order to satisfy his/her own purposes, in answer to a question that
seems important to the pupil, or in order to solve a problem that
the pupil believes to require a solution for some purpose important to the pupil. The content of the knowledge ('school' or
'action') can be identical, for instance the piece of knowledge
concerned might be the freezing-point of ice, or the date of the
Battle of Hastings or themes in the 'Waste Land'. The importance
of 'action knowledge' is that it fits within the unique context of the
individual's existing scheme of thought; it is held in relation to
other pieces of knowledge significant to the individual, and in turn
may stimulate other and sometimes previously unasked questions.

Barnes's student is not, however, isolated in a world of idio-
syncratic thought and non-transferable knowledge. On the contrary, for Barnes the learning context is essentially social and the
medium for learning is talk. Barnes's teacher is a 'facilitator' who
creates circumstances conducive to pupil exploration of problems
in groups. This facilitator recognises that learning is an essentially
individual process, dependent upon the linking of new knowledge
with existing knowledge, and that the major tool for creating this
link is language. The most conducive environment for learning,
therefore, is one which provides the individual with the freedom
and confidence to explore and ask questions. The social aspect is
important here too, in that by working in peer groups individuals
can stimulate and be stimulated by others who are tackling the

same problem at the same time. The peer group also provides an audience for whom embryonic ideas can be articulated, and through discussion refined and developed. As a result of this type of educational experience, the process of knowledge creation is opened up to the pupils who, as a result, come to develop confidence in their abilities to explore and manipulate knowledge. They come to develop a sense of ownership of the knowledge they create, and a faculty for asking pertinent and critical questions. In this approach to education, the distinction between content and method in learning and teaching becomes redundant. The content *is* the method: pupils learn *how* to learn and how to keep on learning what they need to know.

It is suggested here, therefore, that educational approaches which place a high value on the individuality of pupils and permit them full and active participation in the planning and execution of curricular activities, lead to the development of pupil confidence in their skills of manipulating knowledge. Important expositions of this type of approach to education are provided by Carl Rogers (1983), A.S. Neill (1968) and John Holt (1969; 1970). These writers exhibit a strong awareness of the destructive and distortive effects of educational approaches which seek to deny the importance of individual choice. Such approaches, they agree, produce in students feelings of fear and inadequacy, and result in loss of the self-confidence and enthusiasm for learning with which they are born. These seminal educational thinkers stressed the need for educational environments to be places of freedom and discovery for pupils.

The importance of this brief consideration of the importance of the individual in education to the present discussion of school deviance is best summarised in the following key points:

- The courage, confidence and ability to make individual and critical judgements and responsible decisions are necessary qualities for each citizen in any democratic society, if that society is to survive. This provides the core task for educators.
- It would seem that the most effective means of achieving these ends is through providing pupils with the experience of practising these skills in their daily life in schools.
- Pupils who are disaffected and exhibiting behaviour problems are often marginalised and the recipients of treatment which undermines their sense of being valuable and valued individuals (see previous sections of this chapter).

• This perspective on pupil disaffection and deviance draws attention to distinctly educational problems which affect all pupils.
Or, to put it another way, this view suggests that the means for
developing effective preventive and remedial responses to disaffection and school deviance will have much in common with
approaches that are likely to enhance the educational experience of all pupils.

DEALING WITH DISAFFECTED STUDENTS: CHANGING PERSPECTIVES

There have been a number of important changes in the thinking
about how we should deal with schoolchildren with behaviour
problems. It is impossible to consider these changes without looking at the social context in which they have occurred. When we do
this we find that there has been a continuous tension between
meeting the individual needs of the pupils concerned and the
demands of professional groups, policy-makers and other social
forces. The result of this ongoing tension has been to produce
initiatives which profess and at times succeed in dealing with
pupils' individual needs, but which at other times primarily serve
the needs of others and so fail the pupils for whom they were
designed, and may even exacerbate their difficulties. This is not to
say that any one approach is more appropriate or successful than
another. All approaches have their champions and advocates.
What is important to realise is that approaches which have fallen
from favour, such as the use of psychotherapy in residential
settings, may have done so for political reasons, rather than their
inadequacy or otherwise, and they should therefore be considered
on their merits alongside the more fashionable approaches.

Taking as our time-span the era of mass state education in
Britain which began in the last third of the nineteenth century, it
is interesting to note that the earliest formal efforts to cater for the
needs of schoolchildren with behaviour problems were conceived
of as requiring the removal of these pupils from their mainstream
schools into, usually, residential establishments (Bridgeland,
1971). Over this time-span, however, this view has changed to the
extent that residential provision is now often seen as a last resort
(Cole, 1986). An examination of this dramatic change highlights
important ways in which views of the causes and appropriate treatment of behaviour problems have changed. These changes have

shown a welcome recognition of the basic needs and rights of pupils who were hitherto excluded from mainstream schools. They also show a growing sense of the need for mainstream schools to recognise the responsibility they share in the creation of behaviour problems and the remedial effects they can have. This change of perspective is not, however, wholly unproblematic, as we shall see.

In the wake of the Butler Education Act (1944) a system of alternative, mostly residential, schools for 'maladjusted' pupils burgeoned, building on the already fairly well-established tradition of schools created by such pioneers as A.S. Neill, W.D. Wills, George Lyward and an earlier generation led by Homer Lane (Bridgeland, 1971). Many of these pioneers were consciously opposed to what they saw as the dehumanising consequences of traditional approaches to education. Neill and Lyward had been running such alternative schools for fee-paying pupils since before the Second World War, and had made conspicuously good progress with pupils who had been deemed ineducable by other schools. The 1944 Act at last enabled schools of this type to offer provision for pupils newly ascertained as 'maladjusted' under the 1945 regulations (DES, 1945), and this created an opportunity for workers such as David Wills to offer expertise gained working with delinquent young adults and evacuees to this newly-defined group of schoolchildren, at the expense of the state.

These pioneer schools were often shaped out of the vision of an individual, but they shared in common certain values concerning the treatment of pupils. These values have been described by Dawson (1981) as 'four pioneer tenets', and they are here paraphrased as:

1 the showing of unconditional positive regard towards pupils/ inmates;
2 the importance of the inmates' rights to 'free expression', as a means of acting out repressed feelings and symptoms for treatment;
3 the importance of the development of self-discipline through self-government or 'shared responsibility';
4 a psychodynamic orientation in the understanding and treatment of 'maladjustment'.

This approach to the treatment of children, particularly 'difficult' children, was (and perhaps still is) at odds with popular conceptions of the nature and purpose of education. In Britain, Neill

(1916; 1968), Lyward (Burn, 1956) and Wills (1960) were eminent among those heads of schools for 'maladjusted' pupils who rejected what they saw as the rigidity and authoritarianism of state schools. They saw such authoritarianism as contributing to their pupils' maladjustment and saw as central to their therapeutic purpose the use of various forms of structured freedom, which encouraged pupils to express themselves freely and learn to value themselves and others through the experience of living in communities which encouraged them to develop a sense of their individual rights and social responsibilities. In one sense, maladjustment was seen essentially as a form of mental illness, deriving from emotional deprivation and psychological trauma in the early lives of children. Treatment involved placing the disturbed pupil in a 'therapeutic milieu' (Bettelheim and Sylvester, 1948; Bettelheim, 1950) characterised by the removal of constraints to the expression of underlying conflict, the provision of supportive relationships so that the conflicts could be identified, challenged and resolved, and opportunities for pupils to engage in 'ego-building' experiences. This made the need to be free from authoritarian influences of paramount importance.

As Cole (1989) points out, from the outset of state funding of the placement of 'maladjusted' children, the Ministry of Education was concerned with the problem of the segregation of these pupils from their peers in mainstream schools. The official educational line was always to seek community alternatives to segregated provision, on the grounds that the 'maladjusted' pupil would benefit from social contact with his/her peers in the mainstream. The practice of segregating 'maladjusted' pupils (and all other pupils ascertained as having 'handicaps' under the 1945 regulations) continued to be the normal practice. This was owing, in part at least, to two closely related reasons. First, the education of all 'handicapped' pupils was the legal responsibility of the Ministry of Health, rather than the Ministry of Education. Thus it was for administrative convenience, financial and professional reasons that the health professionals sought to create their own provisions with their own medical as opposed to educational priorities. Similarly, this medical approach defined 'maladjustment' in psychiatric terms. It is from this psychiatric base that the dominance of the psychodynamic approach to maladjustment stems. Medical officers, who were responsible by statute for deciding who was 'maladjusted' and what arrangements for their education were appropriate, saw the psychodynamic approach as indispensable in the treatment of maladjustment.

Thus when we come to note the change in emphasis from the psychodynamic orientation to the behavioural approach to the treatment of maladjusted pupils (Laslett, 1983) which occurred in the 1970s, we find this to be related less to the relative merits of these different approaches than to changes in the administrative arrangements concerning pupils with special educational needs. This change was brought about by the Department of Education and Science in 1975, with the publication of a circular (DES, 1975) which stated that the decision to define a pupil as needing special educational treatment should be an educational one, and should be made primarily by an educational psychologist rather than a medical officer. This change was to have major consequences for the treatment of children with behaviour problems.

Laslett (1983) suggests that the inadequacy of the established child guidance system and special-school provision for dealing with the growing scale of disruptive behaviour in mainstream schools, created circumstances which were conducive to the resurgence of behavioural psychology in the treatment of behaviour problems in schoolchildren. The fundamental principle of behavioural psychology is that all behaviour is essentially learned behaviour, and that behaviour can be changed or modified by the manipulation of factors in the environment of the behaver which act as reinforcers to that behaviour. Thus unwanted behaviour can be extinguished by the removal of reinforcers, whilst desired behaviour can be encouraged by the introduction and intensification of reinforcers. Rewards are highly powerful reinforcers, and these can take the form of approval and praise as well as more tangible material rewards. More recently, emphasis has been placed on 'setting events', also referred to as 'antecedents'. These are circumstances which precede or accompany behaviour, such as the time or place at which behaviour occurs, and are seen as having a determining effect on the consequences of behaviour (see Wheldall, 1987).

The advantage of the behavioural model lies in its relative simplicity. Unlike the psychodynamic approach, which demands prolonged inquiry into the internal emotional and psychological state of an individual, the behavioural approach is concerned only with observed behaviour, its observable antecedents and observable consequences. The approach is not concerned with the individual's conscious or unconscious motivations for committing a particular act, but is only interested in the environmental factors which influence the committing of the act. This means that behaviour problems are defined and treated in the context in which they occur, by necessity. The approach recognises the need for educational settings to be 'responsive' to the needs of pupils, by providing them with positive reinforcement, recognition and praise. Although there have been and continue to be a number of residential institutions which employ behavioural approaches (e.g. Bridgeland, 1971; Burland, 1987), it is common for behavioural approaches to be used in the context of mainstream classrooms. The work of Wheldall and Merrett (1984) has been particularly influential in arguing for the use of this approach in mainstream schools, and recent developments, such as the 'Assertive Discipline' programme (Canter, 1990) have found favour with some teachers. The ease-of-use aspect of the behavioural approach also makes it particularly appropriate for use in the light of the Warnock Report (DES, 1978a) and the Education Acts (1980 and 1981), which established in law the responsibility of education authorities to educate pupils with special needs in mainstream settings wherever possible, and to use segregated provision only where no suitable alternative capable of meeting the child's educational needs was available. This integration principle has been further strengthened through the Education Reform Act (1988), which establishes the right of all children to access the National Curriculum, 'disapplication' of which is only permitted in limited circumstances and for specified periods.

There can be little doubt that the work of behaviourist educationists contains much that is of value to teachers and pupils. They stress the need for teachers to present positive models of behaviour to their pupils, and to use rewards and praise as means of motivating all pupils and encouraging positive behaviour. This is sound advice which has been borne out by the work of the school effectiveness researchers (see above), as well as by the rigorous research of the behaviourists themselves. There is strong evidence to suggest that behavioural approaches can help pupils to feel more personally motivated and valued as individuals (see Wheldall, 1987).

Another important approach to behaviour problems in schools is provided by writers who take a systemic approach. This approach arises out of the well-established theory and practice of family therapy, and has been applied in different ways to school behaviour problems by a number of writers (Shuttleworth, 1983; Speed, 1983; Campion, 1985; Dowling and Osborne, 1985; Molnar and Lindquist, 1989; Cooper and Upton, 1990b; 1992). Systemic approaches tend to be less directive than the behavioural approach outlined above, placing considerable emphasis on the importance of individuals' understandings of their own behaviour, and the relationship between their behaviour and that of others. Thus a systemic approach may be used to interpret a child's apparently school-related behaviour problem in terms of: (a) a problem in the family that disturbs the school; (b) a problem at school that disturbs the family; or (c) a problem at school that does not disturb the family (Lindquist *et al.*, 1987). Intervention focuses on the interactional system (e.g. relationships in the family) which appears to be the major location of the problem. Thus what appears to be a school behaviour problem may be solved by intervention in the child's family, without any direct attempt to influence the child's behaviour. An example of this is where a child's misbehaviour at school is covertly condoned by the child's parents, who, unwittingly, act to maintain their child's difficulties by encouraging him not to complete homework tasks. The parents engage in this behaviour as a means of diverting their attention from their own marital difficulties, which become a source of discord when confronted. The child's behaviour problems cease when a psychologist intervenes to provide the parents with a pattern of cooperation which assists rather than hinders their child's development (see Power and Bartholomew, 1985). Less complex though similarly indirect approaches to behaviour problems in classrooms are recommended by Molnar and Lindquist (1989).

An important quality of the systemic approach is the importance it attaches to the perceptions and insights of the individuals whose interactions surround the problem behaviour, and the recognition of the degree to which all the interacting persons contribute to the maintenance of the problem behaviour. Thus the teacher who identifies a pupil's behaviour as problematic must first ask herself why and how she defines the behaviour as such, and whether or not the 'problem' is less a function of the child's behaviour than her own mode of perception. Furthermore, if this line of inquiry fails to produce a solution, the teacher will enquire of the pupil, to see how he/she perceives the situation. Once again the outcome of this enquiry may indicate a particular problem to be solved which may focus on the pupil, the teacher or some other situation in or outside the school. In this way the systemic approach can be seen to share something in common with the humanistic psychology of Carl Rogers (see above), which stresses the importance of empathy and intersubjectivity in the definition and resolution of emotional and interpersonal problems.

Whilst there is some valuable and important work being done using systemic approaches to school behaviour problems, the potential of this approach is limited by the fact that the approach draws on a knowledge base and practice model which lies outside the skills and training of most teachers and educational psychologists. There is evidence of difficulties relating to the interdisciplinary nature of these approaches when introduced into the education service (e.g. Dowling and Pound, 1985).

These developments in approaches to dealing with behaviour problems, and the concomitant decline in the use of residential treatment, have also coincided with important developments in the pastoral care provision in mainstream schools which have taken place over the past twenty years or so. There can be little doubt that the pastoral needs of pupils have continued to appear on the agenda of mainstream schools over recent years. Pastoral care has been defined as that aspect of school organisation which takes account of the personality and individuality of pupils (Hamblin, 1978), and seeks to facilitate the integration of school organisation and pupil needs in ways which engender social and educational development. It has been shown that schools operating effective pastoral care programmes which promote a caring and supportive ethos are likely to have lower rates of disruptive behaviour than schools which do not have such programmes (Charlton and David, 1990).

Powerful advances have been made over the near half-century since the Butler Education Act in the understanding and treatment of behaviour problems in schoolchildren. The various approaches to understanding and dealing with behaviour problems all have their merits, and, as other writers have noted, an eclectic approach is likely to be the most fruitful, since each approach asks a different range of questions and so sheds a light on different aspects of a problem (Laslett, 1983; Charlton and David, 1989). This also is the view taken by the recent committee of inquiry into discipline in schools, chaired by Lord Elton (DES, 1989a).

One could be forgiven, in the face of these developments, for seeing the traditional residential provision for children with behaviour problems as the 'dinosaurs of the education system' (Cole, 1986). The enlightenment which is evident in the development 'of whole school approaches' to disruption (Charlton and David, 1990), the availability of behavioural techniques and other approaches which can be used to tackle problems *in situ*, and the thrust of educational policy towards the integration of pupils with special educational needs, make residential provision appear not only anachronistic, but also a relatively expensive luxury of dubious effectiveness (Topping, 1983). It is tempting to think that schools in general are more responsive to individual pupil needs than they once were, and that systems are in place to ensure that this continues to be the case. This is, of course, a complacent view. Some schools are more responsive to pupil needs than others, but as we have already noted in the discussions of school influences on disruptive behaviour and school effectiveness research, there are many schools which fail to meet the needs of their pupils.

The Elton Report (DES, 1989a) is an important landmark in the history of educational responses to behavioural problems. Though the report contains little that is new, it raises the profile of the issue of school behavioural problems. It offers much good sense and thoughtful advice on the development of whole school approaches to behavioural problems, and in so doing goes some way towards establishing the importance of the institution rather than the individual teacher as the key unit of influence. However, the report's impact is diminished by a lack of theoretical coherence, which leads, in places, to confused thinking of a dangerous kind. The Elton recommendations are at times too eclectic, and found to be sending out contradictory messages when examined with a critical eye. Taken in its totality, the Elton Report reveals that in spite of the considerable advances that have been made over the years in the understanding and treatment of behaviour problems, there is still a dangerous element of authoritarianism lurking in the range of popular opinion on the subject. Thus, in spite of the report's praiseworthy endorsement of the views of the school effectiveness researchers and the behaviourists, that schools need to recognise the role they may play in causing and curing behaviour problems and to concentrate on promoting positive pupil self-images, the report also recommends a number of essentially punitive measures which seem to run against this positive grain. These include: the imposition of civil penalties on the parents of pupils who misbehave in school (Recommendation 74), the legal enhancement of teachers' authority over their pupils (R11), and the dismissal of staff who are judged to be unable to control their pupils (R115.1). On the one hand the report calls for schools to place a greater emphasis on the personal and social needs of all pupils, and on the other hand seeks to undermine this through the use of authoritarian strategies based on threat and fear which serve only to diminish the importance and value placed on the individual (Cooper and Upton, 1990a). What more justifiable grounds for resentment and retribution than that of the pupil whose act of truancy, which he justifies in terms of his ill-treatment at school, is punished by imposing a fine on his parents? What incentive is there for the teacher, invested with legal authority over pupils and with the threat of dismissal for displaying lack of 'control' over his/her class, to relinquish or share 'authority' with pupils? These issues bring the words of the pioneer workers with 'maladjusted' children ringing in our ears from across the decades, with their condemnation of the false dignity of some teachers (Neill, 1916; Wills, 1960), and the 'imprisoning formality' of teacher–pupil relationships (Burn, 1956) which serve only to stunt the social, emotional and educational development of children, and so set the conditions for the production of disaffection.

There are similar flaws to be found with the integration policy in special education and the function of pastoral care systems in some schools. Both of these important aspects of education in our schools have sometimes been shown to be counterproductive as a result of the ways in which they have been implemented. Whilst both the policy of integrating pupils with special educational needs and pastoral care have been long recognised as vehicles for reducing the personal difficulties experienced by some pupils, they have been shown in some circumstances to exacerbate and create difficulties. Reid (1985), in his study of truancy, showed how, in the schools he studied, the pastoral care systems, far from being seen as providing an individualised, caring and supportive service to children, were perceived by pupils in need of such a service to perform a policing and punitive role, being concerned mainly with checking attendance, looking after lost property, and reporting truants to educational welfare officers. For these pupils the pastoral care staff were not only unsympathetic, but were seen as an oppressive force to be avoided and used as a justification for truancy. Galloway (1985b) describes how this negative functioning of the pastoral system in some schools can be related to the way in which pastoral care is seen as: (a) an alternative career path for teachers, and (b) a service to the school as a whole for the control and containment of pupils who prove to be problematic. In such circumstances pastoral effectiveness and professional competence are seen more in terms of the degree to which 'problem pupils' are kept from interfering with the smooth running of the school's academic business.

Galloway and Goodwin (1987) draw attention to the 'de-skilling' effects on classroom teachers of over-specialisation in the teaching profession. They draw on research which shows how the introduction of special education support staff into schools can, in certain circumstances, lead to class teachers relinquishing res-ponsibility for children with special needs and preferring to refer them to 'the experts'. Galloway (1985b) describes a similar situa-tion in relation to pastoral care services in some schools. This also has implications for the integration of children with special needs in schools. As Tomlinson (1982) has suggested, the whole special education service has produced distinctive types of educational professionals, with their own purpose and careers. When one professional establishes his/her particular area of expertise he/she is simultaneously excluding others from that area. By attaching promotion prospects and responsibility allowances to such 'specialisms', the specialism becomes an area to be defended against outsiders. Similarly, 'outsiders' are likely to be discouraged from performing roles and duties for which others are paid addi-tional sums. This begins to help explain why, as Galloway and Goodwin show, the process of integration for pupils with learning and behaviour problems has in some cases been limited to mere 'locational integration' (DES, 1978a), whereby pupils with special needs are placed on the same site as their mainstream peers, but with little or no access to those peers, the mainstream school staff and resources of the larger school. As Galloway and Goodwin suggest, these pupils would be often better served by small special school and off-site units, in terms of resources and quality of educational experience, whilst as it is they experience public stigma before their mainstream peers without the advantages of access to the mainstream facilities. Similarly, a recent HMI report (DES, 1989c) found that a third of the mainstream secondary and primary schools they surveyed failed to give their pupils with special needs adequate access to the National Curriculum. In the same survey, in only half the lessons observed were special-needs pupils judged to be producing work of a 'satisfactory or better' quality.

Another aspect of the integration debate in relation to pupils with behaviour problems has been the heavy reliance placed by some education authorities on off-site units. This trend was at its height during the 1970s, when such units were seen as a cheap and convenient alternative to day and residential special schools (Lloyd-Smith, 1984; Ling and Davies, 1984). This form of provision has been found to be unsatisfactory by many writers and researchers (DES, 1978b; 1989b; Dawson, 1980; Mortimore et al., 1983; Galloway and Goodwin, 1987), owing to the narrowness of the curriculum offered, and the lack of success achieved by such units in returning pupils to the mainstream. Off-site units, like the locationally integrated on-site provision referred to above, are often found to offer pupils a narrower educational experience than that offered by the often much larger, better resourced and better staffed special school (Dawson, 1980).

However, an important quality of these off-site units has often been undervalued or simply ignored. This is the high quality of interpersonal relationships which often exist between pupils and staff and the ways in which this contributes to effective teaching and learning (Dain, 1977; Galwey, 1979; Mortimore et al., 1983; DES, 1989b). In the light of what has been so far said about the importance of relationships and respect for individuality in the creation and treatment of behaviour problems, this would seem an important point. Such relationship factors are repeatedly placed in a subordinate position alongside curricular and resource factors. Thus the special schools and units are often criticised for the extent to which they fail to resemble mainstream schools, rather than given recognition for the achievements they make in forging cooperative relationships between staff and pupils who have been so conspicuously failed in this respect by mainstream schools (see Laslett, 1990). This pinpoints a key issue at the very heart of the problem of school disaffection, namely that it is this very neglect of pupils' individual need for supportive and caring relationships with staff which often hinders these pupils' access to the curriculum and resources of the mainstream school, by exacerbating and sometimes creating alienation and disaffection. So whilst off-site units may be at present 'ideologically unsound' (to some), there is still much that we can learn from them and there is much that pupils can gain from them. It would seem injudicious to dispense with such provision until the problems in mainstream schools which they were set up to counter are more fully understood and solved.

In short, there would appear to be many circumstances which militate against the best interests of pupils who come to be seen as problematic. Whilst pre-eminent among their requirements is the need to be dealt with on an individual basis, for all the reasons outlined above, the systems which have been designed to achieve this have sometimes had the reverse effect and denied individual needs and led to further difficulties.

CONCLUSION

It would seem to be the case that there are still many unresolved problems in the educational response to disaffection, and emotional and behaviour problems in schools. Present educational policy, with its emphasis on the integration of pupils with special needs into mainstream schools, is based, at least partly, on a recognition of the right of all children to receive the same breadth and depth of educational experience that are available in mainstream schools. It is also based on the conviction that there is much mainstream schools can do to mitigate the problems of pupils with special needs. However, as has been shown, the quality of the educational experience of pupils in mainstream schools varies dramatically. Whilst there are many measures which can be taken by schools to inhibit the development of disaffection, not all schools are pursuing these measures. The creation of systems and services is alone insufficient to bring about the changes which are often necessary.

This book attempts to take a fresh look at the problem of disaffection and in particular the measures schools can adopt to tackle it. The study presented here was born out of two important personal concerns of the author. First, the work of the best modern residential schools for children with emotional and behavioural problems is essentially unknown and ignored outside of a narrow field of people working in or with the schools and their clients. Second, that the success of these schools in bringing about positive changes in the outlook and behaviour of many disaffected and disturbed/disturbing children has many aspects to it which should be of interest to many of the mainstream day schools from which these pupils have come.

The study at the heart of this book is based on in-depth interviews with twenty-four boys in two residential schools for boys with behaviour problems, and questionnaires returned by the overwhelming majority of pupils attending both schools. The findings of this study indicate the importance of the following factors in the generation and exacerbation of behaviour problems and disaffection:

- poor staff–pupil relationships and authoritarianism in certain schools;
- low self-esteem of pupils;
- difficulties with family relationships.

The following factors are associated with positive pupil outcomes (in the form of improved self-image, attitudes and behaviour) in the residential schools:

- a high degree of satisfaction with the residential school;
- relationships with staff which are characterised by openness, support, cooperation and high expectations;
- the experience of personal success in a variety of activities and situations provided by the schools, in social, academic, practical and behavioural terms;
- the provision of respite from difficulties experienced in the family, peer group and mainstream school.

The rest of this book offers, therefore, in one sense, an account of some of the factors which have influenced the 'rehabilitation' of a group of pupils with emotional and behavioural difficulties. The following sections also include a critique of what goes on in some (maybe many?) schools, as seen through the eyes of these pupils. In this respect, I hope the book offers reinforcement to some existing critiques, and provides insight into what changes might be profitably made in some schools.

Part II

The experience of disaffection

This part of the book deals with disaffection from the viewpoint of people who have been formally labelled as disaffected pupils or as pupils with emotional and behavioural difficulties. It builds on the theoretical input of the introductory section by focusing on the specific experiences of a group of pupils who have been excluded from mainstream schools and referred to one of two non-maintained residential schools for boys with emotional and behavioural difficulties.

The schools, referred to here as 'Farfield School' and 'Lakeside School' (fictitious names), both conform to a traditional pattern for such schools, being situated in large country houses and providing education and care for their pupils on a twenty-four hour, seven-day-week basis. The staffing in both schools is divided into two distinct professional groups: teaching staff and care staff (sometimes referred to as residential social workers). Both schools profess the aim of presenting a coordinated care and education programme for all of their pupils, whereby their progress and development are consciously fostered and monitored in all aspects of school life. The stated aim of both schools is, primarily, to facilitate the return of pupils to mainstream education through the use of behavioural and therapeutic techniques designed to help them come to terms with and overcome emotional and behavioural problems. To this end also, the staff of both schools are closely involved in pupils' reintegration programmes, by working closely with parents, social workers and mainstream schools to make such programmes successful.

Although they share much in common, the schools differ in certain important ways. Farfield offers some of its pupils fifty-two-week-a-year placements, whilst Lakeside caters for pupils in term times only. The schools also differ philosophically, with Lakeside employing a number of formal arrangements intended to give pupils a sense of community involvement, through the allocation of specific maintenance tasks around the school, and participation in group decision-making exercises. Lakeside also operates a formal system whereby pupils can earn special privileges and responsibilities. Farfield's organisational pattern is less formalised, with decisions depending largely on the will of the school principal. Both schools operate a formal educational curriculum which is based on that of mainstream comprehensive schools, though the Lakeside curriculum places a stronger emphasis on practical and vocational education. (NB. This research was carried out prior to the introduction of the National Curriculum.)

The research involved in-depth, open-ended interviews with twenty-four pupils (fifteen from Farfield, nine from Lakeside) from the upper age range of each school (13–17). The interview findings were then used to construct two questionnaires intended to test the generalisability of these findings across the whole school populations. A total of seventy pupils participated in this interview and questionnaire study, which represents 91 per cent of the combined school populations.

The intention of this study was to represent the experience of disaffection and residential treatment from the viewpoint of the pupils themselves. It will be seen that these boys are highly positive about their residential experience. They feel that the schools have helped them to overcome difficulties which they experienced in their home situations and previous schooling. They indicate that, in their experience, the residential setting provides a necessary alternative to mainstream schools.

The first chapter in this section deals with pupils' accounts of their backgrounds. This includes descriptions of their family and mainstream school experiences, and the bearing these have on their present situations. The second chapter is concerned with the pupils' perceptions of the residential schools and their effects.

Chapter 4

Pupils tell their stories

It may be prosaic to assert that each of these boys is a unique individual, but this is a crucial observation. It wasn't unusual for these boys to say 'thank you' *to me* at the end of the, sometimes lengthy, interviews which I conducted with them. They were perhaps flattered, to be asked for their opinions and views. They clearly appreciated the opportunity to talk and be listened to. There were no pre-taught answers to stumble over, no censures for bad grammar or inappropriate language. Interestingly, the majority of the twenty-four boys who were interviewed were comfortable and open, expressing their views with articulate confidence and self-assurance. They all willingly agreed to participate and did so with enthusiasm. They spoke with great candour about their families, their behaviour, their views of the residential schools and other schools they had attended. In many ways these boys were impressive, both for their insight into their circumstances and their self-effacement. It was clear that the interview process was far more than a research tool; it provided a structure by which these boys pursued and clarified their thoughts and feelings. It was a therapeutic process for some of them, as well as a learning process for them and me. One thing I learned was that there is no such thing as 'the EBD child' (Emotional and Behavioural Difficulties). There are, however, large numbers of children who become bearers of the EBD label, and there are patterns to be found in the life stories of many such children. Some of the recurring themes associated with behaviour problems and deviance have been described in the opening section of this book; the present section offers a more individualised and personal perspective, drawing as it does on the life experience of a small group of boys.

A total of seventy-seven boys provided information on their experience of being pupils with behaviour problems. Twenty-four of these pupils allowed interviews with them to be tape-recorded. There was no shortage of volunteers for interview; however, it was decided to select mainly older children (aged 13–17), as it was felt that these more mature pupils would cope more readily with the open-ended 'informant' style (Powney and Watts, 1987) of the interviews. It was also felt that these pupils, on the basis of their lengthier experience of schooling, would have, in general, more fully developed responses to their circumstances and situations. As a result virtually all of the pupils in the upper age ranges attending the two schools were interviewed, with no pupil refusing or withdrawing. The interviews lasted generally from between forty-five and sixty minutes, though on one notable occasion the interview extended to three hours and filled two C90 tapes! The shortest interview lasted for thirty minutes.

MEETING THE BOYS

In the limited space available it is impossible to give detailed accounts of all twenty-four boys' backgrounds. An attempt will be made in this section to give a flavour of the pupils' family and other personal circumstances, by drawing on representative comments from some of the pupils, and picking out points of particular interest from the interviews.

Clearly, in research of this kind, which seeks to discover the insiders' views of a situation rather than the verification of an existing theory, we find that different pupils talk about different things. Each pupil has his own preoccupations and concerns which emerge from his own special circumstances. Furthermore, some pupils are more forthcoming than others, for all kinds of personal reasons. It will be clear that some pupils have reflected more deeply than others, and some are more articulate and/or talkative than others. Colin, for instance, was a very keen informant whose interview went on for three hours and could have continued for much longer. These factors act as powerful qualifications to what follows. For this reason the substantive conclusions of this study are supported by a questionnaire study, which was based on the interview findings and carried out throughout the two schools. The positive value of this type of research, however, lies in its naturalism. These are real people talking about their real lives.

Inevitably, there are some pupils who emerge as more prominent informants than others. Not only is Colin's the longest interview, he is also the pupil with the greatest experience of residential schooling of this type. At the time of interview he is within six months of statutory school leaving age, and he has spent his entire school career, since his second year of infant school, in residential provision for children with behavioural problems. It is not surprising that he has a lot to say. On the other hand, Colin's status is relatively low in the Farfield pecking order. Although he is a senior, by virtue of his age, he is clearly outside the first rank of the official and unofficial pupil hierarchy. At Farfield the pinnacle of the pupil hierarchy is occupied by the 'Jobbers'. These are senior boys who have high status both among their peers and within the formal organisation of the school. They are seen by the other boys as individuals who can be trusted and sometimes used as advocates or intermediaries with staff. They are also given special responsibilities and 'jobs', sometimes involving the supervision of other boys, and privileges by staff. The chief 'Jobbers' are Ryan and Lewis. These two boys are both in their final year of compulsory schooling. Lewis, who is 16 and one of four black boys in the school, is the senior of the two in age and status. We find that these boys are liked and respected by most of the other boys. We also find that they adopt a caring and responsible attitude to the other, particularly the younger ('junior'), boys. As we might expect, neither of these competent and confident boys is wholly uncritical of the school and its staff, though Lewis is notably the more conformist of the two boys.

The lowest status in the informal hierarchy of Farfield is that of 'squares'. This is occupied, mostly, by boys of junior age who are conspicuous for their poor educational progress and or lack of social skills. These boys also tend to dress in clothing provided by the school which, whilst conforming in type to that worn by other pupils (i.e. training shoes, jeans, tracksuits, sweatshirts), is considered by the boys to be of inferior quality because it often does not bear the coveted designer labels. The apparent callous objectification implied by the term, however, is not reflected in the way the senior boys behave towards the 'squares'. Alan, Colin, Brian and Greg, who are in the interview sample, as younger boys would have conformed to the 'square' stereotype, and whilst they are not among the 'Jobbers', they are 'seniors' and have a sense of progress and status, through the privileges and responsibilities that go with being a 'senior'.

Another identifiable group of boys, at the lower end of the senior age group (aged 14), is composed of John, Alex, Jim, Chris and Ian. These are boys on the fringes of 'Jobber' status. Like Lewis and Ryan, they are identifiable by their fashionable haircuts and clothing and share an interest in pop music and sporting activities. These boys form a friendship group and are considered by staff and often chosen to deputise for the Jobbers. A sixth boy, Dave, who is 15 and a new arrival at Farfield, is a member of this group, though he is older.

The remaining interviewees are less easily pigeon-holed into groups. Malcolm is the eldest of the interviewees (16.2) and is interviewed on the eve of his leaving. He is a tall, strong, quiet and calm boy, well liked by staff and pupils. Malcolm enjoys his own company best, and spends much of his leisure time in solitary pursuits, particularly fishing. He is described by staff and boys as highly trustworthy and dependable. The final boy, Mick, is also something of a loner. He is 14, small for his age, highly talkative and cheerful. He is often decribed by other boys, however, as a troublemaker, and is regarded by the staff as notably cheeky. Along with Les, Ian and Chris, Mick is also regarded as moody and prone to temper-tantrums.

The nine Lakeside interviewees, like the Farfield boys, are from the upper age range of the school, aged between 15 and 17. Like Farfield, Lakeside pupils are divided into junior and senior groups, referred to as 'units'. Four of the interviewees belong to a definable clique: Tim (16), Richard (15), Frank (16) and Fred (15). Frank appears to be the dominant figure in this clique. Tim and Frank are particularly close friends, spending much of their leisure time in each other's company. These boys are generally well liked by their peers, with the exception of Frank, who, outside this immediate clique, is seen as something of a 'troublemaker' by staff and pupils alike. He is believed to be responsible for a number of acts of delinquency, particularly theft, that have taken place in the school.

Larry (15) is a peripheral member of the Tim/Richard/Frank/Fred clique, but regards himself as being somewhat isolated, owing to his middle-class/private-school background. This sense of difference was not apparent to the observer and was not reflected in pupil or staff comments. Larry was seen as a popular and well-integrated pupil by staff and peers. In particular, the staff cited Larry as a pupil of high intelligence, who occasionally shows signs of limited reliability/trustworthiness.

One of the most popular boys in the school is Jock. Jock is, at 17, the oldest and longest serving pupil at the school, having been there for the entire span of his secondary education. He is regarded as a trustworthy and reliable boy by staff and pupils. Like Ryan and Lewis at Farfield, Jock fulfils an important pastoral function among the pupils and is something of an intermediary between the staff and pupil groups. He is generally seen by staff and pupils as occupying the top spot in both the formal and informal pupil hierarchy.

Stan (15) is a quiet, somewhat withdrawn boy, who, according to his own account, has become less withdrawn throughout his time at Lakeside. This account is also supported by staff comments. He is not a member of any particular clique, though he does have at least one particular friend among the boys. Stan is not an unpopular boy, but he is clearly of relatively low status in the informal pupil hierarchy.

The remaining two interviewees, Tom (15) and Arthur (15), are two of seven black boys in the school, but share little else in common. Tom has clearly reflected deeply on his situation, and at the time of the interviews appeared to be very anxious about his future. He presents as a highly dissatisfied and critical customer, determined, as will be seen, to 'rubbish' Lakeside. He expresses very negative feelings about the school, particularly in relation to the quality of the educational provision. He shows faith in his own academic potential, without being arrogant. He also reveals a powerful desire to return to the mainstream comprehensive school from whence he came; he is supported in this, in general, by the staff. Arthur, on the other hand, unlike Tom, is popular among his peers, indomitably cheerful and commends the school, in spite or perhaps because of a chaotic and unstable family life.*

---

* It is important to note that Lakeside employs a far more formalised privilege/status system than Farfield. This system centres on the 'Helpers' List', which is compiled weekly on the basis of staff recommendations. Pupils who are designated as 'helpers' are given recreational privileges and may be endowed with responsibilities. Because of the staff centredness of this policy, however, there is a strongly vocalised resistance to it among the boys, and concomitant confusion about *the desirability of being a 'helper'*.

THE BOYS AND THEIR FAMILIES

Family problems are ubiquitous among this group, and take many different forms; from poverty, marital discord to parental delinquency and rejection of children by their parents. More than half of these boys are from one-parent families, with, in all cases, the mother being the parent who remains. In addition to this there are several boys who describe the parental relationships which are unstable, going through an endless cycle of break-up and reconciliation. Colin, who is 16 and has attended Farfield school for nearly two years, recalls his parents' earlier marital discord, and relates this to his own conflict-ridden experience of mainstream school:

> I was a little brute at school. Y'know they couldn't stand me. They couldn't control me. I was that vicious when I was small. I was like a wild dog. . . . I was really foul-mouthed. . . . I used to start, 'Oh, fucking hell!' and all this crap, y'know. And the teachers used to come in and say, 'Stop that! Stop that! You're only young! Stop it!' I dunno where I picked it up. I don't know if it was when I was in the flat, at my other school, when my mum and dad broke up. . . . They broke up when I was little, and a load of swearing went on. I probably picked it up then. When I came to school I had a mouth y'know. And anyway, the teacher used to say, 'Stop swearing!' And I'd shout foul-mouthly to her to high heavens. . . . They'd stand there, mouths shut. . . . They used to give me the slipper, like, and a clip round the ear. I used to carry on and on. They probably got that sick of me. They must have gone to the authorities and said, 'Sorry, we can't have him with us. You've got to put him somewhere where he'll be tamed down.'

It is sobering to consider that this represents Colin's recollections of his *infant* school-days, ever since which he has moved through a succession of residential special schools, of which Farfield is to be the last. For him, the memory of his parents' marital conflict is inextricably linked with these unhappy recollections of his school-days and the reasons for his referral to residential schooling. It is also interesting to note that Colin's sympathies appear to rest firmly with the staff who tried to cope with him in the infant school, rather than the 'little brute' he used to be.

Colin's story is extreme, chiefly in respect to the length of time he has spent in special schools. Colin's experience of parental disharmony is typical. Alex, a 15-year-old who has been at Farfield for a year, tells of the break-up of his parents' marriage, virtual constant truancy from school, and his own delinquency and frequent brushes with the police, adding:

> I didn't used to get on with my mum and brothers. And I used to argue with my mum.

Fourteen-year-old Jim, who has been at Farfield for just over two years, tells his story succinctly:

> I didn't get on with the headteacher [of his previous mainstream primary school]. I was getting trouble . . . for cheeking, messing around, not doing my work, playing my mum and dad up.

For some boys, home factors are of paramount importance in their personal accounts. Jock, at 17 the oldest and longest-serving (at six years) pupil at Lakeside School, and is glad of the respite the school gives him from an unhappy home situation. For Jock, a major family problem relates to the delinquency of his father and brother. Jock's elder brother is in prison, whilst his father is a regular subject of police attention, the most recent cause of this being his acquisition of 'a dodgy telly':

> The atmosphere at home was horrible. It's usually horrible when our dad's there. He spoils all the fun. . . . Some kids love being at home; I can't stand it! I get on alright with the rest of my family, but not my dad. . . . My dad hates children. . . . I'm always glad to get back to Lakeside.

Jock recalls his own severe behaviour problems in the mainstream primary school he attended, and his own former delinquent tendencies, seeing these as the major reasons for his referral to Lakeside, but it is the family situation which he sees as the persistent problem for him.

For Larry, (15 years old and a pupil at Lakeside for two-and-a-half years), home problems are even more significant than they are for Jock. Larry's situation has many unusual features, when compared with other boys in this study. He describes Lakeside and the boys he lives with there as very different from what he is used to:

> it [Lakeside] was different from what I was used to. It was a different way of life to what I used to lead. When I was living with my parents it was sort of posher than this.

Larry describes his previous attendance at a private (mainstream) boarding school, and his later placement in a state comprehensive school. However, he is anxious to point out that his 'school problems', particularly at the comprehensive, were not the result of any dislike of school. He admits to constantly 'running away' from the schools he attended, not to escape the schools, but to escape family conflict:

> The atmosphere at the ordinary school was OK, but as soon as I got home it was the atmosphere at home which really made me uneasy and nervous all the time. . . . My dad used to get on to me for stupid little things: for not doing the family chores, if I forgot. . . . I got hit around quite a lot.

Larry's main recollections of home life centre around the brutality of his father and the difficult relationship Larry had with his stepmother, who he feels was always finding fault with him. In fact, for Larry, the break-up of his parents' marriage and the introduction of the stepmother are the 'main problem'.

Problems with siblings are also recurrent features of the boys' accounts. With sisters and brothers becoming the objects of anger, resentment and jealousy, and these situations often compounding the already fraught parent–child relationship. Arthur, a 15-year-old who has been at Lakeside for three years, describes the deterioration in family relationships which has taken place since his referral:

> I got put in a children's home. Everything [at home] went to pieces, about a year ago. . . . It wouldn't have happened, if I hadn't been here. . . . Being away from home such a long time and going back. Me brothers and sisters all start playing me up; they start playing up and show-off to you. And your mum thinks, 'Oh no! It's him. He's back. He's caused all this.'

Arthur's perception and experience differ from those of many other pupils, who describe similar conflict and disharmony in the family, but believe these problems to have decreased since being in residential schooling. The following are descriptions of changes that have taken place in family circumstances since becoming pupils in residential schools:

> I've settled down with my mum and dad a bit.
>
> [Jim, Farfield]

It's [his relationship with his single-parent mother] got a lot better, but it's still bad. . . . I think it's got better because we've spent longer times apart. It's nothing to do with what I've been told to say. I reckon it's the break. When I go home for long periods it starts again.

[Ryan, Farfield]

The school's helped me change by helping my mum. . . . By coming here, she can have a rest. Now she's got a month's rest, I can go home now.
[Interviewer:] Do you get on better with your mum now?
Yes, definitely.

[John, Farfield]

It's helped my mum out. Like, when I've been here I've been sorting myself out. And I must be sorting myself out there. . . . Since this last year we've been getting on well. It's got to the stage now where me and my mum have got on well. I can go home every weekend, if I want to. She's given me the front door key, so I can go home if I want to. . . . So it's not too bad now.

[Ian, Farfield]

Since coming here, I can talk to my mum better. We get on now. I think I'm ready to go back.

[Tom, Lakeside]

Another group of children is that composed of boys whose family circumstances are such that they attend children's homes during those periods when they are not in residential school. Fourteen-year-old Les at Farfield, has spent parts of school holidays with foster parents, but does not feel that any of these spells have been successful. Les's own story is that his school and family situation deteriorated after his parents' separation and divorce. An added complication for Les, however, was what turned out to be an ill-advised gesture by his elder brother to have Les live with him and his wife. Les is philosophical about the breakdown of this situation, which he puts down to 'not getting on' with his sister-in-law.

THE BOYS AND THEIR EXPERIENCE OF SCHOOLING

Family life for these boys, for one reason or another, has tended towards the disastrous. Similarly, their experience of schooling highlights many problems. The following is a list of recurrent complaints made by these boys about teachers in other schools they have attended. Teachers were:

- too formal in their behaviour towards pupils;
- too strict;
- 'stuck up';
- unfriendly;
- intolerant;
- humourless;
- uninterested in pupils' personal welfare;
- not prepared/able to give pupils individual attention;
- guilty of labelling some pupils with negative identities;
- guilty of treating some pupils unfairly;
- guilty of conducting boring lessons;
- insufficiently helpful to pupils with learning difficulties;

Already we should begin to see danger signals. Here we have a group of boys experiencing difficulties and conflict in their personal lives; already perhaps painfully aware of the fallibility of adults. School, however, is not only unlikely to compensate for these deficiencies, it is rather, for these children, likely to create further problems. Of course, the precise chronology of events is difficult to untangle. It is often difficult to say which comes first, the family problems or the school problems. What is clear, however, is that together they make a powerful combination of negative forces for the boys.

The diverse experience of schooling that many of these pupils have had gives them a unique insight into the pros and cons of different schools and institutions. Sixteen-year-old Frank, who has been at Lakeside for three years, gives a characteristically blunt and precise account of what he sees as the major deficiencies of staff in mainstream comprehensive schools:

> Teachers in comprehensives are all stuck-up. Here [at Lakeside] they're flexible. Staff are more friendly. You can call them by their first names and everything. Staff will give you more time, if you want to talk to them. Charlie [a teacher at Lakeside] will stay with you, even if he's off duty, until it is sorted out. They have more time for you.

This notion that staff in mainstream schools are aloof and fail to take an individual interest in pupils is a common complaint among the boys. Tom from Lakeside complains that teachers in the main-stream comprehensive school he attended simply refused to listen to him or take him seriously:

> Say if someone shouted out something, and I got blamed for it, and I got kicked out. And I said it weren't me, and they said they're pretty sure it was, and still chucked me out. I was just kicked out and that was all. . . . It's better when they listen to you.

Tom and Frank are here expressing their dissatisfaction at being treated with such disrespect. Tom's use of the expressions 'kicked out' and 'chucked out' recur repeatedly throughout the interviews and exemplify what the pupils experience as the dehumanising effects of their treatment by staff in mainstream and, sometimes, other special schools. It is, however, Arthur, who provides the most graphic description of inhumane treatment, when he speaks of his previous placement in a day special school:

> [the staff at Lakeside are] a lot better. They're more like people! When I was at Rushforth [special school], they were more like robots really. You do something wrong, the first thing they do is grab 'em and stick 'em in a room, and just lock them up!

Arthur reminds us here that mainstream schools do not have a monopoly on dehumanisation. Whatever the type of school, how-ever, the effect of this type of treatment is to make children who may well already feel uncared for and rejected by their families even more unwelcome and neglected; as Tom puts it:

> You didn't get to know them [teachers in the comprehensive school] that well. You're only getting about thirty-five minutes a day with them, with everyone else. I don't think they cared. They said: 'It's your life. It's up to you. You do what you like.'

As well as a condemnation of the uncaring attitude of teachers, there is insight here into the structural constraints of the thirty-five-minute lesson format, which places limitations on both the pupils and teachers.

The belief that staff in mainstream schools are comparatively uncaring and unhelpful is commonly held by pupils in both schools. Brian, a 15-year-old boy who has been at Farfield for two years, praises the opportunities provided by the relaxed atmo-sphere of Farfield for more individual attention from staff and less formal classroom settings:

[at Farfield] the teachers come and help you sometimes with your work here; you don't have to do your work straight away; you can have a talk; you can carry on with your work.

The views expressed above are shared by the majority of pupils in both schools, who, in answer to a questionnaire based on the interview data, agreed with the following statements (number of respondents: 57)

This school is better than an ordinary primary school.
> (72 per cent of respondents agreed [N = 57])

This school is better than an ordinary comprehensive school.
> (74 per cent agreed)

This school is better than a day special school.
> (74 per cent agreed)

Most of the pupils at this school are happier here than they were at other schools.
> (70 per cent agreed)

Pupils here like this school because the staff here are more friendly than the staff in ordinary day schools.
> (86 per cent agreed)

Pupils here like this school because the teachers here give them more help with their schoolwork than teachers in ordinary schools.
> (86 per cent agreed)

Pupils here like this school because the staff here listen to pupils when pupils want to talk to them.
> (89 per cent agreed)

The staff here help pupils if they have a personal problem.
> (74 per cent agreed)

The staff here give pupils more personal attention than staff in ordinary schools.
> (88 per cent agreed)

The staff here are more understanding than staff in ordinary schools.
> (91 per cent agreed)

It is surprising, perhaps, that very few of the boys express the resentment indicated by Frank's dismissal of 'stuck-up' teachers in comprehensive schools. Whilst recognising the deficiencies of their mainstream schools and the failure of their teachers to meet their personal and emotional needs, these boys also tend to express a sense of acceptance, as if they accept the fact that schools are normally not places where one would expect one's needs of this kind to be met. Tom, for instance, recognises that teachers are constrained by the limitations of the thirty-five-minute lesson, and defends what he describes as the uncaring attitude of teachers when he says:

> In my old school there was about as much kids in every class as in this [whole] school, and there's six classes in each year and five years. They hadn't got time to listen to you.

It could be argued, however, that Tom's defence of his former teachers is generous, especially when we consider that the failure of staff to listen to his point of view is seen by him as a major factor contributing to his expulsion and referral to a special school:

> I was always messing around in my old school. Like in lessons. I'd just start playing around and that in lessons. They was trying to make out that I was worse than I was. Half the time, I was just shouting things out; talking, standing up, things like that. Just walking around like. They'd tell you to get out for a little reason, and I'd say, 'I ain't getting out!' And there'd start an argument. And then there starts a fight, with me and a member of staff. . . . Them just dragging me out. They was trying to make out I was worse than I was.

There is a clear sense of injustice in Tom's account. Whilst he does not dispute that he was guilty of misbehaving in class, he feels that staff over-reacted to his behaviour. In effect the more extreme behaviour, that takes the form of his open defiance and physical resistance to staff, is a reaction to the injustice of staff behaviour towards him. This would seem to fall into the category of what Rosser and Harré (1976) call 'reciprocity' (see Chapter 2), and, as such, points to the way in which teachers' control strategies can sometimes exacerbate rather than alleviate problem situations.

Jock (Lakeside) tells of an experience in his former comprehensive school, similar to that of Tom, where he claims he was 'thought of as a bully'. He accounts for his classroom behaviour in the following way:

I used to get bored in class, so I'd throw things.

Jock states his agreement with an educational psychologist who he claims suggested that Jock was placed in classes where the level of work was too far below his level of ability to maintain his concentration. This indicates, again, a boy's perception that a mainstream school failed to meet his educational and personal needs.

It seems that both Jock and Tom are victims of communication problems. They both meet situations in school which they experience as intolerable and respond in ways which their teachers, in turn, find intolerable. In these circumstances both the teachers and pupils are guilty of responding, to what they perceive as problem situations, without knowledge of the way in which their response might be perceived by the other party. It is as if, in these situations, the teachers and pupils are conversing in two different languages: the problem is that teacher and pupil are both monolingual.

The potentially grave consequences of this failure of understanding are demonstrated most strikingly in an incident reported by John, who is 15 years old and has been at Farfield for 13 months. The situation described by John is significant at least because it ends in the nightmare scenario of physical assault on a teacher by a pupil. It is important, however, to consider this event in the context of its occurrence, and to recognise the many contributory factors which might have been usefully considered and dealt with in order to avoid the assault. The situation occurred whilst John was a pupil at a day school for pupils with behaviour problems in his home town. John describes the situation in the following exchange between himself and the author:

PC: Why did you get chucked out?
John: I think I threw a chair at one of the staff, because they got
       me really annoyed. They kept phoning up my mum and
       winding her up, so I threw a chair at them.

Immediately it is clear that John sees this act to be wrong but, according to his own view, justified. He goes on:

> [They kept] phoning up and telling her [John's mother] that, 'John has just run out of school,' and, er, 'just run across the main road.' . . . And that really wound her up.

PC: Was it true?
John: Yes.

. . .

PC: Why did you want to run out in the first place? . . .
John: I just had enough of school: all the bullies there.
PC: What. The kids?
John: Yes.

. . .

PC: What did you do when you got bullied?
John: I used to run out of school and phone my mum. . . . She
        used to come up and really really shout at them [the
        teachers].

. . .

PC: What did they do?
John: Nothing. Well, they couldn't do nothing, could they? . . .
        'Cos there was this big kid there and if I'd gone to tell
        'em, all they say is, 'don't do it again.'
PC: Did you ever tell them that this kid was bullying you?
John: No, or else they'd do it again.
PC: So you were frightened, in case you got bullied more?
John: Yes.

On the face of it, John's behaviour seems difficult to justify,
because he has assaulted a teacher who has merely done his duty
in response to John's obvious misbehaviour. However, when we
look at the situation through John's eyes, and take into account
family circumstances, we find fault with any interpretation which
simply seeks to blame John for the situation. For John, each step
he takes in this apparently irrational chain of events is necessary.
Firstly, we have to consider what he tells us of his family situation.
He lives at home with his unemployed teenage brother and his
single-parent mother. He repeatedly describes the habitually
strained atmosphere which prevails in this setting: he and his
brother bicker constantly and this in turn produces angry outbursts from the mother. Added to this is the fact that the mother
works at nights in 'a club', and consequently sleeps much of the
day at home. John mentions this fact repeatedly, and it is his
mother's unsociable working hours which he believes makes her
bad-tempered and intolerant of her sons' arguing and fighting. In
fact, John sums up family life with the phrase: 'We're always getting
on at each other and arguing.' It seems also that the only times

when John's mother's anger is not directed at him is when those occasions arise when she is forced to go to the school and shout at the staff on John's behalf. The evidence would seem to point to the fact that John uses these situations for the very purpose of securing his mother's advocacy. This is suggested by the fact that he does not approach the teachers about the bullying problem, and by the fact that on occasions prior to the assault incident it was John who telephoned his mother to tell her of his situation. What is different about the occasion on which the assault occurs, however, is that John's *modus operandi* has changed. He does not intend to telephone his mother this time, because she has made it plain to him in the past that she is annoyed at being woken in the daytime. This time John intends to go home and tell her, in person, of what has happened, *after* she has woken up. In this way, it can be surmised, John intends to maximise the benefits he derives from the situation, in terms of what he sees as positive attention from his mother, whilst minimising the cost, in terms of his mother's anger. From John's viewpoint the teacher spoils this plan, and, by telephoning his mother, creates even greater problems for John by causing difficulties in his all-important relationship with his mother.

This essentially systemic interpretation of John's situation (see Chapter 3), enables us to see the logic of and rationale behind John's behaviour. It derives from simply listening to John and trying to understand the way he sees things. One thing became clear very early on in conversation with John, and that was the intense importance he attaches to his relationship with his mother. In fact, he sees his placement in the residential school chiefly as a means of providing relief for his overworked and over-stressed mother. An appreciation of the nature of the parent–child relationship, in this instance, might well have led the teacher to take a different course of action when John absconded, or, better still, could have given rise to a preventive approach which sought to stage situations in which John's mother had cause to give John positive attention, such as through sending reports of John's positive behaviour in school, or inviting the mother to discuss John's problems before they reached crisis point.

Of course, it is easy to identify deficiencies and omissions in teachers' handling of difficult children in stressful situations, when one has the privilege of hindsight. It is equally easy, however, to forget the intense vulnerability of a boy like John, when one is on the receiving end of the difficult behaviour that is associated with this vulnerability. John can be seen as a boy desperately fighting for a sign of his mother's care and attention. His mother, on the other hand, is single-handedly struggling to cope with the basic business of providing for a family. What people like John desperately need is for their cries for help to be listened to, before they explode in the kind of situation described here. This is not to say that the likes of John be given their own way; that would clearly be foolish. It is, however, only by listening to a boy like John's perceptions of a situation that we can begin to understand something of the nature of a problem and so work towards a workable solution. The teacher's solution in this case was certainly not workable, and this fact has to be taken in the context of John's statement that the teachers 'don't listen to you'; a sentiment echoed by many of these boys.

John, like most of the boys, shows little sign of resentment toward the staff of his former school; he says he 'liked a few of them', and he believes that some of them liked him. As has been already noted, there is a sense in which these boys seem to accept the impersonal treatment and distressing situations they have encountered in schools, as if these things were intrinsic to the whole business of schooling. This is shown vividly by Stan, who is 15 and has been at Lakeside for seventeen months. Stan, like several of the other boys, was an habitual truant from the comprehensive school he attended before being referred to Lakeside:

> I just couldn't get there [the comprehensive school], for some reason. I just couldn't face it. . . . I used to get bullied a bit, but not much – just average. I don't know why it was. My sister was the same . . . she's 20 this month. . . . The staff at the school were alright. It wasn't the school's fault, it was me! . . . I think I must have changed quite a bit. . . . I'm not bothered about going to class now.

Stan is certainly an undemanding consumer when it comes to schooling. He is prepared to accept an 'average' amount of bullying, and is happy that the staff are 'alright'. It still remains, however, that he simply 'couldn't face it'. Others describe their inability to 'fit into normal schools' (e.g. Tim, 16, Lakeside), or like Ryan (Farfield) they express the belief that they were simply 'bad' to their teachers. And yet, all of these boys have now found schools which they *can* bear to face, where they can 'fit in' and where their 'badness' is no longer evident. This poses important questions about the experiences these boys have in the residential school and the differences between their present schools and institutions they have formerly attended. This is the subject of the following chapter. What should be clear from this chapter, so far, is that these boys indicate many deficiencies in the schools they have attended prior to arriving at Lakeside and Farfield, particularly in terms of their interpersonal and social relations with staff.

PUPILS AND THEIR PEERS

Before moving onto the residential experience of the boys in this study, it is important to consider the third area of social experience which was discussed in the introductory chapters and which emerged as an important category in the interviews; namely the boys' experiences in their home-based peer groups. As was noted earlier, the peer group can often become a haven for alienated young people whose emotional and esteem needs are not being met at home and in school. Delinquency and other forms of deviant behaviour can become central to the activities of such peer groups, offering a vehicle whereby group solidarity and individual status can be achieved, as well as a form of resistance to the forces of alienation.

Delinquency with peers has featured in the lives of many of the boys of Lakeside and Farfield. When they talk about their experiences of delinquency, however, they rarely speak in terms of resistance or group solidarity. Delinquency is more often seen in terms of pathology. Jock (Lakeside) puts it simply:

> If I had been at home, and hadn't come here, I'd probably be in the same place where our brother is at the moment [prison]. . . . I used to nick things. Now I haven't got the bottle to nick. It's made me soft, but I respect that.

The price of 'softness' for Jock is, however, the loss of his former friends in his home area:

> There's no one to talk to. Nothing to do all day. I just stay in the house and watch the telly.

Ryan's (Farfield) comments on the influence of peers on his own delinquent career:

> If I was at home now I'd probably be inside or something . . . I'd have a record. . . . I know there's a bunch of kids – some old

mates – who if I hang around with, I'll get nicked. Or I'll do a
job, get away with it, then get nicked. But I don't hang around
with them no more, because I know it will bodge up my life. . . .
Before I wouldn't have really thought of it.

Alex, also of Farfield, tells a similar story. Though Alex, rather than
being led describes himself as a 'sort of leader' of a group of
delinquent youths. He claims that the local police were fully aware
of his criminal activities and that they wanted 'to get rid of me'. For
Alex, the residential school was a favourable alternative to some
form of detention.

Although these boys do not themselves make causative links
between their family/school situations and their membership of
delinquescent peer groups, it is clear that for them these factors
are related. Jock describes his delinquency in the context of his
family's criminality, in the form of his brother's stealing and of his
father's receiving stolen goods. For Jock these factors pollute the
atmosphere in his home, and make him glad of the respite Lakeside permits him from this. Ryan, on the other hand, sees his
delinquency as an expression of his almost total 'badness':

I've been bad. A trouble-maker at school, bad to my mum. You
know, about every bad thing.

Alex, in a similar vein, sees his family problems and delinquency as
symptoms of his personal confusion:

I weren't bothered about what I done, probably 'cos I was mixed
up . . .

Furthermore, there is a common belief that when any one of these
problems is overcome there tends to be an improvement in other
areas of difficulty. Thus Alex describes his greater willingness to
reflect on his behaviour and actions, both at home and when he is
in the company of his peers, which he has developed since being
at Farfield. Jock describes the decline in his delinquent tendencies
and his greater interest in schoolwork. Ryan is more guarded
about the improvements he has made, but believes them to be
general. He believes that the fact he now spends large amounts of
time away from home has the effect of reducing his opportunities
for mixing with peers who might have a negative influence on his
behaviour, and also allows periods of cooling-off and recovery in
his stormy relationship with his mother.

Another aspect of peer-group influence relates to acts of disruption in the classrooms of schools these boys have formerly attended. A common theme here is the pupil as clown: performing acts of disruption for the delight of peers. Boys who spoke of this were often bitter. Ian (Farfield) states that he had 'no real friends, at home'. He was merely used and led on by other boys at school to commit disruptive acts. Jim (Farfield) describes an identical experience, and claims that the children who led him into trouble at school also persuaded him to attempt to steal from his parents' shop. Tom (Lakeside) describes the ways in which his acts of defiance towards the teachers at his former comprehensive school were a source of delight to his classmates, who 'were always laughing, and getting me to go on and do worse things'.

A factor which is sometimes linked with this clowning behaviour is low educational achievement. Greg, Les and Mick from Farfield all describe frustration and humiliation in the face of mockery by their peers for poor educational progress. They also, however, speak of antics which created laughter at their teachers' expense. Greg claims:

> They [his classmates] used to dare me to do things. Like shout things out. I did. . . . I didn't care. It was a laugh! We used to have a good laugh. . . . I used to get told off. I didn't care. It was just having a laugh.

In these circumstances, the disruptive behaviour can be seen as an attempt to mitigate the humiliation of low achievement and to obtain recognition from peers in an alternative way.

A third distinctive form of peer-related deviance, which is less commonly referred to by these boys than delinquency and 'clowning', is withdrawal. This takes the form of separation and isolation from the peer group. This takes different forms. We have already noted how Stan (Lakeside) admits to truanting from his comprehensive school. Whilst Stan claims to have no explanation as to why he felt unable to attend school, he admits to having been been bullied to an 'average' degree by his fellow pupils. Alan (Farfield), however, directly attributes his truancy and disruption to bullying by peers in his former schools. Whilst Stan withdrew from a potentially unpleasant situation, Alan's reaction was to absorb the bullying until he felt he could stand no more. This resulted in outbursts of extreme anger and led on one occasion to assault on a teacher. Brian, another Farfield boy, shares in common with Alan a history of being victimised at his former schools. Brian has attended schools for children with learning difficulties for most of his school career, but claims that each placement has broken down because he has been the victim of bullying. In Brian's case withdrawal was not felt by him to be an option, owing to the fact that he was escorted to and from school by a parent. Brian's method of coping was to seek out children who were much younger than himself as playmates. This was observed to be the case at Farfield also, where he named children of age 10 and 11 as his friends, whilst he was 15. In Brian's case, this habit of mixing with much younger children led to difficulties when he was accused, according to Brian unfairly, of a sexual offence against a much younger girl at his former school. The repercussions of this were such that he was forced to leave the school and his home area, where he claims he was victimised by neighbours and local children. He now claims that he has no friends in his home area.

CONCLUSION

This chapter has attempted to show something of the background influences which the boys of Farfield and Lakeside carry with them. It has been shown that, for the most part, the boys arrived at these two schools with particularly negative experiences of schooling (both in mainstream and special sectors), and often with accompanying family and peer-group difficulties. The common theme throughout the boys' perceptions is their repeated failure to enjoy positive and enriching relationships with important adults in their lives (i.e. chiefly parents and teachers). In some cases this problem is heightened by delinquescent and deviant peer-group associations. In nearly all cases, these difficulties are expressed, partly at least, in terms of disaffection from school, by way of disruptive behaviour or withdrawal from the school setting. Many of these boys express a sense of their personal failure to 'fit in' to their schools, or to 'get on' with their families. In contrast they are often surprisingly undemanding of their former institutions. We sense that they locate the deficiencies which have led to their deviance in their own behaviour, rather than in external factors. In the following chapter the focus is shifted to an examination of the boys' perceptions of the residential experience and its effects. Having already established that these boys are often victims of frustration in their emotional, social and educational experience prior to arriving at these two schools, we must now consider the bearing that the residential milieu has on this. The central question is: to what extent, if any, do these residential schools succeed where other schools have failed?

Chapter 5

The residential experience I:
School life

In this and the following chapter we look at the experience of being a pupil in a residential school through the eyes of the boys of Farfield and Lakeside schools. In spite of the relatively long history of this form of provision there is a dearth of research material on this topic. A lack of information about this subject has not, however, hindered the development of generally negative image for the residential sector of special education. In fairness, it should be stated that much educational opinion on the undesirability of residential provision is based upon the well-founded arguments of integrationists (e.g. Galloway, 1985a; Galloway and Goodwin, 1987), whose aim is to identify the measures which mainstream schools can take to prevent and mitigate pupils' educational difficulties. Other educational writers, such as Topping (1983), are more direct in their condemnation of residential schooling for children with behaviour problems, seeing it as a form of provision which is prohibitively expensive and of dubious effectiveness. Topping's conclusions are based on what he admits to be scant evidence, but the opinion stands. A possible reason why such ill-founded opinions tend to survive unchallenged is the strong anti-residential lobby in the wider field of social research. This view is supported by reference to a recent paper purporting to deal with 'issues and developments' in residential schools (Millham, 1987), which draws almost entirely on literature on residential institutions for delinquent children and children in local authority care. Before we can look in detail at the perceptions of residential schooling presented by the boys of Lakeside and Farfield it is necessary to take some account of the issues raised in this range of literature, since it has an important bearing on the way residential schools are perceived by those outside the residential education sector.

IMAGES OF RESIDENTIAL CARE

Popular images of residential institutions for the deprived, disturbed or deviant are often highly negative. This negative view owes much to Goffman's (1961) seminal study of 'total institutions'. Goffman introduced the term 'institutionalisation' into the popular vocabulary. Goffman demonstrates vividly the ways in which institutions, such as long-stay hospitals and prisons, strip away the personal identity of inmates and dehumanise them. He shows how these effects can be related to an institutional culture dominated by the drive for a pseudo-technological efficiency. In this culture the main goal of the institution is its own maintenance as a uniform and predictable organisation. To this end inmates are defined as objects to be controlled and processed; their personal human needs are always secondary to those of the institution.

Shearer (1980) delineates the institutionalising effects of residential care on children. She documents over forty years of public concern with the standards of residential care for handicapped children in our society, and the failure of successive governments to produce effective legislation to remedy this situation.

Research carried out in residential institutions for young people has often reinforced the view that residential institutions are, *per se*, dehumanising and socially debilitating. Tizard *et al.* (1975) and Oswin (1978), in studies of handicapped children in residential care (schools and hospitals), present an image of residential care which emphasises the failure of these institutions to provide the primary experiences on which children depend for healthy social and emotional development. Oswin's (1978) research focuses specifically on the plight of children in long-stay hospitals, and concludes that such institutions are often understaffed, inadequately resourced, with poor standards of hygiene and physical care. These child patients are socially isolated from their non-hospitalised peers, and what limited contact they have with staff is restricted to brief periods of 'body servicing' (washing, feeding, toileting, etc.). The residential experience for the children in Oswin's study amounts to one of multiple deprivation, in social, emotional and physical terms.

Ryan and Thomas (1980), in their study of hospitals for the mentally handicapped, produce findings similar to those of Shearer and Oswin, and stress the social control function of such institutions. They see these institutions as serving a custodial purpose in a society which chooses to disqualify certain people from participation in community life, family life, work and education on the grounds that they are potentially disruptive and difficult to control. This view gains some support from studies which have been carried out into secure residential facilities for juvenile offenders (Millham *et al.*, 1978; Cawson and Martell, 1979).

These negative views of residential treatment have been influential in the general decline in the popularity of residential facilities. In recent years there has also been a raising of the public profile of residential care as the result of a number of highly publicised court cases, involving allegations of the physical and sexual abuse of juvenile residents by staff in the institutions. In 1990 the principal of a non-maintained residential school for boys with emotional and behavioural difficulties received a twelve-year prison sentence, after being found guilty of sexually abusing eight boys who were pupils at his school over a period of several years. In another case the head of a local authority-run children's home was found guilty of sexual and physical abuse against some of the children in his care, over a period of many years. A third case brought to light the 'unlawful, humiliating and degrading' control system employed throughout one local authority, whereby residents who were judged to have exhibited serious behavioural problems and who absconded, were effectively imprisoned, deprived of adequate clothing, and at times physically abused.

These cases have drawn attention to disastrous shortcomings in the monitoring procedures of maintained and non-maintained residential facilities for young people. These shocking examples of unprofessional and inhumane practice have largely gone unnoticed in the past as a result of the lack of adequate inspection procedures, and the neglect of the residents' rights. Measures contained in the 1989 Children Act are intended to remedy some of these shortcomings, by imposing duties on social service departments to carry out regular inspections of non-maintained boarding schools, demanding the careful monitoring of pupils' educational progress in such institutions, and establishing the rights of children in care and their parents access to official records and involvement in the decision-making processes.

These measures are long overdue, and are to be welcomed wholeheartedly. It is important, however, that whilst we must deplore the abuses that have been perpetrated against members of this vulnerable client-group, we do not allow these sensational

cases to cast a shadow over those residential institutions, maintained and non-maintained, which are effective in meeting the
needs of their residents in a humane and caring way. There is, in
the literature on residential treatment, a discernible strand of
opinion which points to the possible benefits to clients of certain
forms of this type of provision, and in some cases this points to the
superiority of this to other available forms of treatment. Millham *et
al.* (1975), in their study of approved schools, were able to differen-
tiate between those schools which adopted repressive and authoritarian regimes, and those which adopted more progressive, therapeutic approaches. They showed that the latter institutions tended
to be associated with lower rates of recidivism. Dunlop (1974)
found that out of 470 boys who attended approved schools, re-
conviction rates were lowest among subjects who had attended
schools which were of a more progressive type, and that placed an
emphasis on trade-training and good quality staff–inmate relationships in their programmes. One of the most detailed accounts of a
therapeutic approach to the treatment of severely disturbed teen-
agers is provided by Hoghughi (1978), who is the director of
Aycliffe School. A cornerstone of the treatment programme described by Hoghughi is a recognition of the pattern of social and
emotional deprivation which often characterises the backgrounds
of the clients of Aycliffe. This leads to a stress being placed on the
creation of a supportive, caring and accepting environment,
highly reminiscent of that described by Bettelheim (see Part I
above), in which the inmates of Aycliffe gradually come to terms
with their own motivations and develop self-knowledge and self-
control. This represents what Miller and Gwynne (1972) describe
as a 'horticultural' approach to residential treatment, which
focuses on the personal growth and enrichment of the inmate,
rather than the 'warehousing' approach epitomised by those
institutions which emphasise the control and containment of
inmates over their care and development.

This move toward a more positive image of residential provision
for people of all ages has been most clearly marked by the publication of the Wagner Report (NISW, 1988). Subtitled 'A Positive
Choice', the Wagner Report attempts to provide a counterweight
to the single-minded pursuit of the replacement of all residential
services with community-based alternatives. The report argues for
residential care to be seen as an important element in the con-
tinuum of total care which should be made available for those who

need it. It is argued that good quality residential care provides a necessary resource for certain groups at times when community provision is inappropriate. One such group identified by the Wagner committee is children. It is argued that residential care can offer facilities which community settings may have difficulty in providing, these include:

- short-term respite care for children of distressed families;
- a stable and caring environment in which a child's needs can be assessed and met in preparation for permanent placement elsewhere;
- the chance for siblings to be kept together when taken into care;
- care, control and therapeutic provision in planned settings.

The central message of the Wagner Report is that residential care, when used in a responsible way and matched to client needs, can operate alongside community provision to cover a wider range of client needs than community care can alone cope with. The report attempts to highlight the positive face of residential care to referral agencies, and to suggest to them more effective ways of utilising this form of provision.

The writers of the Wagner Report share the view expressed by numerous commentators (Davis, 1981; Cole, 1986; Potter, 1986; Ballard, 1987) that residential care for children, when used judiciously, can help to avoid some of the worst consequences of fostering. For whilst the foster family can sometimes be seen as a threat to the natural family, and place confusing demands and loyalties onto a child, the residential home or school can be more easily seen as a helpful alternative or supplement to the natural family. The residential setting is not attempting to substitute the parents of the child, but rather to offer a new range of experiences which, with the cooperation of the child and family, can help to enhance the quality of family relationships.

The subject of residential care raises many complex issues. There can be little doubt that residential provision can, in particular circumstances, have highly negative consequences for its clients; on the other hand it can offer an enriching and healing experience to people in distress. As was shown in Part I of this book, the pioneers of residential schooling for children with behaviour problems were convinced of the positive benefits to be gained from the residential experience. It is also clear, however, that the general drift of modern policy and practice, in the educational and child-care services, is to take a negative view of residential care and to see it as only a last resort. This is, therefore, an opportune moment to turn to the consumer, and to find out just what it is like to be a pupil in a residential school for children with emotional and behavioural difficulties in the late twentieth century.

LIFE IN A RESIDENTIAL SCHOOL

The typical consumer of residential schooling for pupils with behavioural problems is a white boy (making up 92 per cent of the total population), though Afro-Caribbean boys are massively over-represented here, making up 5 per cent of the total population, compared with their level of representation in the general population, where they make up approximately 1 per cent of this age group (Cooper et al., 1991). Furthermore, pupils, once placed in these schools, have a less than even chance of returning to a mainstream school (Cooper et al., 1991), and are likely to experience a curriculum lacking in breadth and balance (Cooper et al., 1990; DES, 1989b).

First impressions

Many of the boys interviewed arrived at their respective schools with little or no knowledge of what to expect. For some, the first they knew of their placement in a residential school was their arrival. Alan describes his feelings on arriving at Farfield thus:

> Well, it did annoy me a bit, because they didn't ask me first. Or they didn't tell me where I was going. I didn't even know where I was going. All I knew was I was going in the country somewhere.
>
> . . .
>
> One day, my old key worker at Spenser House [previous placement] . . . turned up. I said, 'Right, where am I going?' She goes, 'Oh, don't worry about that, just get your watch and clothes ready for tomorrow. Make sure nothing's broken. Get your clothes in a bag.' I didn't know where I was going. . . . I don't normally wear a watch when I go out normally, but she said put my watch on then. So since then I've always kept my watch on, except for night.

Greg, another Farfield boy, tells a similar story:

> I didn't know I was coming to Farfield on the same day. . . . It
> gave me a bit of a shock really. They goes, 'It's quite a few miles
> out.' I goes, 'Where's that?' I didn't know where it was at first,
> when Joe [present 'key worker', i.e. residential social worker
> with special responsibility for Greg] brought me. . . . I thought
> it would be one of those lock-up places.

Colin's move to Farfield was equally abrupt and unexpected:

> One Monday I got up, and as I was lined up for school, Uncle
> Fred [a residential social worker at Colin's former school]
> came over – he was brilliant – he goes, 'Er, Colin, come with
> me.' I says, 'OK. Am I going to the dentist or something?' He
> goes, 'No, I've got a surprise for you!' 'A surprise!' I says. He gets
> in where the head's office is – it's outside, and it smells of
> beautiful brewed coffee. I can't figure it out like. Anyway, it goes
> on. I keep mouthing, 'What's going on? Go on, tell us!' 'Alright
> then. Your dad's coming down.' 'God! Is that all! My dad's
> coming down to see me!' 'No, it's a surprise.' Anyway, my dad
> comes down with this lady in a Citroën. They goes, 'Come on,
> we're going out!' I goes, 'Brill! Where?' 'We're going to visit a
> new school.' I goes, 'Are you trying to be funny? I've been at this
> school for five years and you want to move me for my last year!'
> PC: Who was the person in the Citroën?
> Colin: I don't know. Some social worker from [home town].
> PC: Your social worker?
> Colin: I don't know. Just the school social worker who moves
>   people.

Lakeside boys describe slightly different experiences, in that a
common prelude to placement is an introductory visit. However,
as might be expected, many of the boys face their new schools with
trepidation and uncertainty. Approximately a third of the boys
from both schools claim actively to have chosen to take up placements at the two schools, with an equal proportion of boys from
Farfield claiming to have either chosen not to take up places or not
to have been consulted. Only one Lakeside boy claims that he did
not agree to or choose his placement. They often accept their new
situations with reluctance, believing that they have no real choice
in the matter. For some boys pressure to take up a place comes
from their parents, as in the case of Ryan, John (Farfield) and

Arthur (Lakeside), all of whom speak about the importance of giving their over-stressed single-parent mothers a break from looking after them, and the conflicts that have occurred between them and their siblings. We find other boys, such as Jock, Frank (Lakeside), Greg and Alex (Farfield), believing that accepting a place in a residential boarding school was their only alternative to being placed in a custodial institution. Boys who claim to have chosen their placement for positive reasons all had the benefit of an early visit to their schools. These boys cite a range of reasons for being impressed with the schools. Boys from both schools describe their feelings of relief and pleasure at seeing groups of boys apparently enjoying themselves in a relaxed atmosphere: enjoying recreational activities, or doing jobs of one kind and another. Tom (Lakeside) says:

> I thought it [Lakeside] was good. It looked like a good place. A good atmosphere . . ., the kids were happy.

Ryan (Farfield) describes sensing a similar atmosphere on his first visit to Farfield:

> when I first looked round . . . I thought it was a great place. . . . I thought it was really homely, 'cos when I saw Jane and all that lot [seamstresses and other domestic staff] doing their sewing and that. And they all said, 'Hello.' None of the kids stared me out or nothing, when I come here. They all seemed alright. And the bedrooms: they seemed like actual kids' bedrooms, and not just plain walls.

Other initially attractive features of both schools are described in terms of the promise of recreational activities and privileges, such as holidays and excursions, cinema visits and opportunities to pursue hobbies. At Farfield the following important features are described by pupils as appealing: the 'games room' at Farfield, with its two pool tables and a table-tennis table, the swimming pool in its all-weather housing, the gymnasium and the two pupil ('junior' and 'senior') common rooms with their colour TVs and comfortable seating. At Lakeside, particular attractions are: the 'club hut', with its pool table, dartboard and table-tennis table, and general atmosphere of belonging to the boys owing to its decor, the 'craft hut', with its home-made canoes and evidence of other artefacts manufactured by the boys, and the extensive parklands attached to the school.

Of course, not all initial reactions are favourable. Arthur recalls his first day at Lakeside with disgust:

> When I first come here I couldn't stand it! I came up the front drive, put my bags in the sewing room, went to my bedroom, got changed. The next minute I had to do work and everything! Sweeping! Jobs!

Arthur admits, however, that his attitude has since changed. He now recognises the central importance of this kind of work at Lakeside:

> Then I just got used to it. And it's worth it. . . . It just comes natural. So that when I leave school you just think, 'Oh, work – it's just natural!'

He now concludes that Lakeside is 'just a great place to live!'

Stan (from Lakeside), and Alex (from Farfield), are two other interviewees who describe adverse initial reactions to their schools. For both boys referral to a residential school involved their first experience of being away from home. Alex's anger and distress at discovering that he would not be leaving the school on the day of his first visit is clearly compounded by his sense of having been deceived by his mother and social workers. For Alex, the recreational attractions of the school were no compensation for his being deprived of his home life. Stan's experience, on the other hand, was related to what he sees now as his generally phobic reaction to schools. He believes the main reason for his referral to have been his chronic non-attendance at his comprehensive school. It is not surprising, therefore, that he was highly averse to the idea of living on the premises of a school. Whereas Alex reacted with violent outbursts of anger and swearing at the principal of Farfield, Stan's resistance was passive and silent. Stan remained rooted to the spot at the foot of the drive to Lakeside with his bag at his side. Both boys describe the sensitive and caring response of staff to their reactions. Alex admits to 'over the top' behaviour, and admires the restraint shown by the staff and particularly the principal in allowing him to work these feelings out of his system. Stan describes the patience and fortitude of a member of the child-care staff who stayed with him, 'for hours', at the foot of the drive, simply talking with him until he decided that he was ready to go into the school grounds. For both Stan and Alex these early experiences of conflict and the sympathetic responses of staff are important landmarks in their development. Both use these incidents to illustrate the caring and supportive attitudes of the schools' staff. As will be seen, it is these staff qualities which are highly prized by the majority of boys in both schools and seen as being central to the positive outcomes achieved by the schools.

The quality of staff care is echoed in remarks made about the ways in which the boys greet new arrivals. At Farfield, Ryan describes how his initial apprehensions about the boys were dispelled on his first day, when, to his surprise, other boys did not seek to 'stare him out', as his experience of comprehensive schools had led him to expect. Similarly, Malcolm (Farfield) describes how, on his first day, he found boys with whom he could 'laugh and joke'. At Lakeside, Jock gives a vivid impression of his first days at the school. Like many other boys, Jock entered the school with feelings of fear and trepidation. Jock describes the 'system' by which he was 'adopted', in his early days at the school, by an older boy. According to Jock, it was his senior boy's responsibility to guide him through his first few months at Lakeside. This system, however, was strictly a matter for the boys:

> this was between the boys only. They had a system. It weren't a staff idea. They didn't know nothing about it.

According to Jock, the older boys were responsible for showing their charges:

> what things you can't do and what things you can do. He'd help you out of trouble.

Jock is adamant that the older boys 'weren't bullies, they looked after them [i.e. the younger boys].' To support his point, Jock tells the following story:

> We [11-year-old Jock and another new boy] were messing around in a room and running through the house. And Dave Turner – one of the bigger lads here – stopped us and said: 'You're gonna get told off and get a job, if you don't stop.' As I walked away, the deputy head walked around the corner! So that sort of thing. They stopped you before they [i.e. the staff] got to you.

In both schools we find examples of this kind of support and care from older boys.

Being away from home

Goffman (1961) demonstrates the importance of deprivation in the lives of inmates of prisons, long-stay hospitals and other such 'total institutions'. He argues that total institutions socialise their inmates into accepting as normal the absence of rights and activities that would be taken for granted in the outside world. At one level such deprivations take the form of simple prohibitions and routines which govern aspects of inmates' lives, such as times for eating and sleeping, the clothing worn by inmates, the food eaten, and access to personal possessions. At another level, the institution makes decisions for inmates that in the outside world would be seen to represent a breach of the individual's civil liberties. These include restrictions on individuals' rights of movement inside and outside the institution, opportunities to meet and communicate with persons outside the institution, and the use of institutional control over such matters as a 'privilege system' which requires inmates to 'earn' that which would be considered a right in the outside world. These influences, argues Goffman, can lead to the stripping away of the inmate's sense of personal autonomy and social competence.

At both Lakeside and Farfield the boys provide descriptions of experiences which could be termed 'deprivations' in the sense intended by Goffman. As was shown in the previous section, the sequence of events leading up to a pupil's arrival at Farfield was often notable for its callous disregard for the boy's feelings in the matter. Whatever measures, if any, that were taken to prepare the boys for their new school were clearly inadequate. The boys often seem to have been relegated to the status of an object to be shipped from one location to another. Whilst this was not the same for most Lakeside boys, there is clearly a sense of pupils not always being aware of the nature of the commitment they may have made to the school, and the realisation that the right to withdraw from the school is not available to them.

Homesickness is a common feature of many pupils' early recollections of their life at residential school. Jim describes his earliest feelings in terms of the conflict he felt between the attractions of Farfield and his feelings of fear and loneliness:

PC: What did you think of the place when you first saw it?
Jim: Big . . . there was a lot to do. . . . I thought it was going to be a bad place. When he [Mr Talbot, the principal at

Farfield] says, 'You go to Butlins and Spain [annual school holidays],' it made me think again. . . . When it was the day for me to come here, I got a shock a bit. . . . I was scared. . . . I didn't know how I'd get on with kids I'd never met before.

PC: How did you feel about being away from home?

Jim: I cried a bit. I was upset.

PC: How long did it take to get over that?

Jim: Until I went home really. When I went home and came back and went home. I was just getting less crying and that. I just get used to it now.

Feelings of homesickness commonly diminish after a matter of weeks. Pupils in both schools refer to the way in which induction into each school community is managed gradually. So that, at Farfield, it is common for new pupils to spend their first week, and sometimes more, free of lessons, in and around the house, in the company of residential social workers and ancillary staff during school time. At Lakeside, boys are sometimes placed on a reduced timetable during their first few days. As Stan says:

It's good [having a period of induction] because you get time to settle in. You get used to the unit and that. Then you can start school, when you've settled in your unit. You don't have to get used to everything all at once.

Lewis (Farfield) describes a whole complex of difficulties which he had to overcome in his early days at the school, all owing to the differences between his home life and the life in a residential establishment:

PC: Can you tell me how you felt when you first came here?

Lewis: Well, I suppose I felt like a lot of other kids. When you're first away from home, it's not exactly the best place to be. . . . I hadn't been away from home before, so it made it hard for me. I felt caged-in; as if I did anything wrong I'd get done for it.

PC: Why was that, do you think?

Lewis: I dunno. I just weren't used to a place with so many kids there. And sleeping with kids you don't know – that don't exactly feel right to me. . . . I think you should really have a room of your own, until you get used to knowing the kids; what they are like and who they are, if you know what I mean. So that is one thing that I didn't like about it. But after a while I got used to it. I didn't like having to shower with kids that I'd never known, and that felt bad towards me. . . . It was so far away from home an' all. The only way you could talk to someone was on the 'phone. And when I did that it made me feel worse anyway. . . . I felt weird with the town and that.

PC: Why was that then?

Lewis: Just all different. And that I was the only coloured person in the town. And it made me feel the odd one out.

PC: Yes, the town's a lot different from where you come from. How did you feel about that?

Lewis: It was dead. I wondered where everyone was, because there was only a few people walking down the street.

Lewis shows how the alien nature of the residential school environment is brought home to a sensitive adolescent in so many aspects of everyday institutional life. He is adrift in an alien landscape: a quiet rural town, jokingly referred to as 'Toytown' by many Farfield boys, who, like Lewis, come from homes in densely populated urban and inner city areas. Within the school he is subjected to humiliation and claustrophobic communality in having to wash and sleep in the company of other boys. On top of all this, Lewis is aware that he is the only black person in the town.

Lewis seems to encapsulate a whole range of feelings expressed by different boys in both schools. Boys of both schools commonly complain that the quietness of their schools' locations is the most difficult aspect to come to terms with. Whilst homesickness and the problems of communal living often disappear after a few weeks, for pupils in both schools, the silence of the countryside continues to be experienced as alien and oppressive. This underlines the immense task of adjustment to the new environment which faces many of these boys.

The availability of and access to food is also a source of dissatisfaction to some boys. Ryan (Farfield), Tim, Fred and Bill (Lakeside), all complain about the petty restrictions which prevent them from having access to the food in the schools' kitchens. However, there are differences between the two schools in this regard. At Lakeside, the boys have kitchens in their living units, and a limited range of food is kept here, such as breakfast cereal, milk, bread, tea and coffee. Complaints at Lakeside tend to focus on the fact that the main kitchen, where lunchtime and evening meals are prepared, is kept locked, and the unit food is limited in quantity and variety. At Farfield, whilst the boys have no 'official' access to food and drink outside of mealtimes, the 'out of bounds' rule relating to the kitchen is exercised with great flexibility, and since the kitchen is manned throughout the day and much of the evening by domestic staff, the boys often find they are able to obtain snacks and drinks outside of mealtimes at the discretion of these staff.

Being away from home is by no means a negative aspect of residential schooling for all of these boys. A large proportion of pupils from both schools indicate that they value their residential experience for the *respite* it gives them from problems they experience in their home environments. As we saw in the previous chapter, family, local schooling and peer-group experiences are often described in negative terms by the boys, and these experiences are seen as contributing to their adjustment difficulties. For many of the boys at Lakeside and Farfield the residential experience provides them with much needed *respite* from the destructive pressures of home life, as a brief reminder of some of the quotations used in the previous chapter shows:

> Some kids love being at home; I can't stand it! . . . I'm always glad to get back to Lakeside.
>
> [Jock, Lakeside]

> It's [his relationship with his single parent mother] got a lot better, but it's still bad. . . . I think it's got better because we've spent longer times apart. . . . I reckon it's the break.
>
> [Ryan, Farfield]

> The school's helped me change by helping my mum. . . . By [my] coming here, she can have a rest.
>
> [John, Farfield]

> It's helped my mum out. Like when I've been here I've been sorting myself out.
>
> [Ian, Farfield]

The importance of respite from home-based difficulties is further illustrated by responses to a questionnaire which was administered to both school populations in an attempt to test the generalisability of some of the interview findings, which is also reported in

the previous chapter. It will be recalled that the findings of the
questionnaire survey found large majorities of pupils in both
schools agreeing with the following statements:

- one of the good things about being here is that it gives you a
  break from being at home;
- this school is better than an ordinary primary school;
- this school is better than an ordinary comprehensive school;
- this school is better than a day special school;
- most of the pupils at this school are happier than they were at
  other schools;
- pupils here like this school because the staff here are friendlier
  than staff in ordinary day schools;
- pupils here like this school because teachers here give them
  more help with their schoolwork than teachers in ordinary
  schools;
- the staff here are more understanding than staff in ordinary
  schools.

It is clear that although many of the boys experience irritation as a
result of certain deprivations which accompany the residential
experience, they also, for the most part, find the residential setting
a desirable place to be when compared to other possible locations.
This is so to the extent that we can talk of the residential schools as
providing the boys with respite from family and other home-based
difficulties. This is not to say that the deprivations described are
trivial. The unsatisfactory procedure by which some pupils come to
be referred to the residential schools, and the impersonal and
institutionalised aspects of residential life, are important
deficiencies which make pupils' adjustment to an already strange
environment more difficult than it need be. However, the fact that
the boys come to see the residential experience in a positive light,
in spite of these deprivations, leads us to want to probe further into
the quality of their everyday experience as residential school pupils.

EVERYDAY LIFE IN A RESIDENTIAL SCHOOL

As the boys begin to talk in greater detail about their lives in the
residential schools we find that they become more concerned with
their personal situations. It becomes clear that for many boys the
residential experience provides many sources of personal satisfaction, and opportunities for personal growth and development.

It also becomes clear, however, that, like all institutions, Lakeside and Farfield are subject to constant change. The everyday life of the schools described by these boys can only be taken to represent what was happening at a particular stage in the development of each school. This is an important point to bear in mind, since it draws our attention to difficulties and uncertainties which are often associated with emotional and behavioural difficulties. It also shows the illusive nature of aims of security and permanence.

Status and privileges

You don't have to listen to these boys for long before you realise that these two schools are highly structured environments. Each school has its own distinctive organisational structure which is evident in the language used by the pupils. At Farfield, the boys tend to distinguish quite clearly between 'the school', where the classrooms are and where teaching takes place, and 'the house', where they live, eat and share recreation. Lakeside boys are less consistent in making this distinction, and tend to use the term 'school' to refer to both aspects of life at Lakeside. We find both groups to be concerned with questions of status and its concomitant privilege system. Boys at both schools use the terms 'juniors' and 'seniors' as social and academic categories. These positions bring with them certain privileges, relating specifically to matters such as amount of pocket money, lateness of bedtimes and sleeping arrangements (senior pupils tending to be placed in smaller, less highly populated bedrooms). In addition to these relatively automatic, maturation-related, status positions, there are other means of gaining status.

These additional positions are clearly defined by the pupils and take the form of additional privileges and responsibilities which are awarded to boys who are seen by staff as deserving special rewards. At Lakeside there are junior and senior 'helpers', at Farfield there are 'jobbers'. 'Helpers' and 'jobbers' are rewarded with additional pocket money and wider opportunities to leave the school grounds unaccompanied. At Farfield, and to a lesser extent at Lakeside, these selected pupils engage in supervisory duties over other pupils. Jobbers and helpers supervise other boys at communal mealtimes, each having charge of a table in the dining rooms. At Lakeside, a senior helper is required to accompany a non-helper to expeditions into the local village and nearby city in place of a staff member. At Farfield, jobbers supervise other boys in the completion of certain tasks, such as tidying the common rooms and bedrooms. However, whilst 'helpers' are selected by a formal staff vote on a weekly basis, 'jobbers' seem to hold their positions on a fairly permanent basis, and their selection is less formal. The boys believe that it is the principal, Mr Talbot, who personally selects them to be jobbers.

These status roles form an integral part of the life of the two schools, giving pupils a focus and helping to create a sense of order and stability in the schools. Arthur (Lakeside) puts it like this:

> It's [Lakeside] a great place to live! You know where you stand. You know what's going to happen to you, if you do something wrong. You know what's going to happen if you do something right.

Concern with the rules, privileges and restrictions is common among boys in both schools. However, perhaps surprisingly, it is not the strictness or harshness of the rule systems that boys remark on, but rather the somewhat liberal quality of the rules:

> I've been in so many [boarding schools], I'm up to here with them. . . . But . . . this has been the best school I've had in my life! All the rest have been strict. As soon as I hit this school I felt I was just born and come into a new world.
>
> [Colin, Farfield]

Ryan (Farfield), whose previous school experience has been in mainstream schools in his home area, speaks at length about the quality of life at Farfield compared with that of home and his previous mainstream comprehensive school:

PC: How does this school compare with your last school?
Ryan: The school here is better, but I don't think the home life is as good, because you ain't got as much freedom.

. . .

PC: What sort of things, about this school, are better?
Ryan: Well, it's more relaxed, i'n' it? I mean, at normal schools the bell goes and everyone's gotta shoot off to the next lesson. But here, you can take a bit more time; have an extra hour to finish off something you want to finish.

. . .

PC: When you talk about this school, what do you think of?
Ryan: I'd think of the house, I think.

PC: Can you give me some detail about being here and at your old school?

Ryan: Well, here you can smoke. You do a lot more things here, and get away with them.

PC: Like what?

Ryan: Swear. Get out of lessons. I mean, you can go out of lessons with good excuses, like, 'Oh sir, can I go down town?' and, 'Sir, the laundry's messy, I'd better give Milly a hand.' Or something like that. And you can get off school, just like that, and you couldn't do that in a normal school, could you?

PC: Is that a good thing?

Ryan: Yeah. . . . Because the majority of time you're in school every day, but I reckon it's good to have a break from lessons.

PC: So in a way, there's more freedom here?

Ryan: Yes, in the school. But in the home, no. If you're at home, I mean you can go outside and see your mates, can't you? But here, you have to get permission to go down town. You get the mini-bus going past, with the little ones; you get Mr Talbot, doing his shopping about town. Y'know. You can't really walk around town on Saturday without getting seen, can you?

PC: Do you think that's deliberate?

Ryan: I'm not sure. I think Mr Talbot sometimes goes into town on Saturdays to keep an eye on us, when he's walking round. But not the mini-buses. . . . But you still get seen, don't you? I mean everything you do here, near enough, you have to get permission for, and at home you don't, do you? I mean here, you have to ask for a cup of coffee; at home you can just go and make one. You get 'supper-time' – you have to wait for your meals, don't you? You have to wait for breakfast; wait for lunch; wait for supper. At home you can just get it, can't you?

Ryan's account shows a mixture of satisfaction and dissatisfaction, with a not too faint hint of provocation in his tone. He acknowledges the greater freedom of school life here, as compared to a mainstream comprehensive, but also gives an indication of what seems to be the fine balance which exists in the school between freedom and restriction. Boys can get out of lessons with 'crap' excuses, which usually involve some form of contribution to the domestic needs of the community (e.g. helping in the laundry). In spite of this freedom, Ryan still claims to spend 'the majority of time . . . in school every day'. Furthermore, the 'crap' excuse of 'can I go down town, sir,' has to be contrasted with his later complaint that 'you have to get permission to go down town'. The practice of visiting the town during lessons is justified by members of staff in terms of the social and personal education programme operated for boys in the final stages of their time at the school. These errands are described as taking various forms. For example, on a weekly basis, pupils from one of the senior classes take turns to visit the town shopping centre in order to purchase ingredients for meals they later prepare in their afternoon cookery lesson.

Whilst Ryan complains about the lack of freedom afforded in certain aspects of his life at the school ('the home life'), he also gives us a sense of the feeling of personal control he has in other areas of his life, particularly in school, where he is able to spend time working at his own pace without the tyranny of the school bell. Swearing, getting out of lessons and smoking would seem to most people undesirable freedoms. They must, however, be seen in the context of the whole social structure of the institution, which is geared to offer the boys at least some sense of autonomy. This will be discussed in greater depth later. For the moment, however, it is sufficient to note, for instance, that Ryan still claims to spend the majority of his time in class; that this time is spent productively, and that he is engaged and stimulated by the work he does there. The inference to be drawn from this, on the basis of the rest of his statement, is that this is his choice. This is an important step for a boy who has a history of truancy and school refusal. This indicates something of the effectiveness of the school regime.

Another message underlying Ryan's remarks relates to the inevitably institutional nature of Farfield. In this sense Ryan's detached and critical (even cynical) tone can be seen as a healthy and valuable response: however one looks at it, Farfield School is still an institution; a contrivance with assets and limitations. The school cannot and should not be a replacement for his family home. As Lewis puts it:

> I think there's a lot of effort tried. They [the staff at Farfield] do the best that they can. But you can't make something that isn't your home, your home.

We find Lakeside boys voicing very similar sentiments about life in their school. Larry complains about the lack of freedom:

> The only bit of freedom you get is Saturday afternoons. . . . All the rest of the time you're supervised, apart from when you're having a bath, on the toilet, or asleep. That's the only time you're not supervised.

Frank and Tim complain about what they see as childish treatment for 15-year-old boys:

> Frank: When I'm at home, I go down the clubs and pubs with my brother. Here, you have to go to the boring youth club. It's childish.
>
> Tim: Yeah. I went to the snooker club with Tony [a teacher at Lakeside]. And I wanted half a lager and lime. But no. I was going to get pissed on that, wasn't I? I had to have a Coke instead!

Many Lakeside boys complain about the rigidity of bedtimes, and boys in both schools complain at the lack of availability of food outside of formal mealtimes.

A key feature of the daily routine at both schools is the 'activities' programme. 'Activities' takes place on weekday evenings and at weekends. They involve various forms of leisure activity, and include sports, games and craft activities, as well as visits to local leisure facilities, such as parks, cinemas and sports centres. There is a certain ambivalence among the pupils in terms of their attitudes to these activities. Whilst the activities themselves are seen as enjoyable and attractive, the fact that they are compulsory is often seen as a fault, by pupils in both schools. This relates to a consistently voiced complaint that boys in both schools feel they have insufficient free time. Free time describes periods of unstructured and supervised activity. Pupils in both schools have more free time at weekends and on Friday evenings. At such times they are free to pursue their own choice of activity. Some boys choose to organise their own sporting activities, such as football and tennis. With permission, some boys spend time off the school premises, visiting the local centre of population, for shopping, or specific leisure activities. Boys at Lakeside can take advantage of the twenty-plus acres of parkland, within which the school is set, where many boys spend time walking and playing. Pool and table tennis are popular pursuits among the boys at both schools. During periods of 'free-time' these facilities are in constant use. The difference between 'free-time' and 'activities' is that participation in free-time activities is voluntary; boys have the option to take part in an activity, or a number of activities, or to simply relax. Les, from Farfield, describes one of his favourite free time activities:

PC: Do you usually have a good time over the weekend?
Les: Yes, I usually do; on a long weekend especially. . . . Y'know, when you've got the junior wing all to yourself. It's peaceful. You can crash out and sleep all day long.

When boys are engaging in free-time activities, they are often in the company of members of staff. Though the staff are seen less as supervisors and more as fellow participants. It is a common sight in both schools, to see boys seeking out members of staff to play pool with them, or to take them somewhere, or to set up a particular activity, such as swimming or something requiring school PE equipment.

Rules and responsibilities

In spite of the complaints, the vast majority of boys in both schools describe their daily lives in terms which indicate, in general, a relaxed and untroubled atmosphere. The boys sense that they are busy much of the time, but they are not pressurised. Their lives are rule-governed, but the rule systems in both schools are seen by the boys as being flexible. Boys in both schools talk about strictness, but more often than not it is the lack of strictness on which they are remarking. At Farfield, this lack of strictness is seen by many boys as a positive virtue, whilst, at Lakeside, there is concern voiced by some pupils at the lack of strictness of staff. Boys at both schools speak of the flexibility of the rule system. Several boys suggest that rules can be 'bent' in certain circumstances. Such circumstances are usually described in terms of a particular situation and the reaction of a particular member of staff. Thus we find Lewis describing, with some distaste, the ways in which Ryan 'helps himself to coffee' from the school kitchen, without seeking permission from staff. Ryan's explanation for this behaviour, however, is that certain staff do not mind if he helps himself; only certain staff enforce the rule that permission should be sought. Lakeside boys describe similar experiences:

The staff are meant to crush your cigs, if they find them on you; I've been lucky. They usually get put back in the sleeping-in room, when I've been caught.

[Stan, Lakeside]

If I was smoking, they'd sometimes say, 'put that fag out!' Whereas if I was out of bounds, or say, after activities, when I was supposed to be having showers, and I was fagging it across there, sometimes they'd put you on jobs the next day.

[Tom, Lakeside]

There is also evidence from Farfield pupils' accounts that bedtime and cigarette rules are waived and 'bent' in certain circumstances, so that individual pupils may find their bedtimes extended for specific reasons, by staff, and, occasionally, pupils are rewarded for particular jobs with additional cigarettes. Though these additional privileges are not easily won, and will not be provided by certain members of staff. For instance, the pupils are aware of a strong anti-smoking lobby on the school staff, which manifests itself in reluctance to provide the boys with cigarettes. These staff will only ever provide pupils with the prescribed amount.

Ryan, and a large number of the other boys, see this degree of flexibility in the application of rules as a positive feature of the school. Other boys, particularly Lewis, find this a less satisfactory situation. Lewis believes it to be 'unfair' that boys like Ryan 'take advantage'; he also finds fault with staff who do not enforce rules to the letter. Not surprisingly, Ryan, who is one step below Lewis in the pupil hierarchy, finds Lewis a little too conformist in his attitudes:

Ryan: He [Mr Talbot, the school principal] trusts Lewis. I don't know what he's going to do when Lewis ain't here, to tell the truth. . . . Well, I mean, Lewis, right, he's the top boss, i'n' he, with us. If Mr Talbot tells him to do something, right, then Lewis has got to do it. When Lewis ain't here, he's going to get me. He's going to have to tell me to do things, right. Cos I suppose I'll be next in line. I ain't gonna do it.

PC: Why not?

Ryan: Lewis does a brilliant job as boss, right? I mean, he keeps us all quiet; he never gets us in trouble. . . . The problem is, he keeps us too quiet. We don't have a laugh. Y'know, everything has to be quiet. I know that when I get to

> Lewis's position in jobs, I'm gonna want to have a laugh.
> I ain't gonna be just so, to Mr Talbot, y'know. So prob-
> ably, I'll start losing responsibilities, but I don't really
> give a shit . . .

Here, Ryan gives us an insight into the distinctly personalised
nature of the authority system at the school. The boys' positions in
the hierarchy, the degree to which they hold the principal's trust
and the authority and responsibility that is invested in them, are all
closely-linked factors. Ryan recognises that it is the quality of
Lewis's performance of his role as 'top boss' that encourages Mr
Talbot to give him wide responsibilities. Ryan's unwillingness to
perform the role in a 'just so' manner, will mean that Mr Talbot
will take responsibilities from Ryan.

At Lakeside there is, on the surface at least, a more clearly
defined, and impersonal authority system, whereby boys earn
specific privileges and take on particular responsibilities on the
basis of a formal assessment by staff of their behaviour and progress. The 'Helper' system, however, is a source of some dissatisfaction among the boys, not least because it fails to create
sufficient differentiation with the rule system. Seven out of the
nine Lakeside interviewees expressed dissatisfaction in relation to
the 'Helper' system. The core of the boys' dissatisfaction with the
system, however, relates to the fact that the 'Helper' system has
replaced the former privilege system, known as the 'Leader'
system. These changes took place some eighteen months prior to
the interviews, and were the product of a change of headmaster
and almost complete turnover of staff. The interesting thing to
note is that the new privilege system is part of a whole package of
changes which took place in the school; the general effect of which
is seen unanimously by the boys to be liberalising.

> if you weren't a Leader, you were nothing. . . . . You'd fight to get
> on the . Leaders' list. Now you don't need a Helpers' list to do
> as much as you do. For instance, if you wanted to go into town,
> in them days, you had to be a Leader; now you don't have to be.
> If a Helper wants to take you, you can go with him. Everyone
> gets more privileges. I was a Senior Leader. I had a lot of
> responsibility over quite a few things. Like, if a member of staff
> wasn't there, then you were the member of staff. You used to get
> special privileges. You had to be excellent to get there, in your
> manner; in your way of doing things. Your attitude towards life

I suppose. . . .. If you were coping well [with school work], and doing your best in all areas, then you got on [the Leaders' list]. . . . If you weren't on the list, you went to bed at half-eight. But if you was on the list you'd get later bedtime. You could go for a walk down the village, or go to town on your own. All you get now is an extra 50p [pocket money], and half an hour extra bedtime. But it's not the money, it's the status.

[Jock]

The Helpers' list. I've been on it quite a bit, but I'm not bothering any more. You get 50p extra pocket money, a week; you stay up half an hour extra. But you just get treated the same as normal kids. Other kids don't treat you with any respect. Like, when you was on the Leaders' list, you used to get treated with respect. There wasn't so much cheeking, fighting, or anything like that.

[Stan]

We've got no status now. Before, like, we was in charge of a bedroom; in charge of a table with four other kids on it. Jobs at night. Now you've got nothing. No one is in charge of bedrooms. Staff are in at all meals. No status at all. You had to work hard to get privileges. Junior Leaders took tables; got trips into town. Senior Leaders took trips into town, and they took tea. The staff stayed in the staffroom, and ate their tea there.

[Frank]

Clearly the responsibilities awarded to Leaders were themselves seen as privileges. The authority they exercised over their fellow pupils was also extensive and the source of considerable status. The role of the Helper, on the other hand, is seen as privilege without status, and, therefore, it is not so highly valued.

The demise of the Leader system is also related, by many boys, to a general decline in 'strictness' in the school, and a concomitant lowering of behavioural standards. Boys complain that since the changes in organisation, there has been an increase in the amount of damage done to school property, a decrease in the level of respect shown by younger to senior boys, and a decline in the level of boys' cooperation with and politeness towards staff.

On the positive side, however, the changes have resulted in a decrease in bullying in the school:

They [the staff] didn't think it [the Leader system] was a good system, because of all the bullying that went on. I wasn't a bully. I was one of the ones that was getting bullied, 'cos I was younger then.

[Larry]

In the old days, you'd be punished for swearing at a senior boy. Now we get into trouble for hitting them [the junior boys] for cheek.

[Frank]

This change is also reflected in staff behaviour, according to the boys:

The way it used to be, if you messed around, the staff would hit you. . . . Now they've had new staff; they've stopped that. They've gone soft; they don't hit you. If you swear at them, they say, 'Don't use that language to me!' And that's it! In the old days, it would have been all hell let loose, if you swore at them! They'd hit you; then give you a job, or something like that. . . . But now you can swear your head off, and they don't do nothing. I prefer the old system. The kids didn't used to play up so much.

[Jock]

Bill: It's got less strict.
Frank: It's got softer. You can tell a member of staff to fuck off!
Tim: If you told a member of staff to eff off when Ed [the former head] was here, you'd be put on washing-up, or sent to bed. Now they'd [the staff] probably say sorry!
Frank: It's too soft! . . . The present staff couldn't do nothing. . . . If you're smoking in your room, they can't stop you. We take advantage of the system. If they say you can't do something, we just tell them to fuck off! . . . It was better then, even though it was stricter.

All the boys agree that there is now greater freedom for pupils, and what were once highly-prized privileges for the few are now the commonplace expectations of all pupils. There has been a universally welcomed decline in bullying in the school. And yet, even this change is not altogether without its difficulties:

They [the new staff] didn't think it [the Leader system] was a good system, because of all the bullying that went on. I wasn't a bully. I was one of the ones that was getting bullied, 'cos I was younger then. But you all grew up through that stage. You came when you were young; you grew up through bullying, and then went through it, and so on. . . . I don't know if you call it bullying. . . .. It's just a word that the staff use. Sometimes, it was bullying. There was a black kid who did most of the bullying, Archibald. He used to hit Jim Jones, who's only 13, but so thick in the head that he doesn't know what's happening to him.

[Larry]

It would seem that the established patterns of an institution, however repellent they may appear to the outsider, carry with them a sense of the predictable, which is at least some form of security for the members of the institution. There is a sense also, expressed by Larry here, in which some of the Lakeside boys feel cheated that having served their apprenticeships at the lower levels in the school pecking order, they are now deprived of their chance to be top dogs. The fact is, that in a way, the liberalisation of the school has created new difficulties for some of the boys of Lakeside. There is a sense of dislocation; some of the old certainties have disappeared.

There are positive aspects to the new system that are recognised by some of the boys, though not by all:

Now things are better, because they take you out more. You can go to the youth club, or go to the pictures, if you want to, on your own. Well, that happened once. I suppose you have been given a lot more responsibility to yourself, but not to other people.

[Larry]

Larry's observation about 'responsibility to yourself' sheds a slightly different light on the complaints of Frank, Bill, Jock and Tim, about the 'softness' of staff. These boys (especially Frank and Tim) seem to want to be physically deterred from swearing at the staff; they demand external controls, but seem unwilling to exert any self-control. Once again, Larry provides an insight which suggests that the change of regime is being effective in instilling a sense of autonomy and self-control, at least in some pupils:

It would be better if everybody would try to cooperate more with staff. Instead of thinking that the staff are the screws and we are the prisoners. Some of them have got a prison attitude here; not me! . . . They're trying to break the system all the time. That's what really gets on the staff's nerves, because a lot of the time we do break it.

[Larry]

An important aspect of life at Lakeside is the system of meetings. There are daily 'unit' meetings, which are attended by boys and staff within each living unit, and there is a less frequent 'group' meeting attended by all boys and staff. These are important forums for discussion, which many boys see as an important channel through which they can influence community life:

They're good [i.e. the meetings]. Any problems, like anything gone missing of yours, you can talk about it at the unit meeting, up here. Or if it's anything serious, like windows getting smashed in your bedroom, you can bring it up at the group meeting. You can discuss problems. And staff bring up good points about the weekend and everything. . . . If you want something changed, if it's to do with the unit, the best thing to do is to get Maurice [the deputy headmaster] to come here [in the unit] with all the boys. He listens and tries to get things through.

[Stan]

Every morning there's a morning assembly. Before that, you have a unit meeting. You can bring things up then. Like, if you want something doing, like a window fixing or a lock on your door. Or if there's bullying or something. . . .. The staff usually listen, and discuss our ideas at their Wednesday afternoon meetings. If the staff all agree, then it goes through. I wanted a lock on my door. The staff discussed it, but turned it down, because of the fire risk. I accepted that.

[Jock]

Even Tom, who has a generally negative attitude towards Lakeside, freely admits that channels of communication are available for boys to air their concerns:

I reckon most of them [the staff] do [care]; if not all of them. Some staff have activities that are quite rubbish. Like, when they get in the staffroom, they have quite a big battle with other staff, that we should have better things and that.

Only Larry, surprisingly, voices a negative opinion of the daily meetings:

[the meetings are] a waste of our time, when we could be doing something useful, like having a fag or something. . . . [At unit meetings] you just talk about your area in particular. Things like what damage has gone on; what doors have been bust off; tellies bust; stuff like that. . . . We used to have big meetings when Ed [former headmaster] was here, where everyone talked about one thing. They were useful, sometimes.

This response is quite vociferous and aggressive in tone, and not at all consistent with the kind of perceptive and considered views which Larry gives elsewhere. However, Larry later refers to that very day's group meeting, in which events have occurred which have possibly coloured his professed attitude to the meetings and their value. What emerges most strongly is that he feels indignant that the meeting has been used by a member of staff in a way which may well provoke conflict between staff and boys:

Recently, there's been a whole lot of nicking going on at weekends. And instead of speaking to each kid individually, Hamish [head of care] has to bring it up in assembly, in front of everybody. So it just makes it worse. He doesn't get anything out of it. It's just made the whole school uneasy. He's gained who did some of it, but not who did all of it. So it's made the whole school uneasy. So it wouldn't surprise me if it was a bad night tonight. And Hamish will be asking, 'why was it a bad night?' tomorrow. . . . He talked with a few people, first, individually, and he didn't get anything out of it at all, because nobody would speak to him. So he thought, 'maybe if I put another to somebody, and put two and two together, it might work that way.' He tried doing that and didn't get anything out of that, 'cos everybody kept their mouth shut. Everybody knew about it – what was going on – except the staff didn't.

Larry's frank and complex view of this situation provides a fascinating insight into staff–pupil relations. Larry also shows us something of the 'underlife' of the school, when he goes on to say:

I know who did it, but I'm not going to let on, 'cos I'm not a grasser. I know that sounds stupid, 'cos you'd be helping them, but –. If you don't grass on somebody, you can have a little more trust in somebody, and let them know what's happening. I'm the kind of person who likes to know what's happening. There are some grassers you wouldn't tell anything. Tim and me are the two people who know everything that goes on in this school.

In this instance Larry's prediction of 'a bad night' is seen as a direct response to Hamish's insensitive handling of a situation. A petty-theft inquiry has turned into a battle of the subcultures, with Hamish threatening to challenge the solidarity of the pupil sub-culture, with a full frontal assault on the whole pupil group. At stake, in Larry's view, is individual credibility within the pupil group: breach of the grassing rule, leads to virtual exile. Thus whilst the group and unit meetings are seen by most Lakeside boys as a community event, in which boys and staff air and explore shared concerns, Larry shows how this cooperative atmosphere can be corrupted, through staff insensitivity. Larry does not object to Hamish's investigation of the thefts, he simply believes these should be conducted in a low-key way, and on an individualised basis. Hamish's combative approach creates a 'them and us' situation, which can only lead to conflict.

The value of the group and unit meetings at Lakeside is to give the boys a sense of involvement in the daily life of the community they share. This gives the boys a sense of belonging, as well as a sense of being valued. In the group and unit meeting their views and opinions are listened to by staff and pupils alike. Jock's accept-ance of the refusal of his proposal for a lock on his door (see above), is indicative of the way in which this system enables boys to learn how to cope with not getting their own way. The meetings are, in effect, an exercise in shared responsibility, and this is consistent with the evidence of boys' perceptions of the authority structure of the school, discussed above.

Material matters

At Farfield, as we have seen, the authority structure seems to operate in a less formalised way than at Lakeside. The jobbers clearly play an important role in the organisational structure of the school, but there is no clearly defined route to 'jobbers' status, and neither is there a formalised reward system, like the Helpers' list at Lakeside. There is a far less obviously democratic system in opera-tion at Farfield. Farfield boys, as has been shown, do experience a certain sense of freedom and autonomy, in their daily experiences of school life (too much, for some of them at this time). This sense of freedom, however, is seen by Farfield boys as being a function of the benevolence of the school principal, Mr Talbot. This is an important point of contrast between the two schools. Farfield is seen by the boys as Mr Talbot's personal property: his word is law. A clear distinction is drawn by the boys between Mr Talbot and the rest of the staff, who are employees of Mr Talbot. This distinction has many interesting consequences, but for the present it is sufficient to focus on the way this influences boys' perceptions of school life.

Mr Talbot is seen by all the boys as the most important person in the school. They believe that Mr Talbot runs the school, makes all the rules, and is responsible for all policy decisions. Les puts this succinctly:

> Mr Talbot is the main man.

Mr Talbot's position in the school hierarchy is quite clear to the boys:

> He's in charge. And he tells you, like, what to do, and all this stuff. Like Mr Talbot told me once –. Mr Badger [the head-teacher] told me to do something. Mr Talbot wanted to see me, and Mr Talbot called me over; he wanted to see me first. It would be Mr Talbot first, 'cos he's more in charge.
>
> [Gary]

What is seen by the boys as the quality of material provision, in terms of facilities and activities in the school, is also attributed to Mr Talbot's personal generosity and expenditure. John is very clear about this:

> It's a good school. It's a normal school. It's good for people. People like it here. 'Cos some people hate Mr Talbot, like Mick and Alan. But – it sounds really stupid – all the things he buys for us. I dunno. They're just thick! He bought us tellies; he gives us sweets at night-ime; he gives us free fags. He gives us everything.

The attractiveness of the school's sporting and leisure facilities, and the high quality of school outings and holidays, are constantly referred to by the Farfield boys, as important sources of satisfaction and pleasure:

[Reasons for liking Farfield] All the rooms being decorated; all the [dining] tables being done [i.e. furnished with new table-cloths and floral centre-pieces]; the tellies in the bedrooms. Er, loads of things. . . . Going out on trips; playing football, cricket, table tennis, tennis. That was it.

[John]

I thought it was going to be a bad place. When he [Mr Talbot] says, 'you go to Butlins' and Spain [annual school holidays],' it made me think again.

[Jim]

The boys share a belief that the material quality of life at the school is improving:

The school has got a lot better, facility-wise. Mr Talbot has bought a new pool table, and he's had a proper tennis court built.

[Chris]

Just on a normal weekend, he'll [Mr Talbot] go round and buy a load of sweets; stick it in the supper room, and we'll have a special supper. On average now, that's every three weeks say. . . . Before, we'd be lucky if we got it any time during the year, apart from Christmas. The kids' birthday cakes used to be something the cook has made. Now he goes out and gets gateaux and stuff.

[Ryan]

The significance of this concern with material provision lies in the sense of pride that the boys often display in this area. For the most part, the boys believe themselves to be well cared for, and they see this reflected in the material quality of their surroundings and school facilities:

We have the best. Mr Talbot gets the best for us. He spends thousands on us. The tennis court cost £10,000.

[Les]

Mr Talbot does care a lot about us. He buys us loads of things. . . . I don't think he'd spend as much as that, if he didn't care a lot about us.

[Greg]

There would appear to be a clear effort, on the part of Mr Talbot, to encourage this image the boys have of him as provider. One of the ways in which he does this, is through the 'group meetings' which are held from time to time. These meetings are very different from those held at Lakeside, and indicate important points of contrast between the two schools. The group and unit meetings at Lakeside, as we have seen, are perceived by the boys as vehicles for participation and shared responsibility. In contrast, at Farfield, the group meetings are centred on the person of Mr Talbot. These meetings, according to seven out of the fifteen interviewees who referred to them, consist chiefly of sessions in which all the pupils are brought together by Mr Talbot. During these sessions, no other members of staff are present. The content of the meetings is dictated solely by Mr Talbot. Boys report the meetings to include accounts of recent purchases he has made for the school on behalf of the boys; plans for future development of the school; the raising of issues that have come to his notice via staff or boys; such as incidents of bullying; or educational matters. In addition to this, Mr Talbot also introduces new rules, reinforces existing rules, or simply reviews events of recent weeks. Pupils seldom respond to Mr Talbot's offer of the opportunity to speak publicly on issues of concern to them. Reasons given for not participating in this way include feelings of embarrassment and the belief that Mr Talbot would not act on their suggestions or complaints, anyway.

As ever, this apparent benificence does not escape criticism. Ryan complains:

> To tell the truth, I reckon, myself, that he [Mr Talbot] don't give a shit about us. It's just his name. . . . He'll do anything in his power, right, to have the mums thinking good of him, and to have the people down town thinking good of him. That's why he gets us these clothes. When he says he's buying us trousers, right, he ain't buying us no trousers. Say he buys you a pair of shoes, right. 'Oh,' everyone says. 'Mr Talbot bought me a pair of shoes! Great, i'n' it?' You know what he does? He gets the receipt and puts it in the petty cash [i.e. in order to reclaim what he spent from school funds]. . . . He don't pay for no extra clothes. I don't reckon one thing comes out of his pocket in this place. My old dear hated him . . .; she thinks he just does everything for his name. . . . Every time he gives us something, I can't help thinking, 'Is he doing this because he likes me, or is he doing this so I go home and tell my mum he got me this?'

Ryan's suspicions and insecurities are evident here. He seems less willing than other boys to accept Mr Talbot's persona of bene-volence. Ryan sees less admirable and unstated motives for Mr Talbot's actions, and this creates a distance between himself and Mr Talbot. Having said this, and as Ryan himself suggests, the overwhelming majority of boys accept Mr Talbot's 'generosity' at face value, and this would appear to contribute, for the most part, to their sense of being well cared for and valued.

Lakeside cannot boast of expensive facilities and high-quality furnishings. The visitor's first impression of Lakeside is of a run-down, slightly shabby place. The driveway is potholed; grass and weeds are growing up through the concrete paths. Outbuildings are functional but tatty, reminding one of army surplus Nissen huts. In places there are signs of the need for repairs: to broken windows, crumbling walls, peeling paintwork. Elsewhere, there are signs of such work in progress. The headmaster confides that the main building is really unsuitable for the purpose it serves. It is too big and too expensive to maintain. However, in some ways, a virtue has been made of these difficulties. The lack of funding is com-pensated for by group effort and community spirit. Staff and boys have to work together to help maintain the grounds and buildings. At weekends, and sometimes in the evenings, groups of boys and staff can often be found repairing paths, painting, replacing win-dow panes, or gardening. On the back of the staffroom door there is a 'jobs to be done' rota, with staff names on it, and a corres-ponding list on the boys' notice-board, with their names on it. The staff role is not simply supervisory in these situations, as the observer can see, and as the boys point out:

> Staff are more flexible here. They're different [from those in mainstream schools]. You see them doing jobs, like unblocking the toilets, or something like that. It makes them more ordinary.
>
> [Larry]

These maintenance tasks form an important focus for the com-munity. They are often central to the agenda of unit and group meetings, as we have seen. It is important to note also that it is boys as well as staff who identify jobs which need to be done. In this way, staff and boys are drawn together in a common cause: in the discussion and fulfilment of their shared needs. The involvement of staff and boys in routine maintenance is, therefore, much more than simple expedience, it contributes to the therapeutic purpose of the school, and helps to break down some of the barriers that might otherwise exist between staff and pupils. And it is through these less formalised staff–pupil relationships that some of the more obviously therapeutic processes are enabled:

> Teachers in comprehensives are all stuck-up. Here they're flexible. Staff are more friendly. You can call them by their first names, and everything. Staff will give you more time, if you want to talk to them. Charlie will stay with you, even if he is off-duty, until it is sorted out. They have more time for you.
>
> [Frank]

In the next section, this therapeutic effect will be dealt with in greater detail. What is important to note at the moment, is the way in which the functional aspects of school life at Lakeside – the maintenance programme and the group/unit meetings – contribute to this process.

The maintenance programme is also commonly cited by boys as providing them with a sense of satisfaction and achievement. Many boys speak enthusiastically of the work they have done around the school: pointing to paths they have laid; plants they have cultivated; their achievements in renovating 'the club hut'; the work they have done in decorating their bedrooms, and their plans for further work. Stan shows how these activities have given him an enhanced sense of his own abilities and capabilities, as well as a sense of personal confidence and maturity. He also suggests the way in which the maintenance work and the academic life of the school work consistently to give boys a sense of progress and achievement.

> The school has helped me grow up in myself; helped me to go to school; get on with my classwork. I'm more confident in myself, being able to do things I never thought I could do. Like last weekend, me and another boy: our job was the front drive. There's me and him went off, quite happy, and filled up some pot-holes. I'd have never thought of doing that before, or known how to do it. I've learnt to do quite a few things. Yes, you learn things, and how to do them properly.
>
> [Stan]

This is an important statement from a boy who admits to a history of chronic truancy from his former mainstream school, and the experience of difficulties in relating to other individuals. Stan has a clear sense of achievement and success, and a belief that his experiences at Lakeside have contributed to his progress.

Sanctions

Words such as 'trust' and 'responsibility' recur often in interviews with boys from both schools. In both schools, the shouldering of responsibility is seen as a privilege, and is often conferred as a reward. Similarly, sanctions in the two schools often take the form of the withdrawal of responsibilities and privileges. At Farfield and Lakeside boys who infringe rules have their freedom curbed, by being confined to school grounds and, in some cases, their rooms. Unaccompanied visits home are also suspended for serious offences. The boys of both schools agree that whilst there are certain obvious rules which regulate their daily school lives, the enforcement of rules and sanctions for rule-breaking, depend very much on individual circumstances and contextual matters. As we have seen already, Lakeside boys sometimes dismiss the staff as 'soft' because they do not enforce rules rigidly. Arthur sheds a different light on this, however:

> [the staff at Lakeside] they're a lot better. They're more like people! When I was at Rushforth [day special school], they were more like robots really. You do something wrong; the first thing they do is grab 'em and stick 'em in a room, and just lock them up! Like here, they just talk to you; just tell you what you've done wrong, and have a good go at you. And you know you've done wrong, so you just have to take it. . . . Sometimes, you don't want to listen; they just let you go and have a walk, and come back, and talk to you later.

Under the former regime, there was a good deal of corporal punishment used by staff against rule-breakers, and it is the absence of this that Frank, Tim and Bill complain of. However, as Arthur suggests, the more reasonable approach of the new staff can have a deep impact. Thus, like the systems of rewards and privileges, the sanctions at Lakeside are geared to giving the boys a sense of their own responsibility for their own actions. This leads to some discomfort among the boys, as we have seen already. They complain about the lack of discipline in the school, the softness of the staff, and long for the days of less freedom and draconian discipline. They complain because the current staff do not force them to comply with rules:

> Donald [current head] is too soft. When Ed was here, if everyone was talking in the dining room, as soon as Ed walked in, everyone would be quiet.
>
> [Frank]

> As soon as Donald walks in, everyone carries on – kick the chairs and everything.
>
> [Bill]

> Donald tries to act strict, but no one listens to him. They just give him mouth, and walk off! . . . He doesn't do nothing.
>
> [Arthur]

And yet:

> I think it should be more stricter. But if they get it more strict, I'm going to be the one that's breaking all the rules!
>
> [Larry]

The paradox of Larry's statement says something about the futility of the type of regime that many of these boys claim to feel such nostalgia for. What the boys appear to be engaged in is the painful transition from such a system, which places responsibility for behaviour in someone else's hands, to a system whereby the boys are required to make their own decisions. The step that some of these boys still have to make is to the recognition that the remedy for their dissatisfaction is in their own hands.

At Farfield, we find a slightly different system of sanctions. The boys are encouraged to take responsibility for their actions, and the actions of fellow pupils, to some extent. An unpopular sanction is that which is consistently referred to by the boys, under the umberella term of 'shared responsibility'. This refers to a system of global suspensions of privilege, which follow certain categories of offence. Examples of this are the suspension of smoking privileges for all boys, following the theft of cigarettes from the staffroom; a series of breakages of pool cues and table-tennis equipment is punished by a ban on these activities for a week; the stoppage of pocket money to pay for damage to school property. This aspect of 'shared responsibility' is unpopular, and felt to be unfair by many boys. However, it is clear that boys take an interest and a pride in their school environment, and many claim that rule-breaking of the type outlined here is not worth the effort, both in terms of the inevitable punishment as well as the displeasure it invokes from the pupil community.

Among both pupil groups there is an unstated but clear distinction between those misdemeanours which invoke the kind of punishment described above and those which invoke a therapeutic response. Central to the boys' responses to both schools is the importance of the relationships they enjoy with staff, and the ways in which these relationships impinge on their individual and personal situations. In this way a clear distinction is drawn between those aspects of community life which are regulated by external controls and rules, and the more personally significant individual needs of the boys. Interpersonal relationships will be dealt with in detail in the following section.

EDUCATION AND ACHIEVEMENT

The boys have mixed opinions about the quality of the formal education provided at the two schools. Whilst many pupils claim to have benefited from the educational programmes, there are many who complain at the lack of breadth in the school curriculum and the lack of opportunities to take public examinations. Most of the complaints are voiced by boys from Lakeside, though boys from both schools make complaints. Approximately one-third of the boys in both schools, who replied to the initial questionnaire, agreed with the statement: 'If you were at a comprehensive school, you would be making better progress with your work.' Similar proportions agreed with the statement: 'The schoolwork here is too easy.' Although response rates were low (Farfield: 31 out of 45 boys; Lakeside: 13 out of 32 boys), these views are reflected in the interview data, particularly in the Lakeside sample.

The most vociferous complainant, on virtually all subjects, is Tom from Lakeside:

> I feel I'm getting thicker whilst I'm here. . . . There's less chance to do the subjects everyone else is doing in a normal school.
> . . .
> You're missing out on physics and chemistry. If I go back to my old school, I'll have a lot of catching up to do. 'Cos if I go back, I'll only have a year-and-a-quarter left . . . to get ready for my exams.

Tom's assertion that the school is 'rubbish' is perhaps strongly coloured by his anxieties about his educational prospects. Tom is heavily preoccupied with his desire to return to a mainstream school, in order to complete his education. At the time of the interview Tom was awaiting a reply to a letter he had written to his former school, requesting the opportunity to return. This was clearly a testing time for Tom. His concerns about the quality of the schooling he was experiencing, however, are reflected in the views of other, less obviously troubled Lakeside boys:

> The education here is pathetic! I was doing exams before I came here. . . . My reading age hasn't improved since I was nine.
>
> [Tim]

> It's [Lakeside] helped me in other ways, but not with my education. I was doing 'O' Level maths, before I came here; now I can't even do fractions.
>
> [Frank]

However, not all the Lakeside boys share this view, by any means:

> Before I came to this school, I couldn't do maths or anything.
> [Tom]

These views are echoed by Jock and Stan, both of whom claim to have made much greater educational progress at Lakeside than in previous schools.

Larry offers a more complex picture. He links what he perceives as a lack of strictness in the school with the suggestion that he is under-achieving:

> It's nowhere near as strict [at Lakeside, in comparison with a comprehensive school], and you don't do half as much work here. That's bad, that is. I can't stand work myself . . . it's boring. But when you were at senior school, and you were made to do it, you learned a lot more. I don't want to do it, but sometimes, I think you've got to do it, or you'll regret it when you get older. So I have a go!
>
> [Larry]

These remarks of Larry's reflect many interesting factors present in both schools and, ironically, demonstrate something of the power and success of the schools. The theme of personal responsibility stands out in this speech, and echoes points made in the previous section. It is clear that Larry is not only aware of the need to take some responsibility for his own learning, but he also claims to do so. In an oblique way Larry relates his self-motivation to the lack of strictness which he decries. And it is this very lack of strictness and rigidity which makes their schooling a worthwhile and rewarding experience for many other pupils.

We find both Arthur and Jock claiming that the relaxed and relatively informal classroom atmosphere at Lakeside is conducive to study. Jock claims to positively 'enjoy' going to class, in contrast to his former comprehensive school, which he 'couldn't stand'. He finds the work at Lakeside 'interesting', and believes he has made good progress. Arthur remarks on the helpfulness and attentiveness of staff, who he finds to be more sympathetic and patient than the staff of his former school. These positive views are reflected in the Farfield interviews:

> Well, it's more relaxed, i'n' it? I mean at normal schools the bell goes and everyone's gotta shoot off to the next lesson. But here, you can take a bit more time; have an extra hour or finish off something you want to finish.
>
> [Ryan]

> I've caught up really a lot [with my schoolwork] since I've been here. . . . Really caught up!
>
> [Alex]

> It's [Farfield] helped me a bit with my schoolwork.
>
> [Malcolm]

We also find that the overwhelming majority of pupils who responded to the first questionnaire gave an affirmative answer to the question 'Do teachers here usually give you enough help with your schoolwork?' (Farfield: 30 out of 31 replies; Lakeside: 11 out of 11 replies). The second questionnaire obtained a much higher return rate and strong agreement with the statement: 'Pupils here like this school because the teachers here give them more help with their schoolwork than teachers in ordinary schools' (Farfield: 27 agreed, 6 disagreed; Lakeside: 22 agreed, 2 disagreed).

Schooling, in its narrowest sense, therefore, is the subject of diverse views. The most marked and consistent dissatisfactions relate to what might be termed the rigour of the curriculum. It is perhaps understandable that a small school of less than fifty pupils fails to offer the breadth of curriculum of a large comprehensive. The question of the degree to which pupils are challenged by their schoolwork is less easily answered, though it is clear that this is a source of concern to a subset of both pupil groups. Looked at from a slightly different perspective, however, we find the pupils claiming to face a wide range of challenges and opportunities for achievement, among which education is placed. And it is perhaps more in keeping with the aims and purposes of these two schools to define 'education' in these broader terms.

The Lakeside boys, in particular, give us a clear impression of the benefits they receive from being active participants in a community. It seems that most aspects of their daily life in the school contribute to the development of a sense of personal responsibility. Some of the important vehicles for developing these qualities are: the system of group and unit meetings, the formal 'jobs' programme, and, to a lesser extent perhaps, the formal privilege system (the Helpers' list). Such formalised structures are less evident in the Farfield regime, according to the pupils. However, a central feature of both schools, which contributes perhaps more than anything else to the pupils' personal development, relates to the nature and quality of the interpersonal relationships which exist between the pupils and the staff. It is to a consideration of the interpersonal dimension that we now turn.

Chapter 6

The residential experience II: Interpersonal relationships and personal outcomes

STAFF AND BOYS

A key theme running throughout boys' accounts of their perceptions of their schools, is the importance of staff–pupil relationships. It has already been shown that staff are seen as being friendly, understanding and helpful to pupils. These qualities are often highlighted as points of contrast between the residential staff and the pupils' experience of teachers in mainstream schools. What emerges with great force from the interview data is the trust which pupils place in the staff, and their belief in the dedication of staff. The experience of these relationships is genuinely educative for the pupils, in that it provides the pupils with a positive model of interpersonal behaviour and helps them to develop an increasing sense of their own worth.

The boys express a clear sense of the high level of staff care and support that they receive at the schools in their response to the second questionnaire. We find overwhelming agreement with the following statements, with over 80 per cent agreement from pupils of both schools (Farfield, $N = 33$; Lakeside, $N = 24$):

Pupils here like this school because the teachers here give them more help with their schoolwork, than teachers in ordinary schools.

Pupils here like this school because the staff here listen to pupils, when pupils want to talk to them.

The staff here help pupils, if they have a personal problem.

The staff here give pupils more personal attention, than staff in ordinary schools.

The staff are seen as an important resource, who can be approached in times of personal difficulty. Among the Farfield boys, 68 per cent (N = 31) of the respondents to the first questionnaire claim that they would usually approach a member of the care staff, if they had a 'personal problem', whilst 38 per cent would approach a teacher; at Lakeside, 62 per cent (N = 13) would approach a member of the care staff, and 46 per cent would approach a teacher.

The boys describe many incidents which show the ways in which staff respond constructively to their needs. Larry describes a characteristic situation:

> There was an incident a couple of weeks ago, where I was piling my plate with food, 'cos I was starving. . . . Charlie [a teacher] said, 'Leave enough for everyone else!' And with that, I just slammed my knife and fork down and walked out! He came after me, after about fifteen minutes, when I'd had a good cry in the bathroom, and said, 'Try not to worry too much about what's happening.' I can't remember what he said now, but he gave me new ideas.

Larry relates his emotional upset to the break-up of his relationship with his girlfriend. He clearly appreciates Charlie's supportive understanding, and recalls this sense of the quality of the support, rather than the details of the actual interchange. What is interesting here is that Larry's personal state is treated with seriousness; his superficial 'misbehaviour' is seen essentially as the sympton of an underlying difficulty.

The approachability of staff, and their willingness to listen and counsel boys, help to create an environment in which the boys feel cared for and valued, and where they are able to grow and develop on a personal level. At Lakeside, Maurice, the deputy headteacher, and Charlie, a teacher, are singled out by several boys, for their willingness and skill in counselling and supporting boys, but nearly all of the staff are singled out at some point in this connection:

> The staff are more prepared to sit down and talk to you, and talk your problems out. They'll help you out with anything. There was one member of staff: Fiona – she's left. She used to remind me of my sister and that, 'cos she was the same age as my sister, and everything. I used to be able, if I'd got any problems, to talk to her.
>
> [Stan]

I still respect Maurice, because he's more than fair.

[Tim]

Yes, they [the staff] do [care]. Especially Mo' [Maurice], Hamish [Head of Care], and Charlie. . . . He's [Charlie] a really good talker; he can really talk to you and make you know what's happening. And he gives you new ideas . . . when he's talking to you about your problems.

[Larry]

Jock describes how the openness of staff has helped him personally. Jock, it will be recalled, comes from a family situation which he finds intolerable, dominated, as he sees it, by an uncaring and unsympathetic father:

Before I came here, I never used to speak to anyone about my problems. . . . I used to say nothing to no one, when I had a problem. [Now] I talk to anyone about my problems.

[Jock]

Frank describes what he experiences as the contrast between staff at Lakeside and staff in the comprehensive school he formerly attended:

Teachers in comprehensives are all stuck-up. Here they're flexible. Staff are more friendly. You can call them by their first names and everything. Staff will give you more time, if you want to talk to them. Charlie will stay with you, even if he is off-duty, until it is sorted out. They have more time for you.

[Frank]

In these ways, the boys describe situations in which difficulties they face can be met and dealt with as they happen, rather than being ignored or suppressed, and so a possible source of future difficulty can sometimes be eliminated. Alex (Farfield) describes how the combination of being removed from a difficult home environment and the availability of sympathetic caring adults at Farfield have contributed to an important change in his attitudes and behaviour. Alex's statement is even more interesting when we consider that his initial reaction to Farfield school was negative:

Alex: I went mad! [when he first discovered that he would have to stay at the school]. . . . I told Mr Talbot to go some-

where. I started shouting. I didn't like it . . . being away
from home.

. . .

I thought it [Farfield] was crap! I thought it was stupid!
. . .   I didn't like living with other people. I didn't think I
would get where I am now. . . . 'Cos I've caught up [with
my schoolwork] really a lot since I've been here. . . .
Really caught up. . . .

PC: But obviously, you did manage to settle down, didn't
you? How did you manage that?

Alex: I just worked right into it. . . . I tried as best I could. Put
everything into it.

PC: What would have happened if you hadn't tried as hard as
you did?

Alex: I'd just be bad still, probably. . . . I'd be what I was a year
ago.

PC: So being here has changed you. How have you changed?

Alex: Yeah, a lot. . . . It's helped me a lot. People I can talk to.

PC: People here?

Alex: Yeah, they've helped me. . . . [I've talked about] problems at home. They give me advice sometimes, when they
can help me.

PC: Have you ever had people before you can talk to?

Alex: Yeah, I have, but I never used to say anything, 'cos I was
at home then; I weren't bothered about what I done.
Probably 'cos I was mixed up when I first come here.

For Alex, it is not simply the availability of caring adults with whom
he can talk – he has failed to take advantage of similar availability
in the past – but the fact that this adult help is actually given; he
does not have to seek it. Alex describes the importance of the
relationship he has with his key worker, whom he describes as
'going with me all the way', through problem situations, relating
to his family circumstances and criminal activities he has engaged
in at home. Alex describes how his key worker has persevered
through Alex's initial resistance; always being cheerful and
friendly in spite of Alex's attempts to ignore him and put him off.
Over time, Alex has come to accept and value the help offered by
this member of staff. Specifically, he describes how he took advice
about how to avoid delinquent peers, through engaging in new
patterns of activity at home (which the key worker helped initiate),

and how he has learned to deal with his family in a more constructive manner:

> The school's put me in a different way, y'know. It's made me look at things different. . . . I didn't get on with my mum and brothers, and I used to argue with my mum. That's just stopped now. There's things that I wouldn't do, like say I have a little argument with my mum, I'll say sorry to her after. That's one thing I wouldn't ever thought of doing when I was at home before.

Like Larry at Lakeside, Alex places great value on his key worker's ability to present familiar situations from new perspectives. According to Alex, a decisive event was when the key worker suggested to Alex that he imagine himself to be in his mother's situation. At first, Alex refused to accept any reponsibility for his placement in the school, choosing instead to blame his family, and his mother in particular. His key worker's persistence, however, led Alex, through this act of empathy, to place a value on his family, and to see himself in a new light.

We find Ryan making similar claims to those of Alex:

> Ryan: Farfield has changed me a lot. If I was at home now, I'd probably be inside or something. . . . I'd have a record. . . . I've been nicked, but I've got out of it . . .
>
> PC: Is that anything to do with being here?
>
> Ryan: Yes, I think so. It's straightened me out really. . . . It's made me look at things, I suppose. It's made me think, 'If I do this thing, I'll be stupid.' . . . I think it's made me more sensible. I know there's a bunch of kids, some old mates, who if I hang around with, I'll get nicked. Or I'll do a job, get away with it, then get nicked. But I don't bother hanging around with them no more, because I know it will bodge up my life with the army [which he wishes to join on leaving school]. Before I wouldn't really have thought of it.

Like Alex, Ryan places a great deal of emphasis on his relationship with his key worker, when discussing the ways in which the school has helped him to change for the better. He recounts a particular incident which shows how the quality of the relationship he has with his key worker influences his attitudes and behaviour. The incident centres around an occasion when Ryan returned to school from a home holiday with a quantity of stolen clothing, and sheds light on the special relationship which can exist between key worker and pupil:

PC: Is there anyone here you feel you can go to, if you have a problem?

Ryan: Yes. Mr Brown [RSW], and Miss O'Neill [RSW]. . . . Mr Brown I know I can trust [Ryan's key worker]. 'Cos a while ago, I got in a lot of shit – I didn't exactly get in shit -. But I got a lot of clothes hot [i.e. stolen], right? And I brought them back to school, and Mr Brown sussed on. And he could've had me done, really bad. Y'know, fucked up me going home for a long time; got me in shit with the geezer: Mr Talbot – everyone. But he didn't say a word, and everything turned out alright. 'Cos I got rid of the clothes, and nothing happened. And I promised I wouldn't get no more stuff, and that was it. And I think, if that had been any other key worker, something would've been done about it. But he trusted me. I mean, he didn't go to the Social Services, or nothing like that, saying: 'I'm worried about Ryan.' 'Cos I promised him I wouldn't do it no more, and I'd get rid of the stuff, and I did.

Ryan is quite clear about the fact that he would not have made similar disclosures to any other member of staff, and in his way draws a sharp distinction between his key worker and the school principal, Mr Talbot. Whilst Ryan believes that Mr Talbot would like to be viewed as a father-figure, to be trusted and loved by the boys, for Ryan it is Mr Brown who comes closest to filling such a role, though for Ryan Mr Brown is more of 'a mate' than a father-figure:

PC: . . . How do you think Mr Talbot wants you to see him?

Ryan: As your old man.

PC: How successful is he, in your case?

Ryan: He ain't. He's a good geezer, right. He can be a really good bloke. But everytime he is a good bloke, as I've said, I can't help feeling, is he being a good bloke, 'cos he wants us to go and tell someone that Mr Talbot is good, y'know?

PC: Is there anybody here that you feel could be –

Ryan: Genuine?

PC: I was thinking of someone being a father-figure, like you say Mr Talbot wants to be. Like you said Mr Brown is someone you can talk to and trust; would you say he is more of a father-figure than Mr Talbot?

Ryan: No, he ain't a father-figure. I treat Mr Brown more as a mate. . . . When he sussed out that I'd got these clothes, he got slightly worried about it. 'Cos he knows my old dear can't afford all this stuff. So he come to me, and I give him two stories, right. The first time, it didn't work; the second time, 'This is honest truth, sir. You got to believe me now.' The third time, I let it out. 'Cos he made me feel so bad when he said, 'Right, Ryan, I believe you, but if I find out it's a lie, just don't bother talking to me again.' And I knew, if he found out it was a lie, I wouldn't be talking to him now. It was then I thought, 'Shit! I've had it, haven't I? I suppose I've got to tell him now, and get it all cleared up. And if I get nicked, I get nicked.' So I told him. And he told me he knew it weren't the truth, what I'd told him. And he said he wouldn't say nothing to Mr Talbot, so long as I didn't get no more, right, and I got rid of the stuff.

PC: Is that one of the ways the school helps?

Ryan: I suppose so, 'cos I couldn't have talked to my mum about it.

In Ryan, then, we can see what seems to be a growing sense of responsibility, and a recognition of the need to change his behaviour. This sense of responsibility stems partly from self-interest, in that his ambition to join the army might be foiled if he is involved in delinquent activities. A more important influence, however, would seem to be the relationship with Mr Brown, his key worker, whose patience and trust is so highly valued by Ryan, that he cannot bring himself to sustain the lies he has told him. This is so to the extent that he is prepared to risk being 'nicked' for the sake of the relationship. Ryan's explanation for this is that Mr Brown is simply 'a good bloke', who Ryan does not wish to let down. Thus Ryan is not only exercising responsibility out of self-interest, but also out of liking and respect for another person.

The foundations of these high-quality interpersonal relationships between staff and pupils, are not, however, simply located in the fact that staff make themselves available in times of crisis and difficulty. As has already been suggested, pupils are often, at first, wary and distrustful of staff, particularly when it comes to those areas of their lives which are sources of pain and distress. These boys, for the most part, do not easily relax their defences, and often, when they do choose to confide in staff, they select a particular staff member with whom they feel comfortable. Even when such a member of staff is found, the boys are often selective in what they choose to confide. In the example given by Ryan, it was the high quality of the relationship with Mr Brown that enabled Ryan to disclose the truth about something that he would not have freely confided to a member of staff; in this instance the act of confiding a guilty secret seems to have strengthened the quality of the relationship, by demonstrating the extent of mutual trust between Ryan and his key worker. These relationships do not develop smoothly overnight. Boys in both schools indicate that the relationships evolve, often being marked, in their early phase, by resistance from the pupils and a dogged perseverence by the staff members. Meaningful one-to-one conversations about boys' progress and 'problems' often only begin to take place after this initial phase.

These high-quality relationships are most often born out of, and to some extent sustained through, incidents of informal contact and the sharing of activities. At both schools, boys and staff often seem to mix freely during activity periods, playing pool and other games, or, at Lakeside in particular, sharing maintenance activities. In fact, the majority of contact that boys have with staff, outside of the classroom, takes place in these informal circumstances. In this way the staff give the boys a sense of being valued and respected, and this in turn gives rise to a sense of security that enables boys to call on staff when difficulties arise, or be open to offers of staff help in such circumstances. Stan describes how his teacher at Lakeside has helped him with his difficulties through a combination of formal and apparently informal situations:

> I think he's [my teacher] helped me quite a bit. He's helped me with my work; talked to me quite a bit. Like I never used to like going out anywhere, to do anything; now I feel quite happy to go to snooker clubs. John [the teacher] takes quite a few of us there. We save our pocket money from the weekend to go there.

Greg sheds light on the day to quality of staff–pupil relationships at Farfield. For Greg, the informal 'play' activity which goes on between some staff and boys, in the form of play-fighting and general rough and tumble that sometimes takes place, makes up for an important deficiency felt by Greg when he is away from the school. During holidays and some weekends Greg returns to a small children's home, staffed entirely by female RSWs, who, perhaps understandably, shy away from rough physical contact with an adolescent boy who is nearly six feet tall. Greg admits to gaining great satisfaction from such 'rough and tumble', and cites this as a particularly attractive feature of the school, and a desirable quality in staff. Through such play, inhibitions are broken down and relationships are able to develop.

Relationships based on trust, then, are central aspects of the boys' lives in these two schools. Their therapeutic effect often seems to go almost unnoticed, operating as it most often does through apparently casual encounters and 'chats'; blending seamlessly with the overall social milieu:

PC: And you say you've improved in how you get on with your parents. Is that anything to do with what's gone on here?

Jim: Yes. Me being away from home. . . . The kids here [at Farfield]. . . . They've cheered me up a couple of times, when I've been unhappy. If I've been home for a weekend, and it's gone wrong, they cheer me up when I come back. . . . Staff as well. . . . Miss O'Neill, my key worker, has a chat with me when I come back. . . . What have I been doing; did I see my mates; how's my sister?

For many of these boys, these relationships represent something of a contrast with the kinds of relationships they share with other significant adults in their lives, such as their parents, and the teachers they have had in previous schools. It is not surprising, therefore, that the boys sometimes come to develop a powerful dependence on these professional adult carers; a dependence which is not without its problems.

Attachments between staff and pupils can become extremely strong and create difficulties when they are broken, such as when staff leave. This is demonstrated most graphically among the Lakeside boys. Some eighteen months prior to the interviews there had been a major change in the staffing of the school. The then headmaster, Ed, retired through ill-health, after having been head of the school for over twenty years. The arrival of his replacement, Donald, brought with it many changes in the organisation of the school. These changes were also accompanied by a virtually complete turnover of the staff group. From the pupils' perspective, as we have seen in the previous section, complaints about these changes centre around the formal privilege system which operates within the school, and the transition from the Leader system to the 'Helpers' list. And although these changes have been accompanied by a universally acknowledged liberalisation of the school, they are the focus of intense criticism from many pupils. What becomes clear, however, from listening to the Lakeside boys is that whilst the loss of the privilege system is a genuine source of disappointment, it is accompanied by the much deeper and more heartfelt loss of the much loved former headmaster, and former staff members:

> If you swore Ed'd come over and clout you round the head. But everyone liked him. Everyone respected him.
>
> [Tim]

> There was less freedom when Ed was here, but the whole atmosphere of the school was different. It was a happier place then . . . Ed was good fun. He was very strict. . . . I . . . think he did a good job; he was a good laugh, but he was strict. He knew when to be strict and when to have a laugh.
>
> [Larry]

The sense of loss surrounding Ed's departure is a constantly recurring theme in the interviews:

> The whole place was upset, when Ed left. He was the sort of person who, if you didn't know him very well, you could get on with him. [Since he left] the atmosphere in the school has changed as well. There are more kids messing about: smashing windows and everything.
>
> [Stan]

The intense popularity enjoyed by Ed is clearly a source of difficulty for the new head, Donald, who can never fill the shoes of his predecessor in the eyes of the boys:

> Maybe it's because I wanted Ed to stay; I didn't want him to leave. So it changed my view of the new headmaster. I didn't like the sight of him when he walked through the door, in any case, because he was new.
>
> [Larry]

Ed was great! He was different from Donald. He knew what he was doing. He knew how to manage the money properly. Everyone liked him, everyone got on; everyone respected him. . . . I don't trust Donald at all!

[Arthur]

Donald's too soft. . . . When Ed was here, if everyone was talking in the dining room, as soon as Ed walked in, everyone would be quiet.

[Frank]

As soon as Donald walks in, everyone carries on – kick the chairs, and everything.

[Bill]

Donald is condemned as 'soft', incompetent, incapable of enforcing discipline, but his greatest failing, perhaps, is that he is not Ed.

In spite of these obvious problems, there are indications that the new staff have brought many positive changes into school life which are recognised by the boys. What we appear to be witnessing, therefore, is the inevitably painful severence of old attachments, and the slow development of new relationships. Some boys show a clear appreciation of this process, along with the belief that the changes will be ultimately beneficial to them and the school:

Things will get better. They'll settle down.

[Arthur]

The whole school was upset when Ed left. He was the sort of person who, if you didn't know him, you could get on with him. The atmosphere in the school has changed, as well. There are more kids messing about, smashing windows and everything. In that way, it has got a lot worse. But it will get better, eventually.

[Stan]

I dunno. Maybe it's [Lakeside] changing for the better. If you'd have asked me a year ago, I'd have said, 'No, it's changing for the worse.' But I suppose I'm getting used to the system.

[Larry]

The new relationships, set as they are in a context which stresses self-control and self-discipline over institutional constraint, seem to offer pupils richer opportunities for self-exploration and development. Jock says:

> I couldn't talk to the old staff. . . . I used to be scared of Ed. I couldn't talk to him.

Jock complains that Ed was not prepared to listen to boys when they challenged his preconceptions of them. He recounts an incident in which he claims Ed punished him for bullying, which he had not committed:

> Because I had been thought of as a bully in my old school, he thought I was doing it then. So he didn't listen to my side.

To Jock, Ed's inflexibility seems to have pervaded the entire school regime, making communication with staff difficult; this is a point of contrast between the old and new regimes:

> The old staff were friendly, but not as friendly [as the new staff]. The new staff are friendly and you can get away with murder with them.
>
> . . .
>
> I used to talk to no one, when I had a problem. I talk to anyone now about my troubles.

RELATIONSHIPS BETWEEN THE BOYS

Things that the boys have to say about the relationships they have with one another point to a number of important aspects of the schools, and provide us with deep insight into their daily lives, as well as indicating a sense of the general ethos of the schools. Responses to questionnaires give us insight into the climate of inter-pupil relations in the two schools. Forty-three per cent ($N = 31$) of Farfield respondents and 23 per cent of Lakeside respondents ($N = 13$), claimed that if they had a personal problem they would confide in another pupil. The same proportions of boys stated that other boys were often 'most helpful' in these circumstances. Responses also indicate the importance that is attached to the quality of pupil relationships, with 81 per cent ($N = 33$) of Farfield boys and 92 per cent ($N = 24$) of Lakeside boys agreeing with the statement:

> To do well here, you have to try to get on well with other pupils.

Obviously, relationships among boys are not always cordial, bullying is referred to by a few boys from both schools. At Lakeside, as has already been indicated, bullying is seen to have declined with the change of headmaster, and the dissolution of the 'Leader system', which seems to have amounted to something of a bullies' charter. At Farfield, however, bullying is an issue of current importance to some boys:

Alan: Well, people normally come up and just start hitting you.
PC: Does that happen a lot, Alan? Do you think it happens to you more than it happens to other people?
Alan: I don't know really.

Later, Alan elaborates on the treatment he receives and the way it affects his attitude toward the school:

Sometimes I think: 'I want to get out of this borstal place.' It gets on my nerves, and I start swearing. . . . It gets on my nerves. . . . I just go upstairs and sit down.
. . .
Some people wind you up, and take the mickey out of you and your family – things like that. Just wind you up badly. You just don't know what to do. You just have to stand there and take it. And sometimes they come over and just start punching the hell out of you. . . . [When that happens] I just go sit in my room and keep quiet. Hope no one'll come in, teasing me, punching me – things like that.

This is not a trivial matter, but it is the only such example in the data. 'Winding-up' is a common source of irritation among the Farfield boys, but is not usually equated with bullying by the boys. 'Winding-up' takes the form of verbal banter and personal insults, and acts as a kind of verbal sparring between boys. At its worst extreme, 'winding-up' forms the prelude to physical conflict among boys. At the other extreme it has a playful quality. Other times it appears to take the place of physical violence.

Observational data combined with the boys' accounts indicates that the nature of the insults ('wind-ups') range from generalised attacks on individuals' families ('your family lives in a pig-sty'), to more specific personal remarks, noticeably often directed at boys' mothers ('your mum's a prostitute'). Other 'wind-ups' home in on perceived differences among boys, so that boys with dark complexions (regardless of their actual ethnic origins) are sometimes referred to as 'Paki'. When required, points of difference are hunted down mercilessly, and without concern for consistency or accuracy. Thus we find Colin complaining at being mocked and insulted for wearing 'cut-offs' (i.e. shortened jeans), because they are unfashionable, whilst another boy, Max, who also wore them, is not mocked. (Max, we must note, is regarded as a bully by many of the boys, who greeted his recent departure from the school with relief.) Mick complains that other boys often 'wind him up' by calling him 'Horse': a reference, apparently, to his yellow teeth.

The boys who complain of bullying are, not surprisingly, often those who occupy the lower status positions in the pupil hierarchy. In the case of Colin, Brian and Alan, their low status is associated with their apparent lack of intellectual ability (as perceived by their peers); in Mick's case, his unpopularity is related to his being seen as a 'trouble-maker'. This association with status and bullying is evident in the fact that individual bullies are hardly ever named. With the exception of Max, who clearly is seen as a bully by the majority of interviewees, bullying is attributed to no one in particular.

Of particular interest, in relation to the problem of bullying at Farfield, is the light discussion of this sheds on the positive side of inter-pupil relations. Ryan and Lewis, as has already been indicated, are important figures in both the formal and informal pupil hierarchy of Farfield. Lewis is described by Ryan as 'Top Boss of us kids', and Ryan is seen by himself and others as second only to Lewis. These positions are endorsed by the principal, Mr Talbot, who invests considerable responsibility and authority in Ryan and Lewis. What is interesting here is the high esteem in which these two boys are held by other pupils. Lewis is repeatedly nominated by other boys in the school as a 'friend', and far from being a figure of fear, both he and Ryan are seen as boys who can be trusted and, if necessary, appealed to for help. Brian is one of many boys who describes Lewis as someone who can be approached for help:

PC: Can you tell me something about the other boys at the school?

Brian: Lewis Jones. When you've got something wrong, sometimes I go to him, and he talks to you, and he tells me to go to Mr Talbot.

PC: How do you mean: when you've 'got something wrong'?

Brian: Well. If someone's hitting you, or winding you up, then you go to Lewis. Lewis'll either sort it out or go to Mr Talbot.

PC: So you feel you can trust Lewis?
Brian: Yes.

Repeatedly, Lewis is singled out by his fellow pupils for his trust-worthiness. Ryan is the only boy who is critical of Lewis, finding his willingness to follow rules to the letter a little dull:

> If Mr Talbot tells him to do something, right, then Lewis has got to do it.
>
> . . .
>
> Lewis does a brilliant job as boss, right? I mean, he keeps us all quiet – he never gets us into trouble. . . . The problem is, he keeps us too quiet.

There is a backhanded compliment here, in that whilst Lewis keeps his fellow jobbers 'too quiet', he also, by the same rule, keeps them out of 'trouble'.

Pinning down the precise mechanism by which he achieves what amounts to control over the other boys is difficult. It is clear, on the one hand, that Lewis is identified, in part, by the boys, with the all-powerful Mr Talbot. Lewis is able to 'report' boys to Mr Talbot, and he is trusted by Mr Talbot. At the same time, however, Lewis is not feared by the boys. They seem to believe that Lewis exercises his obvious power responsibly. As we have seen already, Lewis is highly critical of other 'jobbers' who abuse their positions of trust. Lewis is seen by his fellows as being righteous, to the point where he will take up boys' complaints with staff, as well as sort out disputes among the boys without resorting to violence. Another important factor of Lewis's make-up is his compassion. Alex is one of several boys who describes an incident in which he was, in effect, coun-selled by Lewis, after a particularly upsetting weekend at home:

> I was really fed up. . . . I didn't want to talk. I didn't want to do nothing. Lew stayed with me for ages. I didn't want him to. I didn't ask him to. We had a fag. We was talking for ages. I felt really good afterwards. It was like I wasn't the only one; he knew what it was like. Lew's good like that.

We have a first-hand example of Lewis's sense of compassion and justice in his own interview, when he talks about former pupils at the school, and Max, the notorious bully, in particular:

> Max was known as a bully by the teachers, which in a way was wrong. I know a lot of teachers here don't think much of him.

But I think, if they cared for him – I mean, really cared for him here – that he wouldn't be like he is now. 'Cos I think when you're taking a kid from a broken home, it does him worse. . . . 'Cos, I mean, if he was at home. . . . How I can explain it is, why he is like he is, is 'cos no one's cared for him. And I think what makes some kids here so bad, like Fred [a former pupil, renowned for bullying and disruptive behaviour], 'cos no one really cared for Fred here. And Winston [another former pupil, with behavioural problems], no one cared for him. No one really sat down and talked to him about what he was doing. He just used to get told off and sent to bed, or something like that. I think that's what made him more angrier, nastier. But then you get teachers like Mr Badger [the headteacher]. Now, he will pull you aside, by yourself, and he will ask you why you did it, and do you think it's right. And he'll ask you the truth.

PC: Is that good?

Lewis: Yes. It helps you think. You get it sorted out.

It is difficult not to be impressed by Lewis, as a thoughtful and caring young man.

Compassion and thoughtfulness are not, however, the sole preserve of Lewis; we find Ryan expressing similar sentiments:

PC: What do you think of the kids here?

Ryan: I feel sorry for a lot of them, but I don't show it. I mean the kid who I probably feel most sorry for is John Wilson.

PC: Why's that?

Ryan: He's got nothing, has he? He ain't got nothing. I mean, he thinks he's white! [he is of mixed parentage].

PC: Does he?

Ryan: He really does believe he's white, yeah! And . . . he got his hair cut, right, here [by a member of the care staff, who is not a qualified hairdresser]. It got really fucked up, you know. Bodged up! And he knows that, but what can he do about it? How else can he – he ain't got no money. He can't go down town and get it cut himself. He can't go to no one else. He can't go home and say, 'Mum, get us an 'air cut!' 'Cos he ain't got no home to go to, has he? I mean, here is his home. Whatever they do to him here, they can't do nothing about. They could beat the shit out of him, but he couldn't do nothing. If he went to

the Social Services about it, they'd pass it over, because
he's a bit up here [indicating 'mental'], ain't he?

PC: Basically, he's very vulnerable then.

Ryan: Yes. He ain't got no one to turn to.

. . .

PC: Is there any way that you could help him?

Ryan: Yes, I do, sometimes. I buy him cars and things – little
cars. But I found out the next day –. I bought him a car,
right? One of those Dinky things. I found out, the next
day, the juniors had nicked it off him.

PC: So you're a bit of a big brother, then?

Ryan: I dunno [pause]. Some of them. I'd like to be, y'know.
I'd hate to be hated by them; for them to think I'm a
bully, something like that. [pause] 'Cos I know what
being bullied is. 'Cos when Max and that lot was here, I
got it every day. Me, Watson and Philip. We got chucked
about, like a piece of shit. And I can imagine now, how it
would be for the little ones. I mean. The juniors are now
like what we was to Max and that lot: little shits that mean
nothing. Which is what I don't wanna treat the juniors as.

PC: You feel you've got some responsibility to behave in a
certain way to them?

Ryan: Yes. I mean. Some of the little sods, I really hate, right?
But I know, if I saw them getting beaten up down town,
I'd jump in. No doubt! Even though, all the bad things
they done.

PC: Is that because you're all from the same school?

Ryan: I suppose so. But some of them are so defenceless, aren't
they?

PC: When you were a junior, were there any seniors like you
are now [i.e. compassionate]?

Ryan: Yes, there was Joe Smith. He was alright. I could talk to
him. He was the only one really.

Ryan's sense of empathy for the younger boys at the school is
striking here. Far from wishing to inflict on others what he has
suffered, Ryan shows a determination not to allow history to repeat
itself. In addition to his own detailed and consistent account, his
empathic feelings and compassionate behaviour, we have the
testimony of other boys, from across the age range of the school,

to indicate the truth of what he is saying. Also, in this extract, we have a reference to the value placed on having someone 'you could talk to' among the boys; once more stressing the high value that the boys attach to supportive interpersonal relationships.

Another interesting feature of these last two extracts is the fact although both Ryan and Lewis are, in places, highly critical of Farfield as a caring institution, they show by their attitudes, paradoxically, that there is a high quality of care in the school, of which they are integral features. This fact is further underlined by what we can learn about changes in the quality of life at Farfield, which Ryan, in particular refers to:

PC: Has it changed much, since you've been here?

Ryan: Yes, a lot, a lot.

PC: What sort of things?

Ryan: Well, Mr Talbot has. I mean, before he was hard, 'cos he had to be. We had Fred and Wayne [former pupils with reputations for difficult and aggressive behaviour] and that lot here. Nicking going on all the time, and fights. And we couldn't really smoke much, y'know; it was just certain times. And he's much more friendly now than he was before. He was like a proper headmaster before, you know, giving out rules. Now he's slackened off really . . .

PC: Do you think it's as tough now for the juniors, as it was for you?

Ryan: No, I don't think so. Because when Wayne and that lot were here, he was hard on everyone, and now he ain't. He's a lot more friendly. I mean: sweets. These parties he's been having, right? . . . Just on a normal weekend he'll go round and buy a load of sweets, stick it in the supper room, and we'll have a special supper. On average now, that's every three weeks, say. . . . Before, we'd be lucky if we got it any time during the year, apart from Christmas. The kids' birthday cakes used to be just something that the cook has made. Now he goes out and gets gateaux and stuff! [pause] I think he must trust the kids a lot more now, or else he wouldn't have got all the new wallpaper and stuff.

This apparently remarkable change in the principal's approach to running the school is attributed by Ryan to the changes in the pupil population. He believes that Mr Talbot had no choice but to run the school in a more authoritarian fashion because of the presence of difficult boys. Ryan also believes that the privileges and responsibilities enjoyed by himself and Lewis are contingent on their willingness to toe the line:

> I know that when I get to Lewis's position in jobs, I'm gonna want to have a laugh. I ain't gonna be just so to Mr Talbot, y'know. So I'll probably start losing responsibilities, but I don't really give a shit, [pause] 'cos it ain't fair on the other kids, who work for their jobs, yeah. They do the games room, they do the common rooms, and turn all the lights off everywhere, yeah. All they get's a cup of tea and a fag, and that's it, without having a bit of a laugh, y'know.

Once again, however, we find Ryan expressing his concerns about the school in terms of his feelings of compassion for other boys. Perhaps Ryan fails to see the qualities which make him one of the top jobbers. Ryan seems to be suggesting that it is only Ryan and Lewis's docility which keeps them in privileged positions, when it is their demeanour and attitudes, as well as the respect they receive from other boys, that is most striking to the observer. In these ways Ryan and Lewis represent qualities which pervade the school's caring ethos, and which seem to echo the most desirable of the staff qualities.

Many of the points that have just been made about the pupil community at Farfield are echoed in the Lakeside study. In spite of problems of transition, which were a source of distress to many boys, there was still a strong sense of community and loyalty among the boys. To some extent this was even stronger at Lakeside than Farfield, with boys declaring a much greater sense of ownership and control over their community, through the regular meetings and their maintenance work. We also find an example of the way in which the community of boys in schools of this type can develop an ethos of care and protectiveness of one another, which echoes some of the things that Ryan and Lewis at Farfield have reported. Jock tells of his earliest experiences at the school, and describes a 'system' which existed, at that time, whereby younger boys newly arrived at the school were adopted by a senior boy. It was the senior's duty to guide the younger boy through his early days at the school, and to help him settle in with a minimum of difficulty. The interesting thing about this, was that it was an informal and un-official system:

this was between the boys only. They had a system. It weren't a
staff idea; they didn't know nothing about it.

[Jock]

According to Jock, the older boys showed their charges:

what things you can't do and what things you can do. He'd help
you out of trouble.

Jock is adamant that these older boys 'weren't bullies', they simply
'looked after' the younger boys. Jock gives an example of one of
his own experiences of this 'system':

We [11-year-old Jock and another junior boy] were messing
around in a room, and running through the house. And Dave
Turner – one of the big lads here – stopped us and said: 'You're
gonna get told off and get a job, if you don't stop!' As I walked
away, the deputy head walked around the corner! So that sort of
thing. They stopped you before they [the staff] got to you.

Whilst there no longer appears to be a 'system' of this type in
operation at Lakeside, Jock seems to be carrying on the spirit of
these earlier days in his own dealing with younger pupils:

I tell the kids what to do. I don't tell them to smash windows, or
anything like that – I stop them from doing that. But if they're
under-age smoking, or anything like that, I'll tell them to get
away. . . . but I don't hit them . . .

More generally speaking there is a strong impression to be gained
from the boys of both schools of a sense of camaraderie and
mutual support among the pupil groups. In spite of the references
to 'winding-up' and occasional bullying, made by some boys there
is little doubt that for many boys, their peers provide them with
emotional support which is an important beneficial effect of the
schools, as the following Farfield boys state:

PC: Do you think going to a place like Farfield helps you,
          Malcolm?
Malcolm: It helps me [pause] to talk to some people. Some-
          times I have to pluck up the courage.
PC: So how does this place help you to talk to people?
Malcolm: Well, it's the kids here. First time I was here, er, I was
          laughing and joking with other kids. I got to know
          the staff.

PC: Was Farfield better than your old school for that?

Malcolm: Yeah, 'cos at the other school [a comprehensive] you couldn't really call them by their first names. Some of the staff you can here.

PC: So it's more pleasant here?

Malcolm: Yeah. Better than Blackford Comprehensive.

*   *   *

Jim: The kids here . . . they've cheered me up a couple of times when I've been unhappy. If I've been home for a weekend and it's gone wrong, they cheer me up when I come back. . . . Staff as well. . . . Miss O'Neill [RSW], my key worker, has a chat with me when I come back . . . what have I been doing; did I see my mates; how's my sister?

*   *   *

Alex: There's people here with the same problems as me, isn't there? . . . Like, some have got problems and that. Like my family – a couple or more people have got them. You know you're not the only one.

PC: Is that a good thing or a bad thing?

Alex: It's a good thing!

PC: Why's that then?

Alex: Because you can think, 'It ain't just me it's happening to; it's happening to a lot more people.'

PC: Do you ever talk to each other about your problems?

Alex: Well, very small things.

We find Lakeside boys making similar claims; for example:

Stan: When I went home I used to miss chatting to people [at night when in bed]. But now, one of my mates usually stays. . . . Most nights, me and Larry usually have a fag in bed at night, with the windows open. We don't reckon it's dangerous, 'cos we always make sure the fags are out and everything. I'll miss that at home, because my mum and step-dad don't like smoking.

What seems to come across strongest in these extracts is the sense of warmth and belonging that the boys derive from their peer relationships at these schools. Alex makes a poignant statement concerning his sense of relief at finding that there are other boys with the 'same problems' as he has; this is a clear indication of how the school has helped him to overcome the sense of isolation and confusion that he felt before coming to the school. It is also interesting the way in which Malcolm and Jim talk about the ways in which their peers and the staff help, again suggesting that this type of caring behaviour is an aspect of an overall school ethos, by which pupils and staff behave according to a code which stresses the importance of mutual care and understanding.

CONCLUSION: THE EFFECTS OF THE RESIDENTIAL EXPERIENCE

Otto Shaw, one of the great pioneers of residential schooling for 'maladjusted boys', claimed that the only certain way of knowing whether or not the regime at his school (Red Hill, Surrey) had been truly effective, would be to see what kind of adults the children of his former pupils grew into (Shaw, 1965). Underlying this are bold claims for the efficacy of the psychodynamic approach, which Shaw employed at Red Hill school. The interests of the present author are a little less ambitious. This book is about the experience of schooling as it is perceived by pupils. This is not to undervalue the importance of pupils' perceptions. As was argued in the opening chapters, pupils derive their sense of identity from their life experience, and it is, in turn, this sense of identity which influences the way they behave.

So far, we have explored these boys' views of how they came to be at residential schools, and their previous experience of schooling (see Chapter 4), and have juxtaposed these perceptions with their views of their residential experience (Chapter 5 and the present chapter). We have found that many of these boys have embarked upon a residential career, after having had particularly negative experiences of other schools, usually characterised by their being rejected by the schools. These problems are often accompanied by and interact with family difficulties. Whilst the peer group has seemed to offer some boys relief from these difficulties, it has also had an exacerbating effect. As has already been shown, one of the major difficulties experienced by these boys prior to attendance at their present schools has been centred on the poor relationships which they have had with significant adults in their lives (i.e. parents and teachers). For the most part, these boys arrive at Farfield and Lakeside accompanied by a sense of failure and dejection: they believe themselves to be 'bad', out of control, or trouble-makers. After all, they have often been told that they are these things, and their behaviour seems to support the image. The question is, has their residential school experience done anything to alleviate these difficulties? As we have already seen, there is some evidence for an affirmative answer to this question.

There are three main themes which emerge from the boys' accounts which link their residential school experiences with positive personal outcomes and the alleviation of difficulties. These themes are:

- RESPITE from distressing situations;
- RELATIONSHIPS with school staff that are positive and engender a sense of care and emotional support;
- OPPORTUNITIES for participation in a community which enable pupils to develop a sense of self-worth, to experience success and achievement.

Respite

One of the foundations of the residential experience, for many of these boys, is the respite it gives them from problematic situations in their home environments. In response to the questionnaire item: 'One of the good things about being here [at this school] is that it gives you a break from being at home', 62 per cent ($N = 55$) of pupils responding agreed. As we have seen in previous sections of this and earlier chapters, many boys ascribe positive personal outcomes to being away from home:

> It's usually horrible [at home] . . . when our dad's there. He spoils all the fun. . . . Some kids love being at home. I can't stand it. . . . I'm always glad to get back [to Lakeside].
>
> [Jock, Lakeside]

> The atmosphere in the ordinary school was OK, but as soon as I got home it was the atmosphere at home which really made me uneasy and nervous all the time. When I got here [Lakeside] I could relax a bit.
>
> [Larry, Lakeside]

I didn't really like knowing my family. Now I miss 'em, and all that. . . . I didn't get on with my mum and brothers. And I used to argue with my mum. That's just stopped now.

[Alex, Farfield]

I've settled down with my mum and dad a bit. And I think I've improved a bit . . . [as a result of] me being away from home.

[Jim, Farfield]

I think it's got better [his relationship with his mother] because we've spent longer times apart. It's nothing what I've said or what I've been told to say. I reckon it's the break.

[Ryan, Farfield]

The school's helped me change by helping my mum. . . . By me coming here, she can have a rest.

[John, Farfield]

It's helped my mum out. Like when I've been here I've been sorting myself out.

[Ian, Farfield]

Improvements in family relationships are sometimes attributed to the cooling-off period that a residential placement permits, thus enabling both parents and the pupil to reconsider their situation. In other circumstances the respite is simply a relief from a difficult situation which shows few immediate signs of improvement. Either way, these boys claim to experience at least a temporary escape from a highly stressful situation, and with that the opportunity to direct energies that have been sapped by past conflict toward more constructive goals. In some cases this clearly leads to a rekindling of dormant affections and possible reconciliation:

And I must be sorting myself out there. . . . Since last year we've been getting on well. It's got to the stage now where me and my mum have really got on well. I can go home every weekend, if I want to. Mr Talbot says I could as well. So it's not too bad now.

[Ian, Farfield]

I used to argue with my mum. That's all stopped now. There's things that I wouldn't do, like say I have a little argument with my mum now, I'll say sorry to her after. That's one thing I wouldn't even thought of doing when I was at home.

[Alex, Farfield]

Some boys also describe the effects of respite in terms of their decreased contact with delinquescent peers, and lack of opportunity to indulge in delinquent activities:

> If I had been at home, and hadn't come here, I'd probably be in the same place where our brother is at the moment [i.e. prison]. I used to nick things. Now I haven't got the bottle to nick. It's made me soft, but I respect that.
>
> [Jock, Lakeside]

> Farfield's changed me a lot. If I was at home now, I'd probably be inside or something. . . . I'd have a record. . . . I know there's a bunch of kids, some old mates, who, if I hang around with [them], I'll get nicked. . . . But I don't bother hanging around with them no more, because I know it will bodge up my life with the army. Before, I wouldn't have really thought of it.
>
> [Ryan, Farfield]

> [When at home] I don't want to go out much, 'cos I haven't got any good mates. They all gets in trouble. There's only about two or three of them, and I don't hardly see them much.
>
> [Ian, Farfield]

The third area from which their present situation gives them relief is their previous schools. The boys' previous experience of schooling covers a wide range of provision including mainstream and special schools but, as we have already seen, the experience of these settings has been a source of unhappiness, characterised by interpersonal conflict and failure:

> I got kicked out [of a comprehensive school] because I didn't fit into normal schools. . . . I was messing around in my old school. Like in lessons, I'd start playing around and that in lessons. They was trying to make out that I was worse than I was. Half the time, I was just shouting things out. Talking; standing up. Things like that. Just walking around like. They'd tell you to get out. Sometimes they'd tell you to get out for a little reason, and I say, 'I ain't getting out!' And there starts a fight, with me and a member of staff. . . .. Them just dragging me out. They was trying to make out I was worse than I was.
>
> [Tom, Lakeside]

Tom, as will be recalled, has a fairly negative attitude to Lakeside, and actually wants to return to the comprehensive school he is describing in the above quotation, so that he can take public examinations. Even Tom, however, seems to tacitly acknowledge that the distance that has been placed between himself and his former school, by virtue of his placement at Lakeside, has helped him. He has clearly thought a great deal about his situation, and is now trying to exercise some control over his life. He is now determined to show that he is capable of returning to his old school:

> Now I don't mess about so much in different situations. I know when not to mess about. I can't say I've changed a dramatic lot. I suppose I've changed, in that I've grown up slightly.

He states that he now realises the importance of examination passes more so than he did in the past, and that if re-admitted to the comprehensive school he 'will behave a lot differently, because I've got exams coming up':

> I don't think they [the staff] will blame the trouble on me. If I was different in the first place, they wouldn't think it was me.

Other boys' responses to previous schools are less forgiving and more finalised than Tom's:

> Teachers in comprehensives are all stuck up.
>
> [Frank, Lakeside]

> [The staff at Lakeside] they're a lot better. They're more like people! When I was at Rushforth [special school], they were more like robots really. You do something wrong, the first thing they do is grab 'em and stick 'em in a room, and just lock them up!
>
> [Arthur, Lakeside]

> I've improved in everything [since being at Farfield]!
> . . .
> Silliness . . . kept on every minute of the day [at his former school, a residential special school]. . . . As soon as I hit the school [Farfield] it just stopped! Like it was just a bit of wind, like. Just blew away.
> . . .
> It's just the school [Farfield] it's easy-going, it's more relaxed. Y'know you can enjoy yourself. . . . It's more free in this school. At Spencer House [his previous school] you were so blocked in. All together in one common room, you know. When you wanted to watch TV you got two members of staff sitting down,

and fifty kids in a room. This was where me silliness came in. . . .
All packed in. Y'know. Like a package. You're put in and stopped
in there. As soon as I came here, I felt like the wrapping was
chucked away. I was free! Walk out and do anything you like!

[Colin, Farfield]

I just had enough of school [day special], all the bullies there!

[John, Farfield]

Even boys with more neutral attitudes to their former schools
indicate that Farfield and Lakeside have something extra to offer:

I had been thought of as a bully in my old school. . . . I used to
get bored in class, so I used to throw things. Now I could stay in
class all day.

[Jock, Lakeside]

Well, it's [Farfield] more relaxed, i'n' it? I mean, at normal
schools the bell goes and everyone's gotta shoot off to the next
lesson. But here you can take a bit more time, have an extra
hour or finish off something you want to finish.

[Ryan, Farfield]

I just couldn't get there [former comprehensive school] for some
reason. I just couldn't face it. . . . I used to get bullied a bit, but not
much – just average. I don't know why it was. My sister was the
same. . . . The staff at the school were alright. It wasn't the school's
fault, it was me! . . . I'm not bothered about going to class now.

[Stan, Lakeside]

Later, Stan suggests that Lakeside has helped him where his previous school failed:

The school [Lakeside] has made me grow up in myself. Helped
me go to school; get on with my classwork.

[Stan, Lakeside]

There are clearly many different kinds of benefits to be gained by
pupils from being away from their home areas, their former
schools and peer groups. Of course, being away from home is not
a magical panacea for the emotional and behavioural problems.
Colin, who is something of an expert on residential schools, backs
up this point. What matters is the quality of what the school
provides to go with the respite. It is to the effects of school life that
the final two sections of this chapter are devoted.

Relationships

Wilson and Evans (1980), in their study of a wide range of provision for children with emotional and behavioural difficulties
concluded:

> what matters most in the treatment of disturbed children is the
> quality of the relationships offered to them.

[p.157]

This view is echoed in the writings of the pioneer workers in this
field (Bridgeland, 1971), and continues to be a focus for modern
writers and researchers in the field (e.g. Cronk, 1987).

Relationships between staff and pupils in the two schools of the
present study are of central concern to the boys, and are the basis
for many of the positive effects of the schools. The effects of these
high-quality relationships on the boys are evident in the interview
material. We have already seen the ways in which the boys in both
schools value the relationships they share with staff. For many of
the boys these relationships are much better than the ones they
have had with adults in the past. The closeness of the relationships
with staff can have a negative side, as we can see from the discussion of the Lakeside boys' reaction to the departure of their
former headmaster. It is argued, however, that these negatives are
outweighed by the benefits obtained by individual boys.

As we have already shown (earlier in the present chapter), the
boys place a great deal of emphasis on the emotional support that
staff offer them. Boys repeatedly refer the fact that they can talk to
staff, and that staff will listen to them. The singular importance of
this cannot be underestimated. One of the fundamental tenets of
counselling psychology is the view that through talk individuals
both express and discover their personal concerns. The counsellor
acts as a figure of affirmation: showing the speaker that what he
has to say is of interest and so encouraging the speaker to explore
his or her inner world further still (Mearns and Thorne, 1988). In
particular, person-centred counselling (Rogers, 1951; 1980), when
successful, is a voyage of self-discovery, in which the counsellee
learns to accept and understand his/her own feelings and concerns, and is empowered to mobilise inner resources to overcome
difficulties. Whilst there is no formal counselling programme in
operation at either Farfield or Lakeside schools, we can identify
many counselling-like situations and outcomes, which relate to the

pupil relationships. We can also find elements of what Rogers (1980) refers to as the 'person-centered approach' to daily life, which is concerned with ways in which the central aspects of his counselling philosophy can be applied to the routine inter-personal activities of daily life.

Person-centredness

Rogers (1980) argues that people in modern society are often isolated and alienated from one another. This is demonstrated in the way in which power tends to be distributed in accordance with people's economic usefulness. Those who are too old or too young to work, and those who for other reasons without income and employment are the least powerful and least regarded in our society. This value-system pervades western culture to such an extent that people tend to internalise this value system: judging the value of others and themselves in terms which are extraneous to the personal qualities of human beings. One of the mani-festations of this culture, Rogers suggests, is the disaffection, alien-ation and delinquescence apparent in society, and particularly among youth. Rogers's remedy is deceptively simple: give people a sense of their own value and worth and they will learn to value others, and the relationships they have with them: show other people that you respect and care for them and they will respect and care for themselves; in the process they will learn to respect and care for others too.

The mechanism by which Rogers claims we can begin to set this ball rolling revolves around three 'core conditions':

1 *Unconditional positive regard*
   i.e. communicating absolute acceptance of the other person as a person who is worthy of interest and attention;
2 *Empathy*
   i.e. the ability to look at situations through the eyes of the other person, and communicating the understanding of the other's feelings, that stems from this, to the other person;
3 *Being genuine* (sometimes referred to as 'congruence')
   i.e. communicating one's honest reaction to what the other person says: good or bad.

In both interpersonal and institutional terms, this approach amounts to power-sharing. The equal right of everyone to express themselves and to be listened to is guaranteed. No matter what the individual says, the others will never withdraw their acceptance of the individual as a person. The knowledge that others will strive to reach an understanding of the individual's viewpoint, and their promise of unending support, encourages the individual to strive ever harder to self-expression and accurate definitions of feelings. This deep probing of the self can be a painful and distressing experience, accompanied by feelings of low self-esteem. The product of all this, however, is a greater knowledge of self. And because the knowledge is shared with another person, who continues to accept and so validate the person doing the sharing, the feelings of low self-esteem diminish, and the individual moves towards self-acceptance. In the process of searching and confronting the inner self the individual begins to discover their true values, and it is through this discovery that they come to take control of their lives; to change the things they don't like. The process is one in which self-esteem and confidence grow, and the fears and inhibitions which have kept the individual apart from others diminish, and they too can slowly begin to try to relate to others in this 'person-centred' way and form a working part of a person-centred community.

Rogers's theory sounds hopelessly idealistic. Yet, whilst neither Farfield nor Lakeside could be described as fully 'person-centred' institutions, we can detect significant elements of the person-centred approach in these two schools.

As we have seen, in both schools the boys believe that staff care for them and are approachable. They believe that staff will listen to them when they have problems they wish to discuss. In this sense then, the boys, for the most part, believe that there are members of staff who hold them in positive regard, and who they can trust with their feelings:

> Before I came here, I never used to speak to anyone about my troubles. . . . I used to say nothing to no one, when I had a problem. I talk to anyone now.
>
> [Jock, Lakeside]

> The staff here are more prepared to sit down and talk to you, and talk your problems out. They'll help you out with anything.
>
> [Stan, Lakeside]

It's [Farfield] helped me a lot. People I can talk to. . . . They've helped me. . . . [I've talked about] problems at home.

[Alex, Farfield]

Mr Brown, I know I can trust. . . . I treat Mr Brown more as a mate.

[Ryan, Farfield]

[The staff here] they're more like people!

[Arthur, Lakeside]

You can speak to them. They sort out your problems for you.

[Tom, Lakeside]

Staff will give you more time, if you want to talk to them. Charlie will stay with you, even if he is off-duty, until it is sorted out. They have more time for you.

[Frank, Lakeside]

It is clear that boys in these schools have members of staff to whom they feel they can relate as person to person, rather than pupil to teacher. This a sure sign of empathy: a feeling of seeing oneself reflected in the other person. This does not apply to all staff–pupil relationships, but it is clearly present. This person-to-person quality can also extend to situations in which staff are exerting authority:

You do something wrong . . . here, they talk to you. And you know you've done wrong, so you just have to take it. . . . Sometimes, you don't want to listen; they just let you go and have a walk, and come back and talk to you later.

[Arthur, Lakeside]

In Arthur's statement we see an example of the way in which a non-authoritarian approach shifts responsibility to the pupil: he has to listen to staff not because he will be punished if he doesn't, but because he 'knows' he's 'done wrong'. This is an example of a boy employing his own sense of values to regulate his behaviour. We see another striking example of this in Ryan's description of the way in which he admits to his Key Worker that he has been lying to him in relation to the theft of some clothing:

The third time, I let it out. 'Cos he made me feel so bad when he said, 'Right, Ryan, I believe you. But if I find out it's a lie, just don't bother talking to me again.' And I knew, if he found out it was a lie I wouldn't be talking to him now. It was then I thought, 'Shit! I've had it, haven't I? I suppose I've got to tell him now, and get it all cleared up. And if I get nicked, I get nicked!' So I told him. And he said, he knew it weren't the truth, what I told him.

Here, Ryan makes a moral choice. He is prepared to suffer being 'nicked', for the sake of telling the truth to a person he values highly, both in spite of and because the other person has trusted him and taken his earlier lie as the truth. It might be argued that the staff member here is being somewhat manipulative, in that he is trading on his good relationship with the boy, and even implying that he might withdraw his friendship if Ryan proves to be lying. Ryan's description, however, emphasises the choice that he makes, rather than pressure from the staff member; after all, the staff member has already stated that he is prepared to accept Ryan's lie as the truth. So it is Ryan's desire to repay trust with trust that is the key feature of this transaction, even if it means Ryan will have to suffer for it.

This theme of facing up to responsibility for themselves and their actions, is referred to frequently by the boys. As Rogers says, this can be a painful and distressing process, and so it is sometimes resisted. We find many boys describing how their experience of being at one or other of the schools has brought them to an understanding of their personal situations, and some of the things that they can do themselves to change these situations for the better:

> It's made me look at things, I suppose. It's made me think, 'If I do this thing, I'll be stupid.' . . . I think it's made me more sensible. I know there's a bunch of kids, some old mates, who if I hang around with, I'll get nicked. . . . But I don't bother hanging round with them no more, because I know it will bodge up my life with the army. Before, I wouldn't have really thought of it.
>
> [Ryan, Farfield]

> I was at home then. I weren't bothered about what I done. Probably 'cos I was mixed up when I first come here.
> . . .
> The school's put me in a different way, y'know. It's made me look at things different. . . . Like, say I have a little argument with my mum now, I say sorry to her after. That's one thing I wouldn't even thought of doing when I was at home before.
>
> [Alex, Farfield]

When I've been here, I've been sorting myself out. And I must be sorting myself out there. . . . Since this time last year, I've been getting on well [at home].

[Ian, Farfield]

It's [Lakeside] taught me to get on with things and not to argue. Before I came to this school, if someone called me a name, I'd go absolutely mad, and start lashing out. Now I can control it; take it.

[Arthur, Lakeside]

Now I don't mess about so much in different situations. I know when not to mess about.

[Tom, Lakeside]

There are clear signs that for these and other boys the path to their present situations has not been easy; they have had to come to terms with some 'painful and distressing' images of themselves. Ryan describes his pre-Farfield self as:

I've been bad. A trouble-maker at school; bad to me mum. You know, about every bad thing.

From being 'bad' Ryan has progressed to a self-image of one who is 'more sensible', which is clearly an indication of an improvement in his self-image. Similarly, Alex is no longer 'confused', or resistant to change; in fact, he believes that he has 'improved in everything'. Colin describes his transformation from 'brute' to someone, all of whose 'silliness' is now gone. At Lakeside, we find Stan, describing his ascent from being a friendless truant who simply could not bring himself to school, to a person who has 'grown up', and now confident in ways that he never was before:

The school has made me grow up in myself. Helped me to go to school; get on with my classwork.

He is in no doubt of how he has been helped:

I think he [his teacher] has helped me quite a bit. He's helped me with my work. Talked to me quite bit. Like I never used to like going out anywhere, to do anything. Now I feel quite happy to go to snooker clubs. . . . John [the teacher] takes quite a few of us there. We save our pocket money from the weekend to go there.

Wherever there is this sense of improvement, there is an indication of an improved self-esteem.

Of course, there are still some boys who have some way to go. We find Chris (Farfield) still struggling with low self-image, not unlike the one that Ryan had to start with:

> I've been a trouble-maker all my life. I expect I'll always be a trouble-maker.

But this could represent a beginning of the gradual process of self-acceptance. We see this process taking shape more clearly among a number of the Lakeside boys, particularly Larry, Frank and Tim. These boys are all critical of the 'softness' of the Lakeside regime, and claim to prefer the 'strictness' of the former regime, where staff would hit children for swearing and where disobedience was summarily punished:

> The present staff couldn't do nothing. . . . If you're smoking in your room, they can't stop you. We take advantage of the system. If they say you can't do something, we just tell them to fuck off!
>
> [Frank, Lakeside]

> If you told a member of staff to eff off when Ed was here, you'd be put on washing-up or sent to bed. Now they'd [i.e. the staff] probably say sorry!
>
> [Tim, Lakeside]

This strong sense of dissatisfaction is interesting, mainly because although it is ostensibly directed at the school staff, its true target is the behaviour of the boys themselves. They do not think they should be allowed to swear at staff, etc. They clearly dislike the disorder that is represented by their misbehaviour, but they are not yet ready to take the responsibility to make the situation more comfortable by their own efforts. There are, however, glimmerings of the necessary self-knowledge:

> I think it should be more stricter. But if they get more strict, I'm going to be the one that's breaking all the rules!
>
> [Larry, Lakeside]

Larry's recognition of the paradoxical nature of the situation is close to a recognition of the responsibility he needs to take, but still falls short of the necessary level of self-knowledge:

It would be better if everybody would try to cooperate more with
staff. Instead of thinking that the staff are the screws and we are
the prisoners. Some of them have got a prison attitude here.
Not me! . . . They're trying to break the system all the time.

[Larry, Lakeside]

Tim also seems to be beginning to move towards a shift in values,
for he says that in spite of disliking the softness of the new regime:

I still respect Maurice, because he's more than fair.

At last Tim is placing a value on fairness alone: strictness is no
longer a necessary condition for the bestowal of respect. So maybe
the optimism of some of the Lakeside boys is going to be rewarded:

Things will get better. They'll settle down.

[Arthur, Lakeside]

It will get better eventually.

[Stan, Lakeside]

I dunno. Maybe it's changing for the better. If you'd have asked
me a year ago, I'd have said, 'No, it's changing for the worse.'
But I suppose I'm getting used to the system.

[Larry, Lakeside]

One of the most encouraging and impressive aspects of the interpersonal relationships in both schools is the quality of empathy
which is evident among the boys. This was dealt with in some detail
in an earlier section. The importance of it to the present discussion is the way in which it shows, albeit on a restricted scale, a
sense in which the humanistic values which characterise staff–
pupil relationships are reflected in some of the relationships
among the boys. Here we see demonstrated the strength of some
of the older boys' sense of their own worth. They are strong
enough to support their fellow pupils in the same caring and
empathic way as they perceive some staff to behave. This,
combined with the image of staff that is presented, suggests that in
both schools there are strivings, on the part of some pupils and
some staff, to promote an ethos which places a high value on the
individual, and is to a large extent truly 'person-centred'.

Positive signification

The experience of these boys demonstrates the extent of the influence that interpersonal relationships can have on the self-image and behaviour of individuals. Just as deviant identities can be socially constructed and attached to individuals, as in the processes of 'typing' or 'labelling' (Hargreaves *et al.*, 1975; Rist, 1977), so, as we see here, can positive images be created by the same mechanism. These boys are treated by staff in ways which communicate the staff members' view of them as worthwhile and important people, who are capable of positive behaviour; this is the antithesis of many of the boys' previous experience of people, who have treated them in ways which communicate a view of them as 'bad', worthless and deviant. The impact of this positive experience is to cause the boys to internalise these positive views of themselves, and so to develop images of themselves as worthwhile and capable individuals, who have the power to control their behaviour and act on the difficulties they encounter in productive ways. In short some of these boys have gone through a process of *positive signification*, whereby the characteristics by which they come to define themselves are associated with positive, as opposed to negative attributes. As Matza (1976) puts it:

> To signify is to *stand for* in the sense of representing or exemplifying. An object that is signified, whether it be a man or a thing, is rendered more meaningful. To be signified a thief does not assure the continuation of such pursuits; but it *does* add to the meaning of a theft in the life of that person in the eyes of others . . . signifying makes its object more significant. . . . The object enjoys or suffers enhanced meaning. To be signified a thief is to lose the blissful identity of one, who among other things happens to have committed a theft.
>
> [p.127]

Many of these boys have been signified as 'deviant' or 'maladjusted', prior to placement in these schools, and they have come to accept this view of themselves and even live up to it. The experience of these schools, particularly the interpersonal relationships, has offered them new significations: new and positive identities. The boys who are most advanced in this process no longer define themselves in terms of their 'badness', but now see their 'badness' as something either of the past or at least within their control. Their defining features are now their positive achievements and successes.

Whilst interpersonal relationships are the central feature of this mechanism of change, there is one other area of school experience which is vitally important for the exercise and development of these growing, positive identities, and that is the area of 'opportunities'.

Opportunities

Respite from home-based difficulties creates a sense of relief, which enables boys to reflect on their situations in an atmosphere of relative calm. Good quality interpersonal relationships provide the boys with the necessary support as well the impetus and confidence to face and contend with their personal difficulties. The social organisation of the schools provides a third important ingredient, in the form of various opportunities, which help to promote and reinforce positive pupil development. It is in considering the range and types of opportunities that schools make available to their pupils that we can gain a sense of the values (or ethos) which underly the school. In these schools we find a common ethos which places a high value on pupils' individuality and their need for experiences which will build self-esteem and confidence.

We have already seen evidence of the ways in which boys are incorporated into the organisational structures at the two schools. At Farfield, senior boys can attain the status of 'jobber', at Lakeside boys can become 'helpers'. Both of these roles offer all boys the possibility of achieving an enhanced status, though at Lakeside, as we have seen, there is some dissatisfaction (for historical reasons) at the lack of responsibility which accompanies the helper role. At Lakeside, however, there are opportunities for involvement in the running and organisation of the school through the system of group and unit meetings. The involvement of boys in the maintenance programme at Lakeside serves a similar function.

Each of these facets of school life make available to boys situations in which they can perform and explore the new and positive sense of self that they are beginning to develop. A useful way of thinking about this is provided by Davies (1984), in her study of deviance among girls in a comprehensive school. She employs the concept of scripts to describe the ways in which personal identities are developed. A script is defined as:

the way an individual makes a statement about their identity and their definition of the situation. . . . It is the result of a person formulating a certain interpretation, combination or selection of wider type scripts. . . . A person's script . . . indicates where that person stands in relation to what he or she perceives to be going on.

[p.96]

The individual's choice of scripts is, however, limited:

A person's repertoire of acts and statuses originates in, and must be validated by, the social group.

[p.98]

At Lakeside and Farfield, therefore, we can see examples of the way in which certain scripts are made available to boys, through the routine patterns of institutional life. From what we have seen in earlier sections, these scripts can be said to include:

• active and valued participant in community life;
• 'helper';
• 'jobber';
• befriender of younger boys;
• worthy of trust and care;
• critic of care practices;
• peer counsellor/counsellee;
• successful student/worker;
• master of one's own problems.

Each of these 'scripts' is facilitated by the organisational patterns of the schools. Each script enables pupils to perform behaviours which provide a source of pride and a sense of ahievement, capability and self-worth.

An important aspect of the range of opportunities lies in their diversity. Questionnaire returns and interviews indicate that boys believe there to be many different criteria by which to judge their progress and success at the schools. Over 70 per cent ($N = 57$) of responding boys from both schools agreed with the following statements (figures in brackets refer to level of agreement):

You don't have to be good at schoolwork to do well here.

(80 per cent)

Your behaviour is more important than your schoolwork here.

(75 per cent)

To do well here you have to try to get on well with staff.

(75 per cent)

To do well here you have to try to get on well with other pupils.

(83 per cent)

To do well here you have to show that you can be trusted.

(86 per cent)

To do well here you have to try to do well in your school work.

(70 per cent)

To do well here you have to try to do your jobs well.

(70 per cent)

These findings are reflected in the interviews where boys describe themselves as 'improving' over a range of areas, including in their educational attainments, their abilities to relate to other people, their attitudes to schooling and work:

When I first come here, I couldn't stand it! I came up the front drive, put my bags in the sewing room, went to my bedroom, got changed. The next minute I had to do do work and everything! Sweeping! Jobs! But I got used to it. And it's worth it. It just comes natural. So that when you leave school, you just think, 'Oh, work, it's just natural.'

. . .

Before I came to this school I couldn't do maths or anything.

. . .

It's taught me to get on with things and not to argue. Before I came to this school, if someone called me a name, I'd go absolutely mad, and start lashing out. Now I can control it; take it.

[Arthur, Lakeside]

Now I don't mess about so much in different situations.

[Tom, Lakeside]

This school has given me a bit more understanding of life.

[Larry, Lakeside]

The school has helped me grow up in myself. Helped me go to school; get on with my classwork. I'm more confident in myself. Being able to do things I never thought I could do.

[Stan, Lakeside]

[Being here has] calmed me down. . . . It's helped me with my school[work].

[Malcolm, Farfield]

I think I've improved in my behaviour.

[Jim, Farfield]

I've improved in everything!

[Colin, Farfield]

It's straightened me out, really.

[Ryan, Farfield]

It seems that boys feel they are given the scope to develop in areas which are of particular importance to them as individuals, rather than having to conform to a narrow ideal which may not encompass their individual strengths.

Opportunities to develop are closely linked with the quality of interpersonal relationships at the schools. In fact, these relationships present substantial and important opportunities of their own, as we have already seen. We find Ryan, Alex, Malcolm (Farfield), Jock, Arthur and Stan (Lakeside), in particular, describing their own progress in terms which indicate a complex interaction between these two areas of influence. The staff relationships provide a basis of confidence and support, whilst the opportunities serve to reinforce the boys' strengthening self-images, by giving them situations in which they can take responsibility and make decisions. From filling potholes on the school drive, or taking on a protective role in relation to younger boys, these are confidence-building experiences, which are enabled by the schools' patterns of organisation.

Another important factor present in both schools is a sense of attachment which many boys express towards their schools. At Lakeside and Farfield, there is a sense of ownership expressed by boys. They are distinctly aware of their personal and shared spaces: bedrooms and bed spaces are personalised; boys make clear distinctions between their own rooms or 'units', and those of other boys. The Lakeside boys also show pride in their maintenance activities and the fruits of their building skills. The sense of ownership is further extended for Lakeside boys, through their involvement in day-to-day decision-making in group and unit meetings. Whilst Farfield boys do not have such formal involvement in decision-making, they do express a sense of ownership in their pride in the facilities that they see as having been provided *for them*. These various experiences all contribute to boys' feelings of self-worth, and indicate something of the support that the school environment can provide. These are important factors which help to build boys' confidence, and thus promote their ability and willingness to face difficult personal situations from a position of strength.

Similarly, the classroom experience at both schools is characterised by individualised work programmes and a degree of flexibility which permits pupils the opportunities to make their own decisions and choices. Staff play a supportive role here too, encouraging pupils, helping pupils and allowing pupils flexibility and space to develop individually, and the chance to work at their own pace. Interestingly, this is an area of some disagreement among the Lakeside boys, who resent the 'softness' of staff who refuse to force them to work. Here, again, there is evidence of a developing sense of self-discipline:

> It's nowhere near as strict [as a comprehensive school], and you don't do half as much work here. That's bad that is. I can't stand work myself . . . it's boring. But when you were at senior school, and you were made to do it, you learned a lot more. I don't want to do it, but sometimes, I think you've got to do it, or you'll regret it when you get older. So I have a go!
>
> [Larry, Lakeside]

Larry's determination to 'have a go' seems to sum up an important quality common to both schools. It is, at its best, a sense of autonomy and self-worth which derives from the experiences of being valued, of belonging and of responsibility that the schools provide. For many boys, their previous experience of people and schools has been such that 'having a go' has often been limited to aggression. These are boys whose self-confidence and self-esteem have been constantly undermined by failures in school and in interpersonal relationships. They have often lacked any belief in their capacity to 'fit in' or to 'get on'. These residential schools have helped unlock, in many of these boys, suppressed potential which enables them to 'have a go' in a positive way. For the first time, some these boys are able to say that they have achieved something positive, and be proud of what they have done. However, just as self-images can be built up so they can be broken down again. For these boys who have reached some sense of mastery over themselves and those who are taking their first steps along this path, there is at least the knowledge that they are not thoroughly bad or intrinsically deviant.

We don't know what will happen to these boys when they leave these schools. We don't know what influences they will come under, or whether they will continue to develop in ways set in motion at Lakeside and Farfield. We have, however, had some insight into what they think and demonstrate to be circumstances that are conducive to the kind of positive outcomes that are of interest to all those who are concerned about problems of childhood deviance and disaffection from school.

Part III

School effectiveness, disaffection and mainstream schools

This book is concerned with the ways in which environment and social relationships can influence attitudes and behaviour. It is argued that schools can have a significant effect on the ways in which pupils behave within the school context. Specifically, this book has presented evidence which shows how two groups of pupils have found their experience of schooling in two residential schools to be enriching, rewarding and a basis for positive personal development. This is in spite of the fact that these same pupils have been labelled as disruptive and unmanageable by some schools, and have found their previous experience of schooling in other institutions distressing and damaging. Having explored some of the ways in which these schools achieve these ends, mainly from the pupils' perspective, we now turn to the question: can any of these insights be applied to mainstream schools? Chapter 7 considers the findings from the residential study from the perspective of research on school effectiveness, and links concepts drawn from this research with the outcomes observed in the residential schools. Chapter 8 takes a brief look at the current policy issues surrounding state education and schools in England and Wales, and considers some of the possible implications of this situation for disaffected and disruptive pupils. The remainder of this chapter gives an account of one mainstream secondary school's attempt to tackle the problem of disaffection.

Chapter 7

School effectiveness

The idea of school effectiveness, as it is generally understood today, began its life during the mid-1970s. It was born, in part, out a dissatisfaction with the then dominant idea, that schools had little or no effect on pupil performance characteristics in the face of cultural and social determinants (Reynolds, 1985). In the intervening years an ever-growing body of research has developed which indicates that schools can and do have a powerful effect on the social behaviour, attendance and achievement of pupils. This research has shown that schools with similar pupil and catchment area characteristics, achieve remarkably different outcomes, in social and educational terms (Rutter *et al.*, 1979; Reynolds and Sullivan, 1979, 1981; Mortimore *et al.*, 1988; Smith and Tomlinson, 1989). Much of this research has been of a large-scale quantitative type. Researchers have employed increasingly sophisticated statistical techniques in order to provide accurate measures of pupil progress and behaviour (Mortimore *et al.*, 1988; Smith and Tomlinson, 1989). In addition, researchers have collected data on a wide range of variables including: pupils' attitudes to school, teachers and peers; pupils' self-concepts, peer group relations; head and deputy headteachers' perceptions of school organisation and policies; teacher views on class organisation and policies, and teacher strategies; parents' views of the school and their children's progress; as well as observational data. The task of identifying those school factors which are critical to outcomes is, understandably, extremely difficult, as the researchers acknowledge:

> it is alarming rather than helpful to find such a large number of relationships, unless there is a way of understanding how they all fit together.
>
> (Smith and Tomlinson, 1989, p.25)

The identification of 'key factors' in effective schools, then, is less a product of statistical analysis, and more a product of theorising on the basis of the statistical findings. Such theories are:

> derived from a combination of careful examination and discussion of the statistical findings, and the use of educational and research judgement. They represent the interpretation of the research results by an inter-disciplinary team of researchers and teachers.
>
> (Mortimore *et al.* 1988, p.248)

The important thing to recognise about this research, then, is that its product is theory, albeit well-grounded and rigorously supported theory. And like any theory, we must beware of taking it for granted, or assuming that it is 'proven'.

This is not to say that school effectiveness research is in any sense diminished or devalued by its theoretical nature. On the contrary, the discovery of theory is a stimulus to debate and re-appraisal, and provides a basis for informed innovation and further evaluative research. Smith and Tomlinson (1989) argue for future school effectiveness research to 'concentrate on testing clearly articulated theories in a more focused way' (p.26). Whilst this is desirable, it must be remembered that too much emphasis on the verification of theory can lead to a neglect of the means whereby theories are generated. This has been a criticism levelled at earlier generations of educational researchers, on the basis that research which is limited to theory testing is resticted by the quality of the proposed theory (Glaser and Strauss, 1967).

The present book is very much concerned with looking at school effectiveness from a comparatively unusual viewpoint, namely that of the pupils. The central section of the book has dealt with pupils' perceptions of schools. In this way the book fits in with a tradition of broadly ethnographic educational research which includes important studies by Hargreaves (1967), Hargreaves *et al.* (1975), Sharp and Green (1975), Willis (1978), Ball (1981), Schostak (1983), Davies (1984) and Cronk (1987). This is the first book to be centrally concerned with the perceptions of children in residential special schools for school pupils with emotional and behavioural problems. From a school-effectiveness point of view, this is an important focus for study for the following reasons:

1 School effectiveness researchers have employed measures of disadvantage as elements in their comparisons of schools, and have used behavioural measures and attendance levels in assessing school outcomes. The pupils from Lakeside and Farfield speak from the perspective of children who are perceived to have emotional and behavioural difficulties, and many of them describe a history of truancy. 'Disadvantage' is a difficult concept to operationalise, but in terms used by school effectiveness researchers (i.e. low family income, absence of one parent, involvement of Social Services), we find many Lakeside and Farfield boys coming from 'disadvantaged' backgrounds. In this sense these boys represent a critical group. They are pupils for whom particular mainstream schools have found themselves unable to cater. This is not to suggest that such schools are, by definition, ineffective and necessarily to blame for these pupils' difficulties. What is of interest here is what the boys have to say about their previous school experience, and how this might relate to their difficulties.

2 Each of these pupils has experience of a number of different schools, and many have attended a range of different types of provision (mainstream school, day special school, residential school, primary, secondary, off-site unit, on-site unit). This enables the boys to offer an informed comparative perspective.

3 The most interesting thing about what these boys have to tell us is their broad agreement with the school effectiveness researchers. These boys show us that they too believe that schools make a difference. By and large, they find their residential schools to be effective, in their own terms. The importance of these perceptions lies in the fact that these boys have often had unhappy and distressing experiences in previous schools. What they have to tell us about the differences between their present and former situations is, therefore, of particular interest. The boys are able to exemplify and account for this effectiveness in terms of school factors, in ways which give us insight into the meaning of school effectiveness.

This focus on the pupils' perceptions of effectiveness is vitally important. It is only by trying to develop a construction of the school environment through the eyes of pupils that we can begin to understand the ways in which aspects of that environment impinge upon them. By learning about what matters to pupils in their schools, we can start to understand the mechanisms for producing and reducing disaffection, and then employ this understanding in the development of a whole-school approach. It must, however, be remembered of course that these pupils are speaking for no one other than themselves. We cannot generalise, from what these pupils say, about what all pupils think or might think. These pupils simply offer their view of their situation, and so give us an insight into a very particular set of circumstances. The value of such an account is that it provides us with a living context in which we can explore important issues.

It is now necessary to develop our interpretation of what the pupils have told us in the light of school effectiveness work, and to see what bearing this might have on our understanding of effectiveness in mainstream schools. It is important to note, before embarking on this analysis, that the research presented in this book is not as focused as the existing school effectiveness research. Its origins lie in an attempt to obtain pupils' firsthand accounts of their experience of schooling. Thus they were not questioned systematically about issues of relevance to school effectiveness, they were simply asked to talk about those aspects of their school lives which they felt to be significant. Given these differences between school effectiveness research and the present study, it is pertinent to ask two questions:

1 What commonalities are there (if any) between the components of effective schools, as they are identified by the boys from Lakeside and Farfield, and those identified by school effectiveness researchers?
2 What if anything can be added to our understanding of school effectiveness by the boys of Lakeside and Farfield?

Before we can address these questions directly, it is necessary to highlight some of the differences between the present research and that of the school effectiveness researchers in greater detail.

TWO DIFFERENT APPROACHES TO RESEARCH IN SCHOOLS

It is important first of all to make some clear distinctions between the nature of the evidence which is derived from the study of Lakeside and Farfield, and the school effectiveness research. The school effectiveness studies have developed out of a positivist tradition of educational research which asserts that social phenomena can be usefully understood through the use of research techniques which are equivalent to those used by researchers in the natural sciences. Educational research in this tradition proceeds from the basis of hypotheses which are tested through the accumulation and analysis of statistical data. In education, this type of research often takes the form of 'process-product' studies (e.g. Wittrock, 1986), of which school effectiveness work is an example. In the case of the school effectiveness research, the aim has been to explore possible relationships between school outcomes (in the form of measures of behavioural and educational attainment) and school processes (in the form of physical and organisational features of schools). Different researchers in this field have found, repeatedly, that when the characteristics of the intake characteristics of their pupils and other environmental factors are controlled, school processes, in the form of aspects of social organisation have a statistically significant association with the outcome measures. They found that differences in school outcomes are positively associated with particular process variables, so that Rutter *et al.* (1979) were able to conclude that:

> children were more likely to show good behaviour and good scholastic attainments if they attended some schools than if they attended others. The implication is that experiences during the secondary school years may influence children's progress.
>
> (p 178)

This view has been supported consistently in other major studies (Reynolds, 1976; Mortimore *et al.*, 1988, and Smith and Tomlinson, 1989).

The thinking which underlies the study of Farfield and Lakeside is rather different. This type of research is born out of an ethnographic tradition (Hammersley and Atkinson, 1983), which rests on certain key assumptions about the nature of social reality, and the relationship between the researcher and the researched. Ethnographic research attempts to develop a description of a social setting which is based as far as possible on the perceptions of the people who are involved in that setting. The ethnographer takes the view that the detached observer's understandings of a setting are necessarily limited by his or her own preconceptions and assumptions: such an observer will only see what he or she is ready to see. The ethnographer, therefore, seeks to develop under-standings by encouraging the research subjects to share their thoughts. This sharing makes the research process a social situa-tion, in which the researcher and researched are interacting and, obviously, having an effect on one another. Unlike the positivist researcher who takes up a disinterested stance, the ethnographer seeks to engage with the research subject in a way which facilitates the subject's sense of ease and willingness to share his/her feelings and beliefs. A key tool of the ethnographer is 'reflexivity', which refers to the researcher's ability to monitor and adjust his/her influence in the social relationship that is formed with the subject (Hammersley and Atkinson, 1983). The ethnographer must avoid leading the subject to supply responses that simply fulfil the researcher's expectations or preconceptions. The ethnographer, therefore, does not develop hypotheses prior to entering a research setting, but rather begins the research with a few general and open-ended questions. The subjects provide the answers to these questions and the researcher's role is to motivate the subject to be explicit and to elaborate. It is the subject's responses which fill in the detail and complexity of the developing description. And it is from such description that theories and hypotheses can then be developed (Glaser and Strauss, 1967), and later verified in accordance with more positivistic methodology.

Chapters 5 and 6 of this book reported an ethnographic study of two residential special schools for boys with emotional and behavioural difficulties. These chapters presented an account of the ways in which these boys perceived their circumstances as members of these two schools. It is important to stress that the content of this description represents the researcher's inter-pretation of what the boys told him, and that the categories of concern that are presented are claimed to be the chief concerns that were expressed by these boys in answer to the central ques-tion: 'What is it like for you to be a pupil at this school?'

The new research presented in this book, therefore, depicts the views of a particular group of pupils about what is important to them about their schools and schooling. This is a very different claim to that made by the school effectiveness researchers. Their research identifies important features of schools on the basis of externally imposed criteria. We do not know the views of the pupils in, for example, the Rutter *et al.* or Mortimore *et al.* studies, on the effectiveness of their schools, or the most significant features of their school experience. On the other hand, the conclusions that have been drawn from the Lakeside and Farfield studies have been based almost entirely on the perceptions of the pupils who attend these two schools. The school effectiveness researchers and the present researcher draw inferences about the effects of schools on pupil motivation and behaviour, though they base their inferences on views taken from quite different vantage points.

SYSTEMS AND INDIVIDUALS

One of the great achievements of school effectiveness research has been to provide evidence to support the view that schools can have an effect on pupil behaviour and achievement. Thus, it is argued, whilst pupils from disadvantaged circumstances are, by and large, likely to fair less well in schools than pupils from more privileged circumstances, schools have been found to produce remarkably different outcomes, even when allowance has been made for levels of disadvantage. As Rutter *et al.* (1979) show:

> In short, it appears that in a part of inner London known to be disadvantaged in numerous ways, some schools were better able than others to foster good behaviour and attainments.
>
> (p. 93)

Mortimore *et al.* (1988) go a step further:

> we have shown that, in general, schools which were effective in promoting progress for one group of pupils (whether those of a particular social class, sex or ethnic group) were usually also effective for children of other groups. Similarly, those schools which were ineffective for one group tended to be ineffective for other groups . . . school effectiveness does not seem to depend on pupils' backgrounds. . . . By attending a more effective school all pupils will benefit, even those who are at an initial educational disadvantage because of their particular background characteristics. . . . Even though overall differences in patterns of pupil attainment are not removed in the most effective schools, the performance of all children is raised and, as we have demonstrated, disadvantaged children in the most effective schools can end up with higher achievements than their advantaged peers in the less effective schools.
>
> (p. 217)

The fundamental message of the school effectiveness work is that it is the system that counts. It is not the individual acts of teachers alone that are associated with positive outcomes, but rather it is evidence of people working in concert towards common ends that is most clearly associated with effectiveness:

> the association between the combined measure of overall school process and each of the measures of outcome was much stronger than any of the associations with individual process variables. This suggests that the cumulative effect of these various social factors was greater than the effect of any of the individual factors on their own. The implication is that the individual actions or measures may combine to create a particular ethos, or set of values, attitudes and behaviours which will become characteristic of the school as a whole.
>
> (Rutter *et al.*, 1979, p. 179)

These findings have struck a chord with many educationists. Reid *et al.* (1987), for example, suggest that earlier efforts to facilitate school improvement have failed, because of a past tendency to place too much emphasis on improving the skills of the individual teacher. Reid *et al.* reject this 'cult of the individual' and argue for its replacement with an approach to school improvement which takes as its focus the needs of the school as a whole rather than those of individual teachers. Burden (1981), in advocating a whole-school approach to behaviour problems, describes a 'systems approach' which:

> seeks to understand how the explicit and implicit organisational structure of the school affects the perception and behaviour of its pupils in a way that leads them to be seen as problematical or disruptive by those faced with the task of maintaining that structure.
>
> (p. 35)

He also states that:

> a piecemeal approach centred on problems is nonsensical when seen within the framework of such organisational complexity, since the intricate relationships of parts cannot be treated out of context of the whole.
>
> (p. 31)

The point being made here is that the actions of individual teachers and pupils are constrained by the school system.

It is an obvious, but nonetheless important point to make, that if we want to improve whole schools, then we must intervene in schools in ways which take account each school's individual institutional identity. On the other hand, it would be a mistake to assume that the individual is merely a pawn of the overarching system: an automaton programmed by the system. 'Ethos' might well be the defining characteristic of the school as a social institution, in that the term refers to the dominant values underpinning the behaviour of school personnel, the goals they seek and their images of themselves. It is also true to say, however, that 'ethos' cannot exist in isolation. School ethos does not have an existence which is independent of the thoughts and perceptions of the individual pupils and teachers of the school. In this way school ethos, as the term is used here, can be equated with 'the hidden curriculum', that is, the agenda of values and beliefs that pupils and teachers actually employ in their everyday interactions, as opposed to those they simply profess. Individual teachers and pupils are socialised into the prevailing ethos of a school, and through their individual behaviour they each help to maintain and develop the ethos. It follows that the professed ethos may or may not coincide with the 'lived' ethos of the school, since the lived ethos necessarily develops out of the individual's interpretations of the experiences he or she undergoes. For example, as Galloway (1985b) has shown, variations among schools' pastoral care policies do not correspond to variations in pastoral effectiveness; it is the extent to which the espoused policy is enacted throughout the school that is critical in relation to outcomes. And this is best assessed 'by reference to attitudes throughout the school and to educational and behavioural standards' (Galloway, 1985b, p. 78).

When we take into account the relationship between the perceptions of individuals and the systems they inhabit, as outlined above, it becomes clear that the type of micro-level inquiry presented earlier in this book has an important contribution to make to our understanding of school effectiveness. This importance can be summed up by saying that since schools are concerned with producing particular effects in pupils, one of the ways by which we might ascertain school success is by examining pupils' perceptions of school effects. Having presented a fairly detailed account of a group of pupils' perceptions of the effects of their experience of schooling, we can now turn to an examination of the relationship between these boys' perceptions of effectiveness and those of the school effectiveness researchers.

PUPIL EXPERIENCE IN EFFECTIVE SCHOOLS

The studies of Lakeside and Farfield, it will be recalled, showed that boys in these two schools identified a number of positive personal outcomes. Strongest among the impressions conveyed by the boys was the sense of personal achievement that many boys expressed. In many cases boys felt that they had arrived at the schools with highly negative identities, which had, over the course of their stay in the schools, been reshaped to the extent that they now defined themselves in positive terms and had a clear sense of self-worth. Recurrent aspects of this development are: boys' perceptions that they have overcome behavioural and emotional problems, and have an improved sense of self-control; their claimed mastery of particular social skills; their improved ability to reflect on their actions constructively; their claimed mastery of practical and (in some cases) academic skills. These outcomes are, in turn, related to three broad categories which were perceived by the boys to be instrumental in helping them achieve these outcomes. These are: **Respite** from harmful influences, in the home/neighbourhood/former school setting: **Relationships** with teachers and peers in the school, which have a therapeutic and supportive effect; and **Opportunities** to practice and develop new aspects of themselves in a supportive environment. Each of these categories will now be discussed with reference to school effectiveness studies.

RESPITE

In some ways 'respite' seems the least likely of the three categories to find any correspondence among the work of the school effectiveness researchers. After all, the key element of respite, as expressed by the boys of Lakeside and Farfield, rested on the fact that the schools were residential establishments far removed from their home towns. When we begin to look closely, however, at the anatomy of 'respite', as it is experienced by these boys, we find important links with the characteristics of effective schools.

The pinpointing of 'respite' as an important quality, arises from the repeated references made by boys to the value they place on being temporarily removed from stressful home situations (which might include family problems, peer-group associations and school difficulties). The residential experience is seen to provide an environment which gives boys the time and space to reflect on these difficult circumstances in an atmosphere of relative calm. Furthermore, boys whose home lives are characterised by disputes and conflict often seem to find their school circumstances inter-acting with home problems, to the extent that difficulties they experience in one setting exacerbate and are exacerbated by difficulties in the other setting. John (Farfield), it will be recalled (see pp. 60–3), provides an example *par excellence* of this phenomenon. John's admitted assault on his day-school teacher is closely associated, in John's mind, with the difficulties that surround John's family circumstances, and particularly his fraught relationship with his mother. The teacher's (understandable) act of contacting John's mother, when John plays truant from school, is seen by John in terms of the further damage it is likely to inflict on this already problematic relationship. Similarly, delinquency among peer groups is associated with family and school difficulties, seeming to offer boys who are deprived of positive identities in their homes and schools opportunities to obtain high status. Again, the residential setting offers respite from these undesirable opportunities.

An examination of research findings shows that effective mainstream school seems to offer similar opportunities for respite. The chief agent of 'respite' in the mainstream school appears to be the somewhat misty quality of school ethos. School ethos, or 'climate' as it is sometimes called, refers to the particular atmosphere of the individual school, which resides in values and attitudes that are implicit in the behaviour and interactions that are characteristic within the school. Ethos is the code by which pupils and staff operate in schools. As was noted earlier (see Chapter 3), Reynolds and Sullivan (1979) identified two contrasting patterns of school response to the problem of eliciting pupil compliance, which they term 'coercive' and 'incorporative' (elsewhere termed 'cooptive'). Coercive schools were marked by:

high rates of institutional control, strict rule enforcement, high rates of physical punishment and very little tolerance of any

'acting out'. . . . Pupil deviance is expeditiously punished . . .;
therapeutic concern would have little effect because pupils
would have little or no respect for the teacher–therapist.

(p. 51)

Incorporative schools, on the other hand, were characterised by
the fact that they incorporated pupils into the organisation of the
school, and by their successful efforts to elicit parental support for
the school:

Pupils are incorporated within the classrooms by encouraging
them to take an active and participative role in lessons and by
letting them intervene verbally without the teacher's explicit
direction. Pupils in schools which utilise this strategy are also far
more likely to be allowed and encouraged to work in groups
than their counterparts in schools utilising coercive strategies.
Outside formal lesson time, attempts are made to incorporate
pupils into the life of the school by utilising other strategies.
One of these is the use of numbers of pupil prefects and monitors, from all parts of the school ability range, whose role is
largely the supervision of other pupils in the absence of staff
members.
   Another means of incorporation into the values and norms of
the school is the development of *inter*personal rather than
*im*personal relationships between teachers and pupils.

(ibid., p. 50; original emphasis)

Reynolds and Sullivan were able to conclude that the
incorporative schools achieved higher rates of academic success,
significantly lower rates of delinquency, and higher rates of attendance than their 'coercive' counterparts. Given that the schools
were all drawing on catchment areas of highly similar socio-
economic and cultural make-up, the researchers attributed these
marked differences between the schools to:

differences in the ideology, consciousness and beliefs of those
participants who together made up the social world of each school.

(ibid., p. 50)

For present purposes we need only to consider the 'incorporative'
school in terms of the global impact of its ethos, rather than
dealing in detail with the components of incorporative strategies.
We will return to these in later sections.

If we consider the incorporative/coercive dichotomy in relation to the concept of respite, we can see that it bears many characteristics which we have already considered in this context. The coercive school tends to reflect many of the negative qualities which the boys in the present study identified in their personal home circumstances, and in their former schools. It is also important to note that similar negative qualities have been shown to recur frequently in the family backgrounds of young people who are delinquent and who exhibit behaviour problems (see Chapter 2, above). These negative qualities can be summarised in terms of experiences of rejection by significant others (particularly teachers and parents), interpersonal conflict, and intolerance of acting out behaviour. In such circumstances the individual is seen as an object to be manipulated and controlled, and expressions of individuality are outlawed and punished. These are experiences which serve to undermine the individual's sense of self-worth. The person who is subject to such a regime is facing constant demands for self-negation and docility. The lack of reward and incentive inherent in this situation, when coupled with an individual's strong drive for affirmation, is likely to motivate the individual to self-assertion, and the search for a contrary set of values. In such cases conflict is an inevitable outcome. Over time, where patterns of oppression become entrenched, so too do the responses, and so there develops a culture of resistance which, in turn, can motivate the oppressors to evermore oppressive measures.

The incorporative school, by contrast, offers circumstances which make the pupil a centre of positive adult interest. There are many opportunities in such schools for pupils to achieve success, and to enjoy the rewards that follow from this. In such schools pupils are encouraged to believe that the staff actually want them to be there, and want them to express themselves. Certain pupils in such schools may well, therefore, be offered opportunities that are not available to them in their family situations (as is the case with some of the boys at Farfield and Lakeside). Whilst the coercive school will serve to reinforce the negativity that flows from disadvantaged home circumstances, and may even exacerbate the problems that flow from this (see systems theorists such as Campion, 1985; Dowling and Osborne, 1985; Power and Bartholomew, 1985; Cooper and Upton, 1990b; 1992), the incorporative school offers respite from these difficulties, as well as a possibly restorative counterbalance, in the form of opportunities to establish a level of self-esteem which is not engendered by experiences obtained outside the school.

The ideas expressed in the previous paragraph are well supported by experiences described by the boys from Lakeside and Farfield schools. Negative attitudes to former schools (both mainstream and special) are often justified in terms of the qualities of interpersonal relationships that they have experienced. Teachers are seen as distant, uncaring, 'stuck-up', and often failing to consider pupils' perceptions of situations. These views are also echoed in the work of other writers in the field of pupil disaffection, as we have already noted (e.g. Schostak, 1983; Tattum, 1982). Many of the positive characteristics of the incorporative school, on the other hand, have been consistently associated with positive pupil outcomes. Positive behavioural outcomes have been associated with low incidence of punishment, and an emphasis on praise and rewards (Rutter *et al.*, 1979; Mortimore *et al.*, 1988; Smith and Tomlinson, 1989). Similarly, Rutter *et al.* found that schools in which a high proportion of pupils held positions of responsibility tended to perform significantly better on measures of behaviour and examination success. Another of the findings of the Rutter *et al.* study, was that where working conditions of pupils were assessed by observers to be pleasant (in terms of the quality of maintenance and decor of buildings and classrooms), pupil behaviour and attainment tended to be better than in those schools where conditions were not so pleasant.

These positive aspects of the effective schools coincide well with the views of those residential boys who repeatedly draw attention to the quality of care that they receive in the residential setting. The importance of the physical and material environment is underlined by Farfield boys, who show pride in and a sense of ownership of their school. Common to the studies of Reynolds and Sullivan, Rutter *et al.*, and Mortimore *et al.* are references to the quality and extent of communication between pupils and their teachers. Both the Rutter *et al.* and Mortimore *et al.* studies suggest that in the more effective schools teachers spent more time communicating with pupils than in the less effective schools. It is perhaps surprising to note that in the more effective schools there was a greater incidence of teachers communicating with groups of pupils rather than individuals. However, as Mortimore *et al.* point out, the value of teachers' interacting with groups (not necessarily whole class groups) lies in the fact that it enables larger numbers of pupils to have more frequent contacts with teachers, than pupils who enjoy only individual contacts. Rutter *et al.* (1979) also found that the availability and of teachers to talk with pupils at any time (i.e. not just in lesson time) varied considerably between schools, and was associated with positive outcomes. Both the Rutter *et al.* study and the work of Reynolds and Sullivan describe a positive association between outcomes and the degree of collaboration between teachers and pupils, in the form of shared activities in and out of the classroom. This finding again is endorsed by the views of the residential boys, particularly those of Lakeside, who attach importance to opportunities they have for being with staff in shared activities (both recreational and work-oriented). From this we develop a sense of the ways in which such activities help to forge harmonious relationships between teachers and pupils, and avert possible conflicts. Such relationships would seem to be particularly valuable to pupils who may have developed highly negative attitudes towards teachers and other adults: seeing them as alien and even inhuman.

The various positive features of schools identified above are most effective in relation to the full range of measured pupil outcomes, when they appear together in the same school, along with a number of other variables which indicate an academic focus to school and classroom life. Rutter *et al.* (1979) were first to point out that the total effect of the various components of effective practice is greater than the combined measures of the individual effects of each variable. And it was on the basis of this finding that the concept of 'ethos' was presented. In the context of the idea of 'respite', as developed from the residential boys' perceptions, it is logical to suggest that the significance of school 'ethos' in the daily experience of school pupils, is likely to reside in the extent to which the school ethos expresses to pupils a sense of their value and importance. In the effective school pupils find school a useful and valuable place to be, as a result of the concerted effort of school staff. The experiences provided by staff in such schools repeatedly reinforce the very message which the boys of Farfield and Lakeside did not receive in the schools they formerly attended, namely that: pupils are welcome; pupils are centrally important, and the school and staff are there to promote the interests of pupils. The pupils' working conditions, the quality and extent of communication between teachers and pupils, the emphasis on praise rather than blame, the extent of pupil participation in lessons and school organisation, and the prevalence of cooperative/collaborative behaviour among teachers and pupils can all be viewed in terms which stress the value and importance of pupils.

It was noted in Chapter 2 of the present book that among the problems associated with adverse family circumstances are unstable family circumstances and a punitive emphasis among some parents. This gives a particular importance to the consistency and stability of the effective school, with its emphasis on reward rather than punishment. This is not to say that punishment is not a feature of effective schools. Rutter *et al.* (1979) found that the most effective schools in their study had a disciplinary approach to pupil misbehaviour, rather than the therapeutic approach identified by Reynolds and Sullivan (1979) in the 'incorporative' schools of their study. What appears to be important is the extent and frequency of punishment, and the degree to which it is balanced with the frequency of rewards and incentives. Rutter *et al.* noted, that in the most effective schools the use of punishment, although prescribed, was a relatively infrequent occurrence when compared with the level of praise and reward; Mortimore *et al.* echoed this conclusion. This sheds an interesting light on the views expressed by the residential boys, who stated a general acceptance of the limits imposed by the rule structures of their schools, and, in the case of some of the Lakeside boys, a dissatisfaction with the absence of effective sanctions against rule-breaking. We might interpret the preference for counter-balancing reward with punishment as indicating a desire for the imposition of clear and secure behavioural parameters. For some of the Lakeside boys, the staff members' authority to give boys rewards was undermined by their apparent lack of ability to apply effective sanctions. For these boys the value of rewards was to some extent contingent on the severity of possible punishment. This might suggest that the perceived need for such parameters might well be greater among pupils who have experienced negativity and aggression in their previous relationships with adults.

It must be remembered that the dissatisfaction expressed by the Lakeside boys with the absence of sanctions was related to the relative disorder which had ascended on the school after the abolition of the draconian 'Leader' system', and, more especially, with the loss of the former, much loved headmaster. For these boys, therefore, the abolition of the more severe degrees of punishment was associated with a loss of order and emotional security. This point underlines the central importance of consistency and order which is present in those schools which researchers have defined as effective. For example, in these schools there is consistency in what different teachers expect of pupils behaviourally and academically; when pupils are in class lessons are focused on the learning task and minimal time is spent on in-lesson preparation (Rutter *et al.*, 1979); lessons are carefully structured so that pupils are kept constructively occupied (Mortimore *et al.*, 1988); teachers arrive at lessons promptly (Rutter *et al.*, 1979). The sense of order which is implied by these measures, is tempered, however, by the encouragement of pupil participation and opportunities for pupils to exercise initiative, which are also features of these schools. For certain of the Lakeside boys the paucity of sanctions was experienced as a threat to their security, facing them with a need to shoulder responsibilities for which they felt themselves to be unprepared. This would indicate the possible dangers inherent in the structured environment which limits opportunities for pupil participation.

We can conclude this section concerned with 'respite' by indicating that effective schools, as identified by earlier researchers, can be seen to offer their pupils positive experiences which are in contrast to the home circumstances of pupils from disadvantaged and unstable home backgrounds. These experiences can be usefully viewed as reflecting some of the beneficial experiences identified and valued by the boys from Lakeside and Farfield, and attributed to the geographical separation between their residential schools and homes. What is significant here is the presence of circumstances in the 'effective' schools which would appear to contrast dramatically with those circumstances described by many of the residential boys as being prevalent in their former schools, and instrumental in exacerbating their adjustment difficulties. We cannot say if the boys from the residential schools would have avoided referral to schools for pupils with emotional and behavioural difficulties had they attended such 'effective' schools. What we can say is that the points that these boys express in their evaluations of schools reflect some of the qualities of the 'effective' schools. It can also be said that the effective school, almost by definition, provides a degree of respite for those pupils who may come from disadvantaged backgrounds.

RELATIONSHIPS

The residential boys placed a high value and importance on the
the relationships they shared with staff in the two schools. It was in
the residential setting that these boys, often for the first time in
their school careers, came across adults who were sympathetic;
approachable and dependable. Qualities which were particularly
prized included staff members' willingness to listen to pupils when
they wanted to talk about personal matters, and the positive regard
in which staff held them as persons. For many of these boys, their
previous experience of staff in schools has led them to expect staff
to be authoritarian and unsympathetic, the residential setting,
however, provides them with experiences which confound these
expectations. These relationships become an important vehicle
that helps bring the pupils to new understandings of themselves
and their situations. The residential setting gives these boys the
opportunity to develop a sense of themselves which does not focus
solely on their 'problems' or negative qualities. We find these
themes reflected in the school effectiveness literature, particularly
those aspects of the work that relate to interpersonal and social
relationships.

As Hastings (1992) points out, the importance of 'good relationships' between teachers and pupils has long been acknowledged by
teachers as a vitally important ingredient in the classroom process,
and particularly in relation to the prevention and resolution of
behavioural problems. The boys of Lakeside and Farfield would
seem to endorse this view wholeheartedly. Hastings attempts to
bring some clarity to this often vague notion of the 'good relationship'. In defining what is meant by a 'good relationship' Hastings
emphasises the importance of reciprocity, arguing that:

> In a good relationship each party feels that they are important
> to the other and that the other is important to them. They feel
> that what they say and do matters. . . . One feature of a good
> relationship is that each party's behaviour is affected by the
> other's in both pleasing and, at least potentially, displeasing
> ways. Each has the experience of their behaviour being of
> consequence to the other – because they see that to be the
> case. . . . In a 'good relationship', each feels that what they do
> affects the other and that what the other does is of consequence
> to them – and each is right!

(p. 85)

A good relationship provides affirmation to the people involved. In the case of the residential boys, their teachers and care workers acted towards them in ways which encouraged the boys to think of themselves as worthwhile individuals. The ways in which this was achieved in the residential setting are many and varied, as we have seen, ranging across classroom, living accommodation, educational and welfare contexts. An examination of the school effectiveness research reveals that the most effective mainstream schools can be observed to create circumstances which are conducive to good staff–pupil relationships.

Reynolds and Sullivan's (1979) typology of 'coercive' and 'incorporative' schools is, as we have already seen, centrally concerned with the climate of social relationships in schools. The more effective 'incorporative' schools were notable for the emphasis they placed on 'interpersonal rather than impersonal relationships between teachers and pupils' (p.50). Reynolds and Sullivan suggest that teachers in incorporative schools try to influence pupils' value systems by winning the respect of their pupils. Central to the desired value system are notions of individual worth and respect for persons. By demonstrating to pupils that they respect and value them, the staff are living the values they wish to transmit. The experience of being valued in this way triggers the kind of reciprocal process described by Hastings (see above), in which the pupil enjoys the experience of being responded to in a positive way and so learns to perform in ways which serve to maintain this situation. Some of the practical measures which are associated with the incorporative approach are echoed in the work of other school effectiveness researchers, as well as the work of those concerned with effective teaching.

Many of the teacher actions associated with effective schools can be accounted for under the heading of 'group management' (Rutter *et al.*, 1979; DES, 1989a; Hastings, 1992). It is important to understand, however, that effective group management involves an acknowledgement and avoidance of the anonymity and objectification which group settings can sometimes create. A central feature of effective group management appears to be a deliberate awareness of the ways in which the teacher's actions are perceived by the pupils. Thus, the effective teacher behaves in the classroom in ways which are calculated to produce positive responses from individual pupils. At the same time, skilled teachers monitor their own responses to pupil behaviour and make the most of opportunities to to respond to pupils in positive ways. It is only through effective group management that teachers, faced with twenty or thirty pupils at a time, can be responsive to individuals in their classes.

A key feature of 'good relationships' is positive responsiveness. In effective schools teachers are responsive to pupils in a variety of ways. They focus more attention on creating learning situations which hold the pupils' interest, than teachers in less effective schools. Teachers in effective schools arrive in their classrooms before their pupils, are well prepared for their classes and do not waste lesson time with setting up equipment or other organisational matters (Rutter *et al.*, 1979). These teachers are aware that their pupils, like anyone else, will be bored by inactivity and too much of the same kind of activity. To prevent boredom periods of aimless waiting are avoided, and a variety of stimuli is employed. Where periods of waiting might be necessary, teachers provide productive and purposeful activities to occupy pupils (Rutter *et al.*, 1979; Laslett and Smith, 1984; Mortimore *et al.*, 1988). However, teachers such as these are not only brisk and business-like, they also take great care to plan lessons that pupils find challenging, though within their capabilities (Rutter *et al.*, 1979; Mortimore *et al.*, 1988). As Smith (1992) points out, whilst variety and the maintenance of a brisk pace are important, these are not effective strategies if the content is not appropriate to the specific learning needs of the pupils. The effective teacher, therefore, particularly in the mixed-ability context, keeps all pupils fruitfully occupied by selecting whole-group tasks which all pupils can tackle with confidence, and that enable all pupils to display the best of their abilities, whilst also, when necessary, providing alternative and supplementary materials, which extend the more able and support the less able. In these ways the teacher is responding to the individual differences among the pupils, by providing each pupil with opportunities to succeed at the given task.

The maintenance of the focus of the lesson on the work task is also an important feature of the effective school and classroom (Rutter *et al.*, 1979; Laslett and Smith, 1984; Mortimore *et al.*, 1988). Mortimore *et al.* describe effective schools as having a work-centred environment in the classroom, where pupils enjoyed their work, were keen to begin new work, and where the work was challenging. The work-centred environment is contrasted with the least effective schools, where schoolwork appears to play a less central role in the classroom situation. In such schools lesson time is limited by the teachers' use of it for routine matters, the setting-up of equipment and management of resources (Rutter *et al.*, 1979; Mortimore *et al.* 1988). Another point of contrast between more and less effective schools is the amount of time taken up with disciplinary matters, with teachers in less effective schools repeatedly interrupting the flow of lessons to administer rebukes or punishment. Teachers in effective schools, on the other hand, tend to use punishment sparingly, and rely more on the liberal use of work-related praise as a means of motivating their pupils (Reynolds and Sullivan, 1979; Rutter *et al.*, 1979; Mortimore *et al.*, 1988). These characteristics of effective schools all point to the responsiveness of staff, and their efforts to create for pupils an ordered and positive classroom experience.

Teachers in effective schools know their pupils well, and spend more time than their colleagues in less effective schools communicating with their pupils. Rutter *et al.* noted that the teachers in the effective schools tended to spend more time communicating with groups of pupils rather than with individuals. This clearly implies that pupils in such schools experience more direct teacher communication than pupils in the less effective schools. This is borne out by the research of Mortimore *et al.* and that of Galton and Simon (1980). There is no single scheme of classroom organisation that is associated with effectiveness. Reynolds and Sullivan (1979) found that pupils were more likely to engage in group work in the cooptive schools than in the coercive schools, but in general it seems that flexibility of teaching approach is the most common feature. Such flexibility depends upon the teacher's knowledge of the pupils, an awareness of the organisational patterns that are appropriate to those pupils in a given situation, and the willingness to adapt the teaching approach accordingly (Laslett and Smith, 1984). The use of group seating arrangements, where pupils face one another, is clearly facilitative of pupil interaction, and therefore appropriate to tasks requiring such interaction. There are times, however, when the seating of pupils in rows is more appropriate and effective, such as in whole-group teaching (Wheldall and Glynn, 1989). Effective classroom organisation, then, can be seen as a correlate of good teacher–pupil relationships in that it reflects teacher responsiveness to pupils' individual and group needs.

Many of the ways in which teachers relate to pupils that have been discussed so far can be seen as measures likely to prevent classroom disruption, in that they ensure that pupils are not bored by inactivity, or uninvolved owing to the excessive or inadequate demands of the work set; pupils are not distracted or confused by lack of focus to lessons, frequent interruptions to the flow of lessons, or inappropriate classroom setting. One of the more direct ways in which teachers relate to pupils in effective schools is in the willingness of teachers to accept and encourage pupil verbal intervention in lessons, as part of a general policy which encourages pupil participation in lessons (Reynolds and Sullivan, 1979). In line with this finding is the observation made by Mortimore *et al.* (1988) that teachers in the most effective schools asked a higher proportion of open questions, suggesting the teachers' willingness to entertain pupils' perceptions, rather than demanding simple recall. Teachers in effective schools are also more likely to make themselves available to pupils outside of lesson time, should they wish to speak to them about personal matters (Rutter *et al.*, 1979; Mortimore *et al.*, 1988). It is easy to see how this emphasis on interactive teaching styles helps to develop the teachers' knowledge of who each pupil is, as well as knowledge of pupils' capabilities and interests. It is on the basis of this accumulating knowledge that the teacher is able to create a classroom environment which is responsive and rewarding to all pupils (Wheldall and Glynn, 1989), helping each to feel valued as an individual, as well as giving the individual a sense of personal educational progress.

By relating to pupils in positive ways teachers do much to prevent the development of behavioural problems and disaffection. It has long been held that when teachers behave towards pupils in ways which indicate negative expectations, that pupils come to 'live up' to those expectations (Hargreaves *et al.*, 1975). It would also seem to be true that when teachers behave as though they have positive expectations of their pupils, pupils come to live up to these too, as the school effectiveness researchers repeatedly suggest. The operating principle of the effective school is to make the lives of pupils as rewarding as possible. Pupils from across the age and ability range, in these schools, can receive public rewards for their achievements both in and out of class. In class, individual teachers contribute to this by giving pupils liberal amounts of praise when they deserve it, and also by creating circumstances which give pupils opportunities to deserve it. Pupils also receive praise and recognition when they are awarded responsibilities, such as through prefect and monitor schemes. By being given responsibilities, pupils are shown trust and given opportunities to display initiative. The rewards which go with the successful performance of responsibilities, such as enhanced social status and praise, help to incorporate pupils into the formal value system of the school (Reynolds and Sullivan, 1979). There are also important applications of pupil responsibility, which have wider benefits, such as the social and educational improvements that can stem from peer tutoring and peer counselling programmes (for example, see James *et al.*, 1991), whereby pupils are trained to assist their younger peers with learning tasks and affective needs.

The other side of the group management coin is the range of penalties incurred by pupils who misbehave. Rutter *et al.* (1979), with some surprise, noted that teachers in effective schools tended to adopt a 'disciplinary' approach to behavioural problems when they occurred. However, whilst the praise of pupils was given a high profile, reprimands and punishments were found to be firm but generally low-key so as not to disturb the smooth flow of lessons. The discipline systems of the most effective schools were noted for the consistency of behavioural expectations throughout each school. In this way, whole-school approaches to discipline matters can be seen to avoid the problems which sometimes arise when pupils encounter variable standards of behavioural expectation from one class/teacher to the next. Such circumstances can be perceived by pupils to indicate the arbitrariness of teachers' expectations, and leave teachers open to accusations of favouritism or victimisation (Tattum, 1982). The whole-school approach to discipline can help the teacher to preserve order without this interfering with the good relationships that have been developed with pupils.

In summary, it can be said that research shows that teachers in effective mainstream schools relate to their pupils in ways which stress their positive regard for pupils. There is a clear sense of continuity between the interpersonal and social relationships throughout the school. When teachers relate to whole groups of pupils they are taking careful account of the individual differences among their pupils and catering for these. Where pupils require individual attention, teachers make efforts to make themselves available to pupils. Such teachers are also more likely to set up patterns of classroom interaction that encourage pupils to participate, and thus display their interests and capabilities. Teachers also communicate their positive regard for pupils through the use of praise and by creating conditions in the classroom that help to encourage pupils to perform well. Such conditions include the quality of the learning environment which, in effective schools, often gives the impression of being cared for as well as being educationally stimulating, through the use of wall displays (Mortimore *et al.*, 1988). As some of the residential boys indicated, the degree to which the setting is cared for can be equated with the degree to which the pupils feel cared for. Furthermore, the teachers in these schools present their pupils with positive behavioural models, through their manner of relating to pupils, which encourage pupils to develop similar patterns of behaviour in their interactions with others (Rutter et al., 1979), and so, in this way, contributing to and perpetuating the positive ethos of the school.

OPPORTUNITIES

Boys from the residential schools found that Farfield and Lakeside provided them with a wide range of opportunities to achieve success. For some boys these opportunities were of an academic nature, for others they were chiefly of a practical or social type. Some boys claimed to have benefited from a range of such opportunities. The function of these opportunities was to enable the boys to discover new and positive dimensions within themselves, and so help to build up and strengthen their often weakened self-images. In many ways the respite from home-based and other difficulties afforded by the institutions, and the good quality of the relationships they shared with staff in the schools, can be seen to represent vital elements of the setting which enabled the boys to take advantage of these opportunities. Of course, the relationships are not only to be seen as a background feature of these schools. It is through the relationships with their staff that these boys first begin to see their own positive potential. The relationships also continue to be an important continuing resource that many of the boys refer to in times of trouble or when seeking affirmation. In this way the relationships are a source of support to the boys as well as a framework in which trustworthy guidance can be sought. It is the security of reliable and supportive relationships that enables the boys to take the risk of possible failure that is always inherent when opportunities are presented.

The school effective researchers show repeatedly that the more effective schools tend to offer pupils a greater range of opportunities for achievement and success than their less effective counterparts. In fact, one of the striking features of the least effective schools tends to be an emphasis on denial and negativity which can be interpreted as an absence of opportunities for pupils (Reynolds, 1976; 1984; Reynolds and Sullivan, 1979). It would seem that the least effective schools have a greater tendency to exhibit practices which act as obstacles in the paths of many of their pupils. For example, in the least effective schools: pupils' classroom learning is more likely to be disjointed and subject to interruption and delayed starts, with teachers being less than well prepared for the lesson (Rutter *et al.*, 1979); opportunities to achieve academic success and public praise are likely to be limited, and not made available to vast numbers of pupils; opportunities for recognition, success and achievement outside of the formal academic curriculum are unlikely to be available to most pupils; teachers' expectations of pupils are likely to be low, and the staff–pupil relationships are likely to be dominated by a coercive disciplinary approach of the staff which has the effect of limiting pupil involvement in the formal life of the school (Reynolds, 1976, 1984; Reynolds and Sullivan, 1979; Rutter *et al.*, 1979). One of the most depressing educational portraits in the school effectiveness canon must be that of the 'disaffection-prone school', supplied by Reynolds (1984). This school is dominated by high levels of disruptive and delinquent behaviour, which the school staff attempt to tackle through the imposition of a coercive regime, revolving around a highly proscriptive rule system. Social control is enforced through constant punishment:

> the organizational and rule strictness is precisely how one would expect a school with major problems to behave – a reactive, defensive strategy that seems likely to increase the amount of misbehaviour exhibited by the pupils.

> (Reynolds, 1984, p. 173)

In this school there is a significant proportion of the staff composed of '"old timers" who have survived the school by turning to instrumental motivation and to cynicism' (ibid., p. 173). The remainder of the staff tend to be young, inexperienced, 'professionally insecure' and prone to a high turnover. It is easy to see how such a vicious circle of problems and failed solutions can lead to the kind of desolate, hostile environment, devoid of positive opportunities, of which some disaffected pupils complain (see Woods, 1990).

The unifying feature of the extreme example of the dis-affection-prone school is its negativity. Such a school rests on a knife-edge between order built on repression and chaos. It is the fear of the chaos that might be (and sometimes is) released if the resentful and resistant pupil subculture is left unrestrained, that urges the staff to evermore restrictive and repressive control strategies. The greatest threat to such a school is perceived by the staff to be the energy and the vitality of the pupils. Such a school attempts to subdue and repress pupil expression and constantly enforce the dominion of the school over the individual. Such a school can, therefore, be seen to represent the absolute antithesis of the effective school, since a common feature to these schools is a fostering and utilisation of pupil energy and vitality.

Effective schools offer means of detecting pupils' enthusiasms and capabilities, by providing conditions which are positively responsive to the emergence of these qualities. Thus incentives and rewards are made widely available in effective schools, and schools where pupils are subject to higher rates of personal teacher praise tend to have higher levels of academic performance and lower rates of behaviour problems (Rutter et al., 1979; Mortimore et al., 1988). Similarly, the opportunities for success and achievement outside of the formal academic curriculum are greatest in schools which measure high on effective ratings. Such opportunities include: the availability of formal recognition and prizes for sporting achievement (Rutter et al., 1979); opportunities across the ability range to hold positions of responsibility, as monitors, prefects, or members of school decision-making bodies (Reynolds and Sullivan, 1979; Rutter et al., 1979; Mortimore et al., 1988). The provision of rewards for non-academic performance reaches a significant proportion of the school population that is unlikely to achieve high academic honours. Though these pupils will also receive recognition for their academic progress and achievement, in class, for example, through teacher praise and the display of pupil work (Rutter et al., 1979; Mortimore et al., 1988). Similarly, the most effective schools in Mortimore et al.'s and Rutter et al.'s studies were found to be marked by their academic emphasis and the intellectual challenge of classroom teaching. Both of these indicating a tendency in these schools to provide pupils with opportunities to extend their academic achievements.

The importance of creating opportunities for all pupils to become incorporated into the mainstream life of the school cannot be over-emphasised. Of particular significance here are the measures that schools take to cater for pupils who experience learning difficulties. As Smith (1992) points out, all too often learning difficulties if mishandled can soon develop into adjustment difficulties. Hargreaves (1967), for example, demonstrated the way in which the demotivating effects of rigid streaming could be witnessed in the close association between low-stream membership and anti-school values: the lower the stream the greater the proportion of pupils who subscribed to anti-school values. Deprived of opportunities to obtain positive status in the formal school culture, pupils in the lower streams rejected their low status and sought to meet their esteem needs in a counter-culture. What is becoming increasingly clear is that the means by which schools can best prevent the development of such negative outcomes for their less able pupils are identical to those which promote the learning and achievement of the brightest and most able of children. In short, these measures involve extending the opportunities for success and achievement that are made available to some pupils to *all* pupils. As Smith (1992) argues, the transmutation of learning difficulties into behavioural problems can be prevented if teachers and schools have high expectations for all of their pupils, offer curricula which enable pupils to find learning experiences which are stimulating and well matched to the abilities of individuals, and provide pupils with support, in terms of a responsive setting and expert help where needed.

An important issue here relates to the ways in which support staff are used in classrooms. It is generally agreed that support teachers are most effectively employed when they act as consultants to class teachers, rather than simply as classroom assistants. As consultants, support teachers should still work alongside class teachers, but relate to class teachers as equals rather than juniors (Galloway and Goodwin, 1987; Smith, 1990). The support teacher's involvement should begin at the planning stage of lessons. At this stage the support teacher can advise class teachers on ways of making learning experiences accessible to pupils with special educational needs, and so help to develop mainstream teachers' appreciation of special educational needs. This kind of collaborative working also enables unexpected difficulties to be met promptly, such as when pupils who have not previously been thought of as 'having difficulties' presents with a specific learning problem. Where this kind of responsive, stimulating and supportive provision exists for all pupils, positive pupil behaviour is often produced as a by-product (Galloway and Goodwin, 1987). Or to put it another way: the failure of schools to provide these kinds of opportunities in equal measure is an important contributory factor in creating behavioural problems and disaffection.

This view is supported by the findings of HMI, which have stated repeatedly that pupils with special educational needs benefit from their placement in mainstream classrooms, in terms of the range of learning opportunities that are made available to them (DES, 1989c, 1991). HMI have also stressed, repeatedly, that teaching which is effective for pupils with special needs is effective for all pupils, depending on: the teacher's detailed knowledge of each pupil's performance levels; a sufficient level of differentiation in each pupil's work programme to facilitate a good match with current performance level, and:

> organisation and classroom management focused on supporting a positive pupil self-image to enable realistically high performance expectations to be achieved.
>
> (DES, 1989c, para. 34)

HMI also note the often negative consequences of extraction of pupils with learning difficulties from mainstream classes, which often results in discontinuity or duplication in pupils' work programmes as they move from one context to the other (DES, 1989c). They also found the unsatisfactory practice observed in some schools of placing large groups of low-attaining pupils in the same class, owing to the way this often entailed narrowing the breadth of the curriculum to which the pupils were exposed, as well as restricting their access to specialist staff (DES, 1989c). This latter point receives considerable support from Galloway and Goodwin (1987) in their review of research on the education of pupils with educational and behavioural difficulties. They conclude that SEN pupils who are merely locationally integrated in a mainstream school (i.e. in segregated provision on the site of a mainstream school) often have access to a narrower curriculum than was available to them in special schools and off-site units.

They conclude that, wherever possible, nothing short of the full integration of special-needs pupils into mainstream classes will be necessary if these pupils are to be given their rights of access to the full curriculum. This requires appropriate patterns and levels of support. As we have seen, the skills involved in dealing with this sort of situation are already very much in evidence in some schools and classrooms. It would also seem to be the case that if opportunities for achievement and success were extended in this way to a wider range of pupils in the first place, there would be at least some pupils who are now deemed to have 'special educational needs' who would be so labelled.

CONCLUSION

Earlier chapters of this book revealed what a group of pupils in two residential schools for boys with emotional and behavioural difficulties had to say about their experience of schooling. It was shown that for many of these boys the residential experience provided them with positive experiences which contrasted with their negative experience of previous schools. For many of these boys, the residential school has provided an ordered and stable setting where they feel valued by their staff; where they are able to exercise responsibility and experience the trust of others; where staff relate to pupils in ways which stress a respect for the individual, and where opportunities are provided for individuals to achieve success across a wide range of areas. In the present chapter it has been suggested that many of the values espoused by these pupils are reflected in the concerns of the school effectiveness researchers. It is suggested that what these pupils appear to value and require in their schools are the very things that some schools are already beginning to achieve. The implication of this is that 'disaffection from school' may well be something much more to do with the effects of particular schools on particular pupils than it is to do with the individual's rejection of schools *per se*. More importantly, it is suggested that when pupils are conscious of being respected, cared for and valued by their teachers, they experience benefits to their individual self-images, which in turn help to motivate and sustain their efforts to strive for further achievement. As Dessent (1987) suggests, there is still a long way to go before most British mainstream schools will be able to cater effectively for all pupils. We cannot, therefore, assume that had the boys of

Lakeside and Farfield attended some of those schools which have been described as being measurably effective, that they would not have found their way into segregated special-needs provision. What can be said with confidence is that some of the problems which these boys claim to have faced in their previous schools, and that they believe to have a bearing on their special-needs status, are being addressed in some mainstream schools, and that where they are being addressed there is a lower incidence of the kind of the disruption and disaffection that these boys have exhibited.

In the following chapter we will examine a school where practical efforts have been made to tackle the problem of disaffection.

Chapter 8

Tackling disaffection in the mainstream school: One school's experience

In this penultimate chapter consideration will be given to the practicalities involved in meeting and preventing disaffection in schools. One way of doing this might be to abstract characteristics from school effectiveness research and offer suggestions as to how these might be implemented in a fictitious school. Such an exercise would offer scope for a comprehensive coverage of the relevant points, but would be lacking in other important respects. One of the problems with school effectiveness research in general is its tendency to present an idealised picture, which might mislead readers into thinking that by simply aping the characteristics of those schools identified by researchers as 'effective', that the same measures of effectiveness can be achieved. This book is not intended to create such an impression. School effectiveness researchers have never claimed to be in a position to make claims about the links between school outcomes and processes, on anything other than an (albeit well informed) speculative basis. This book has so far attempted to introduce the pupil perspective more centrally into the debate, and in so doing offers a small degree of further support for the speculations of these researchers.

The introduction into the debate of the views of pupils who have been excluded from mainstream schools, has the advantage that these pupils are able to reflect on real schools, and to describe the ways in which their difficulties and the resolution of their difficulties might be related to school experience. The conclusions that might be drawn from this discussion, concerning effectiveness in mainstream schools, remain at the level of speculation. The only links that can be made between the perceptions of the residential boys and the findings of the school effectiveness researchers are conceptual. In this chapter, therefore, brief consideration will be given to a real school where attempts have been made to improve the school's effectiveness, particularly in relation to pupil disaffection. The main focus of the chapter will be on the firsthand accounts of staff who have been involved in this process, and an exploration of some of the key mechanisms that have been utilised. This chapter in no sense represents an exhaustive study of the school concerned. On the contrary, it is best seen as a limited exercise which attempts three things:

1 to give an insight into the way in which the problem of effectiveness was approached by one school in its particular context;
2 to illustrate some of the practical measures that the school has implemented;
3 to illustrate some of the effects that have been attributed to these measures.

Of particular importance to this exercise is the fact that these three areas will be considered within the living context of the school: its history, its location and its internal and external relations. Throughout this account we will see echoed the concerns which have been aired earlier in the book under the categories of, 'respite', 'relationships' and 'opportunities', which were generated from the interviews with the residential boys. It will be seen that these concepts can be applied to the school in question and highlight many important features of its successful campaign against pupil disaffection. The many unanswered questions that will arise from this chapter will hopefully provide a stimulus for more detailed research.

(It should be noted that, as with the residential study, the identities of the school, its staff and pupils of the school where this study took place have been disguised through the use of fictitious names; certain other details have also been altered in order to protect the privacy of those concerned.)

FACING UP TO THE PROBLEM OF DISAFFECTION

Valley Comprehensive School exists, like every other school, within a particular setting. Some aspects of that setting are unique; others are common to some other schools; still others are common to the vast majority of schools in England and Wales. Before dealing with those features which are most particular to Valley Comprehensive, attention will be given to some of the broader issues which form an important part of the context within which the majority of schools have to operate at the time of writing (i.e. the early 1990s).

STATE SCHOOLS IN THE ERA OF THE EDUCATION REFORM ACT

The 1988 Education Reform Act (ERA) has imposed a range of dramatic changes on schools in England and Wales, which have far-reaching consequences for teachers, pupils, parents and local education authorities. The three main features of the ERA are the introduction of the National Curriculum, changes in the manner in which schools are funded and their budgets managed, and an increase in the degree to which important educational decisions are taken out of the hands of local education authorities and given over to parents of pupils in schools and the governing bodies of schools. These changes have placed significant new duties and responsibilities on schools, and introduced a new range of concerns for schools to consider. An important consequence of these changes has been to increase the importance of the individual school, as the critical unit in the delivery of state-funded education (Beare *et al.*, 1989). Local management of schools (LMS) has forced school management teams into developing the skills of financial management, whilst the pattern of formula funding (whereby schools are funded on the basis of their pupil numbers and the average pay bill of schools of similar size) has led some schools having to fund part of their salary bill with money that would otherwise have been spent on other resources. Thus whilst some school managers have felt liberated by the freedom which the new legislation has granted them in deciding their own funding priorities, others have found the changes restrictive and inhibiting (Smith, 1991). Similarly, the increased power of parents to select or deselect schools for their children has been greeted by popular schools and feared by the less popular.

Proposals, contained in the Citizens' Charter, published recently by the British government, for the publication of 'league tables' describing the performance of schools in relation to such things as examination pass-rates and pupil attendance levels, exemplify the ethos of competition and accountability that characterises the current educational climate in England and Wales. Whilst the National Curriculum has been heralded by the government as representing a prescription for the educational entitlement of all state school pupils, there is some disquiet that the entire package of 'reform' may well benefit some schools and pupils more than others, and those who benefit most are likely to be those already possessing considerable advantage. Large schools housed in well-maintained, modern purpose-built accommodation, that are well equipped, that have a staff group with a more than average proportion of staff at the lower end of the pay scale, are the winners in financial terms. Smaller schools which are already deprived of good quality modern facilities, with a long-serving, generally older staff, set in areas where there is little history of parental support, have reason to be anxious about their future financial viability.

It is too early as yet to assess the full impact of the ERA on our schools. At the time of writing, mechanisms are being proposed which are intended to function as performance indicators for schools. These indicators are intended to be easily read by parents and politicians. They claim to offer clear data which will enable the interested observer to distinguish, fairly quickly, between the good schools and the bad schools. Good schools will have the highest levels of academic achievement that can be measured in terms of GCSE and GCE grades, and through pupils' progress in National Curriculum attainment targets. Good schools will also have the lowest levels of truancy. It is difficult to imagine any circumstances in which such a crude comparison could be justified. The fact that some schools are more effective than others, as this book has shown, is a longstanding concern among educational researchers. The complexities, however, involved in distinguishing school effects from catchment area and other effects not within the control of schools are immense. To simply ignore these complexities is to do a disservice to those schools which are succeeding in making headway in disadvantaged circumstances.

A more disastrous consequence of this situation is that some schools may put less effort than before into catering for the needs of pupils who are unlikely to contribute to their performance profile, and may actively seek to exclude pupils who might have a negative impact on their ratings. Suspicions have already been voiced that claimed increases in exclusion rates can be attributed to increased competition between schools. Recent articles in *The Times Educational Supplement* referred to 'dramatic increases' in exclusion rates in Birmingham, Sheffield and inner London, and reported the 'alarm' expressed by the Association of Educational Psychologists at this state of affairs (Pyke, *TES*, 4/10/91; Merrick and Manuel, *TES*, 25/10/91). There is also concern that LMS arrangements act as a disincentive to schools to buy in additional help for non-statemented pupils who display behavioural problems, since such funding at present comes out of the school's existing budget. If a pupil is excluded, however, the local education authority foots the bill for the pupil's education, whilst the school continues to receive income for excluded pupils (Merrick and Manuel, *TES*, 25/10/91).

There is a danger, then, that access to a broad and balanced curriculum in a mainstream school may be being limited, for some pupils, rather than enhanced, as a result of ERA. As it stands at the moment, the schoolchildren with special educational needs can have their entitlement to the full range of the National Curriculum waived (modified, disapplied or an exemption made). When we consider this fact in the light of the increased demand for pupils to be statemented (O'Grady, *TES*, 25/10/91), as a means of securing the necessary resources to provide for pupils' needs which cannot be afforded within the school's existing budget, we might begin to see a pattern emerging which does not look to be in the best interests of some of our most vulnerable and disadvantaged pupils. Pupils who will fall into this category will include those who are the central focus of this book.

What follows is an account of one school's attempts to improve its effectiveness, particularly in relation to the problem of disaffection among its pupils. The basis of this account rests on the perceptions of the headteacher of the school, and certain other staff. With some limited input from a small group of pupils. The interviews that form the substance of this chapter all took place in 1991, and so can be placed firmly against the backdrop of the early period of the implementation of the 1988 Education Reform Act.

THE VALLEY COMPREHENSIVE SCHOOL

Valley Comprehensive School is a mixed comprehensive school, catering for approximately 750 pupils aged between 13 and 19. The school is situated on the Valley corporation housing estate, which is on the outskirts of a medium-sized English city. The school's traditional catchment area draws on the local council estate, the nearby city, as well as pupils from rural communities outside the city. In the year 1990–1, 19 per cent of pupils came to the school from outside the catchment area. The sixth form is open entry and accounts for 25 per cent of the school roll. The school is also a regional centre for pupils with learning difficulties, and this caters for forty pupils, who are integrated into the curriculum.

The local education authority maintains a mainly selective system among its secondary schools. Valley School is the only comprehensive school within the city boundary, all other city secondary schools being grammar schools or secondary modern schools.

The visitor to the school in 1991 is impressed by the school's setting within its own extensive playing fields. The school buildings themselves form an interesting collection, representing a range of architectural styles from the 1950s to the 1980s. The buildings tend to be single or two storeys in height, and fall into a number of discrete 'blocks', which are spread over a fairly large area and are connected by a series of covered walkways. Within this area there are a number of hard-surface tennis courts, an open-air swimming pool, and a purpose-built sports hall. The school also boasts modern and well-equipped science and design/technology/art blocks. The visitor is, at first, somewhat confused by the complex geography of the site, but cannot fail to be impressed by the quality and range of the facilities, and the state of care and repair of the buildings, which appears to be of an equally high standard in the oldest and newest buildings. Classrooms are carpeted throughout the school, and are centres of pupil activity at breaktimes and lunchtimes, as well as during lessons.

Putting the physical appearance of the school to one side, however, it would seem that Valley School is a very different school from what it was in 1984, when the present headteacher (Eileen Lincoln) took up her post. Ms Lincoln found the school to be in a very bleak condition when she arrived. She describes something of the background to the situation she inherited, emphasising the particular pressures which surrounded the school, virtually from its inception as a comprehensive school:

> I came here in 1984, and inherited a school that in 1977 had been put together – made into a comprehensive on the three-tier system: first school, middle school, upper school. . . . It had originated from two single-sex schools on this site . . ., with two heads who were, I think, very anti what was going to happen

anyway. Both applied for the headship of the new school. The head of the girls' school got it. . . . There was a reluctance of staff on both sides to mix. . . . Then . . . because of the local political scene [i.e. the presence of selective schools] the newly appointed head of the amalgamated comprehensive school, in my view, set this school up, as near as possible, aping the grammar schools. Now that's not the way I would have done it, but that's the way she did it. Now . . . there were many attempts at reorganisation of [the existing selective schools which are located in the south of the city], which failed. Because, you've got a very vocal middle class in the south of the city and a number of people who know what to say and they know how to say it! So what happened was that during the reorganisation campaigns, when it got very hot, the head here got involved politically, and what happened was, there was a great divide and a great antipathy between the north of the city, where we are situated, and the South. To the extent that, when they adver- tised housing in the south of the city, they also put 'grammar school catchment area'. So what you've had then, in this area, the people who've moved in here have been people who either don't hold grammar schools in the same esteem, or have come from comprehensive areas, who believe that what they had was very good. But you haven't got the same [social] mix on this side of the city, perhaps, as what you've got in the south of the city. Because you've got the inflated prices in the south, and you're actually buying your child the chance of a grammar school education. Of course with the new Acts they can apply for those schools from here.

From the start, then, Valley Comprehensive School was a victim of the internal hostilities of its staff, and subject to the external pressures imposed by the presence of selective schools, which clearly felt comprehensivisation to represent a threat. The response to this threat was to publicly belittle the comprehensive school.

The first headteacher's apparent desire to 'ape' the grammar schools can perhaps be understood as an attempt to compete with the selective schools. Though Ms Lincoln believes this approach to have been a mistake, which she took immediate steps to change:

the first thing that I decided to do [when I got here] was to cut out anything that aped the grammar schools. And just to point to people we were futuristic in our thinking, and we were proud to be different.

The chief victims of this uncomfortable situation were the pupils of the Valley School:

> Now, the pupils, when I came: there was little self-respect; damaged buildings; graffitied buildings. You asked them what they thought of their school –. I'd been for many years [a deputy head] in a super school, and to hear children run their school down, and run their teachers down, as they did here, was a real eye opener. I couldn't believe it. And it made me very sad, because I'd been used to children being really proud of their school, and wanting to be at school; enjoying school.

In addition to the picture of disaffection painted here, Ms Lincoln refers to the poor examination results (less than 10 per cent of pupils entered for GCSE obtaining pass grades); a high level of truancy, and a high delinquency rate (with between ten and twenty pupils per year being subject to criminal prosecution). Staff morale was low, in the face of what were seen as insurmountable problems:

> Ms Lincoln: They [the staff] knew the curriculum was wrong, but they didn't know how to put it right. . . . They could see that what they were doing was not successful. Nobody comes into work to do a bad job, but they were going home, feeling very dis-satisfied with what they had done, because they were not winning.
>
> PC: Was that because of poor exam results?
>
> Ms Lincoln: Disruption in the classroom. They believed you didn't really look for results in a comprehensive school. Because they were so indoctrinated against it, by what happened locally. Their expectations were very low.

The climate among the staff meant that the new headteacher came into a situation where there was a dearth of new ideas, but where there was already a perception shared by staff that things had to change. Ms Lincoln admits that in many ways this was an advantage to her, offering, as it did, a willing audience to the ideas she would propose.

CHANGING THE CURRICULUM

Ms Lincoln's immediate response to the depressing situation that she met upon arrival at the Valley School was to examine the way in which the school might be seen to contribute to these difficulties. At no time does Ms Lincoln reach for defeatist explanations for these problems which might refer to the individual characteristics of pupils. It is clear that she felt from the start that the school had been failing its pupils. One of the key areas in which the school was failing, according to Ms Lincoln, was in the inappropriateness of its curriculum for its pupils:

> everybody coming into the school at 13 had to do two languages: French and Spanish. Now, that was because good grammar schools are known to offer two languages. But you had within that, no special needs set-up. So for some children English was already a foreign language. So you were saying not only are you going to fail at English, but we'll make darn sure you fail at French, and even more, you'll fail at Spanish too.

Ms Lincoln is not opposed to the principle of diversification in language teaching; her complaint is against the way in which all pupils, upon entering the school, were met with a curriculum which failed to take account of the needs that pupils had for support in the curriculum. As a result, the first year of many pupils at the Valley was marked by the experience of failure. The school's response to such failure was, instead of providing curriculum support in areas of weakness, simply to remove the pupils who were most conspicuous in their failure, to more practically oriented subjects. Even the more able pupils were following programmes of study which were lacking in breadth and balance. In short, the curriculum was something of a mess: failing to offer pupils opportunities for achievement outside of a very narrow range. One of its most alarming features being the practice of asking pupils at the age of 13 what job they wished to do as adults, and asking them, on the basis of this, to choose five options from a range of over twenty subjects, which would make up the major part of their school programme for the next three years:

> There was no balance and breadth in the options that pupils were steered into. There were quite a few who were doing no science at all; quite a few who were doing no humanities at all. And of course, as was usual at that time, many of the least able

were doing everything that tired them out: metalwork, wood-work, tech. drawing, car maintenance and PE.

As a result, one of the first decisions that Ms Lincoln made was that the curriculum required considerable reform.

The decision to change the curriculum was an integral part of a broader strategy, designed to raise the aspirations of pupils and to give them positive experiences of schooling which go beyond the merely instrumental needs that pupils have:

> I believe deeply that if the curriculum is right, and the relation-ships are right, then everything else falls into place. But you've got to have children wanting to come to school, no matter how bad things are at home, or no matter how unsuccessful they feel in being taught. You've got to entice them to school, and let them see school as a way forward; an enjoyable place to be; something they're going to get something out of; and some-thing that perhaps in many cases is going to help them forget the horrors that they live with at home. A sanctuary.

Here Ms Lincoln is referring to the affective needs of the pupils, which appeared to her to have been a fairly low priority for the former head. It is an area of particular importance, however, to many of the pupils at the Valley, living as many of them do in circumstances of relative deprivation, compared with their counterparts in other areas of this county. The areas of the city served by the school include some of the most deprived areas of the city, with relatively high unemployment rates, high pro-portions of single-parent families, and high concentrations of families receiving income support. Locally, the Valley estate has a seedy reputation, which Ms Lincoln sees as undeserved. According to Ms Lincoln some of this reputation is a product of the demono-logy of some of the local middle class who believe that places such as the Valley estate are necessarily populated by muggers and worse. Ms Lincoln recognises that a significant proportion of her pupils do come from measurably disadvantaged backgrounds, and that this disadvantage is compounded by what she perceives to be an unfair stigma that is attached to their place of residence by people from other parts of the city.

Difficult living circumstances, social stigma, a divided staff, and an inappropriate curriculum, might seem quite enough for the pupils of the Valley School to have to cope with, but there was more. Not only was the former headteacher attempting to build a school with inappropriate aims in mind, but she was doing so, according to Ms Lincoln, pretty much singlehandedly. The management 'team', of head and two deputies, not only did not work as a team, but had problems of its own:

> I inherited two deputies. One, very good, very dynamic, who'd applied for the headship and not got it, because he was just a little bit underexperienced and a little bit young. And another one who had serious health problems. So I could see there: I had an effective deputy – a curriculum deputy – who had not really been given enough experience under the previous head. If there had been any curriculum ideas, it came from him, but very often they were also blocked by the head. And I knew he was going to move on pretty quickly: a couple of years and he was going to be away. And I had this other male deputy in ill-health –. And I was used to a senior management team that was bright, sparkling, innovative. We had worked as a team; we hadn't worked as individuals.

The structure through which the new head might work to initiate change, therefore, was itself in need of reform. It is interesting to note here, Ms Lincoln's implied concern that the school should provide opportunities for development to its staff, as well its pupils.

Ms Lincoln's aspirations for her new school are recollected in terms which suggest that she felt as if she were starting from scratch. She knew what the school ought to be, and could see that in almost every respect it was failing. She wanted a school where pupils were given a broad and balanced range of learning opportunities; where pupils were proud to be; where pupils were happy to be, and where they felt safe and welcome. One of the few positive aspects that she recalls from her initial period at the school is the wholehearted support she received from the school governors:

> The governors were totally behind me, in that we set out to be different: to be a good comprehensive school; a quality school. And they have backed me all the way on that. Even to the extent that one of the first things we did was we got rid of the traditional school uniform and tie. Because you know and I know that there's two ways of wearing a tie: one is, 'I'm proud of this school', and the other is down here, which says, 'Two fingers up

to this place! I loathe it!' And they even backed me into going into schoolwear, rather than uniform, which was a very dicey move to make in an area which is so uniformed on the other side. But they backed me on that, and they wouldn't change it for the world now.

The previous head had tried to cope with the peculiar situation of the school by blending in with the existing setting. Ms Lincoln's decision to celebrate the uniqueness of the school in relation to its immediate neighbours was clearly a bold step, in that a school which was already seen as something of an oddity might well have become even more stigmatised. This initial step, therefore, was clearly something of an act of faith which the governors, to their credit, were prepared to support.

The abolition of the school uniform might also be seen as a symbolic gesture: a shedding of the old, unloved school, and the birth of a new and quite different school. This break with the past was important not only for the sake of the pupils, but it was also a signal to the parents of many the school's prospective pupils, who were former pupils of the school and its predecessors. This point is underlined in a document that is provided for helping pupils and their parents select year 10 and 11 options:

> Parents who remember the 'Options' system that prevailed in the school since the establishment of the Valley Comprehensive School may wonder what has become of it and what effect the new situation will have on pupils' career prospects.

> Some may not remember the old system with pleasure, posing as it did the problem of selecting five 'Options' subjects from a list of twenty-plus and the fear of making a mistake in the choice.

This clearly demonstrates the importance, in school improvement, of coping with the existing situation, rather than attempting to impose some disembodied blueprint on a school.

Similar radical changes were imposed internally. One of the measures Ms Lincoln took fairly soon after joining the school was to alter the management structure. This might be seen partly as an expedience to overcome the deficiencies in the existing management team, but it was also part of a broader plan to create opportunities for school staff to have greater involvement in decision-making processes, and contributed to the development of an 'open' style of management:

I opened up the senior management team, and brought in three senior teachers . . . and that opened up the senior management team. And the staff saw that as a way of people actually working towards promotion. They were the people with the right ideas; the bright ideas. And eventually the deputy who had been ill took early retirement, because he realised his health meant he just wasn't up to the job. And that ended very amicably, because there was nobody pushing him, because he realised that what was being demanded of him he wasn't capable of.

In many ways the demands that were being made on this particular deputy head, as well as the rest of the staff, were onerous. They were being asked (if not told) to begin to think of their work in a way which ran contrary to the practice that many of them had lived with for many years.

Central themes in the new approach, sponsored by Ms Lincoln, were: the need for teachers to raise their expectations of pupils, both in academic and social terms; the need for ways to be found of raising pupils' sense of self-respect; the need for pupils to be given wider opportunities for success, achievement and active participation in their studies and the school community; the need for aspects of the local community to be reflected, in positive ways, in the life of the school; and the need for staff to recognise the importance of creating a caring environment for pupils. These themes are articulated clearly in the school's prospectus for 1990–1:

Our aims for ALL students are:
1 To help them acquire knowledge and skills (both practical and academic) abilities and the motivation to utilise them to their best advantage.
2 To help them develop mental, physical and spiritual qualities.
3 To help them to appreciate the breadth of human achievements, aspirations and creativity in art, science, mathematics, technology and literature, and, where possible, to give pupils firsthand experience of these.
4 To help them to understand language and numbers, and to use them effectively.
5 To help them to understand the social, economic and political order.
6 To help them develop a reasoned set of values and beliefs

and to instil in them respect and tolerance for the beliefs and values of other religions, races and ways of life.

7 To help them leave our school at 16, 17 or 18, well prepared for the adult world they will meet in their personal and working lives, and ready to make a full contribution to the local as well as the wider community.

8 To help them develop a sense of their own self-worth, the ability to be self-reliant, to have lively and enquiring minds, to be able to question and argue rationally, whilst being active and constructive participants in society.

9 To help them find pleasure in learning and give them the experience of success and personal achievement.

There is nothing remarkable about this list of aims. A similar list might be found in a wide range of school prospectuses. What is interesting here is that these aims declare an intention to overcome many of the difficulties that Ms Lincoln has acknowledged. What follows is an account of how these aims are being approached at the Valley School.

THE NEW CURRICULUM

The curriculum, which evolved into its present form in 1988, anticipated well the National Curriculum. In order to overcome the over-specialisation, which was a problem of the pre-1984 school, a curriculum was devised that was intended to provide all pupils with a broad and balanced programme of study which would give them continuous experience of a wide range of sub-jects. Following some of the principles laid down by the govern- ment's Training and Vocational Education Initiative (TVEI) and prefiguring the National Curriculum, the curriculum (for years 9–11) is organised around a compulsory core of ten subject areas which are taken up to GCSE level. In addition, at the end of year 9, pupils are required to choose an additional subject. There is also a range of 'top-up' options. The core is composed of the following subjects:

- Maths
- English
- Humanities
- Science
- Expressive Arts
- Design Technology

- Community and Industrial Studies
- French
- Physical Education.

The optional subjects are:

(one from):
- A Second Science
- Business Studies
- Travel and Tourism
- PE
- Home Economics

In addition, pupils deemed to be 'most able' in French are given the opportunity to study GCSE German as a second foreign language.

There is also provision for 'top-up courses'. These enable pupils to sit for additional GCSEs by doing further study in certain subjects (Geography, History, Art, Music or Drama), and adding this to the work that they are already doing in the integrated courses (Humanities or Expressive Arts), thus counting some of the work done in the integrated courses twice.

The 'top-up' options are:

(one from:)
- A Humanities subject (from History, Geography or Religious Education)
- An Expressive Arts Subject (from Art, Drama or Music) Child Care
- Fashion and Textiles

This curriculum allows for the students to take up to eleven GCSEs.

There is a strong emphasis on coursework throughout the curriculum, with English (double award), Humanities, Community and Industrial Studies, Expressive Arts, Design Technology, French and German GCSEs being awarded for 100 per cent coursework. Maths is assessed on 50 per cent coursework, and science (single and double award options) is assessed on the basis of 45 per cent coursework. Modular courses are provided in all subjects, except English and Maths, and there is a strong emphasis placed on giving pupils firsthand experience of real-life situations, and encouraging pupils to reflect about themselves and their environment. Community and Industrial Studies, which leads to GCSE in Social Science, is based wholly on the study of the community local to the school and its local industry, and includes a two-week placement for each pupil with a local employer.

The values and aspirations declared in the curriculum focus very clearly on the problems that faced the school in 1984. That there is a strong commitment to these aspirations is underlined by the management's decision to proceed with their curriculum development, along TVEI lines with its emphasis on student-centred learning approaches, without the additional funding that was given to the schools which piloted the scheme:

> We wanted to be part of the TVEI, but they didn't choose our area, because our colleagues in the rest of the area were so far behind. Which grieved us enormously. . . . But we thought . . . there's no point in depriving these children any more; we'll go into it a year early, if we have to, even without the money, because this is what we feel the children need. This is what they need; this is what they want. So we went into it a year early, without the money.

INTEGRATING SEN PUPILS

This commitment to these values of student-centred learning and the raising of pupils' levels of self-esteem is further demonstrated by measures which were taken to ensure that all pupils in the school were provided with opportunities to benefit from the new curriculum. A major hurdle to overcome in this regard was the degree of division and stratification in the organisation of teaching groups, which meant that when Ms Lincoln arrived some 10 per cent of the school population were not receiving the full range of the existing curriculum, because they were considered to have learning or behavioural difficulties. First, there was a group of forty statemented pupils with learning difficulties:

> In '84 there were four mobile classrooms out there, and that was called the MLD [Moderate Learning Difficulties] Unit. Again, that was a thing that we inherited. When they put up a unit for children with moderate learning difficulties, for the whole of this area, where did they put it? Here. I wouldn't have agreed to that, if I'd have been head at the time. Of course what that did was skewed us, as Rutter would put it, by giving us a much higher proportion of pupils with learning problems than most other

schools. And of course, what the other children did, they called them 'thickies', 'dimbos', 'dimdums', 'muppets', you name it. And those [forty] children, the programme of education they had was really rather inadequate. They got English, English, English; maths, maths, maths. They didn't integrate with the other children at all. So it was just locational integration, on the same site, which actually stigmatised them, even more. . . . And if you took into account the children at the bottom end of mainstream, who had never been statemented, for whatever reason, but should've been . . ., and we had more than our fair share of those anyway, just because of the social mix [i.e. more than the 18 per cent expected in the normal population]. . . .

Second there was a group of twenty-five non-statemented pupils, who were segregated within the mainstream school, owing to their learning and/or behavioural difficulties:

And in mainstream school there was this thing called 'ALP Group'.And I said, 'What's this?' 'Oh, it's the Alternative Learning Programme Group.' 'What's that mean?' 'Well, they do a different course from the rest of the school.' 'Why do they do a different course?' 'They're the naughty ones.' 'What do you mean "they're naughty"?' So when I investigated that: it was . . . a combination of the least able in mainstream, who should've been statemented, and hadn't been, and the ones just above that, for whom school meant nothing and had just turned off and were disruptive. So it was like a beargarden in there. . . . There was a class of about twenty-five of them . . . of years 4 and 5 [i.e. 10 and 11 in National Curriculum terms]. . . . They were a recipe for disaster, because whereas you'd got these very well behaved children in the unit, then at the bottom of the school you'd got these children who'd been stigmatised: 'You are the no-hopers! You are the naughty people aren't you!' And, by golly, they lived up to the reputation. They didn't integrate with other children, they were taught separately. They didn't have a full curriculum, they had a very narrow curriculum, and they could only put the very strongest teachers [in the sense of control] in to teach them. So I stopped that at the end of the year I came. I said, 'There's no way!' And we got into talking then about integrating children.

In 1984 these two segregated groups represented the school's total provision for pupils with special educational needs: statemented pupils were in the MLD unit, mainstream pupils perceived to have difficulties were in the ALP group; mainstream pupils had no learning support provision. Ms Lincoln adds wryly:

> It was little wonder that they [pupils in the ALP group] weren't surviving: they'd failed so often, they'd turned to misbehaving to try and show themselves successful at something – drawing attention to themselves.

The integration issue was a tough nut to crack with the staff, with a period of five years passing before all the segregated groupings were completely absorbed into the mainstream.

Ms Lincoln's account of the way in which she tackled the integration problem illustrates important points about her management style, and gives us some indication of how she has managed not only to initiate change, but how she has, at the same time, attempted to elicit staff commitment to the changes. One problem that she did not have to face was that of convincing staff that problems existed. When she arrived at the school she found general dissatisfaction among the staff with matters such as levels of pupil achievement, behaviour and commitment to the school, as well as a shared feeling that the curriculum was inadequate for pupil needs. There was a sense among the staff that they were barely coping with a worsening situation. However, the solutions proposed by Ms Lincoln and her management team did not meet with such ready agreement:

> They saw the problems, but what they didn't perhaps agree with was my way of leading them forward on that. They didn't believe it was possible, or it could be successful.

On the integration issue there was resistance from both the staff in the unit and the mainstream staff:

> I had to change the staff's attitude towards integration; that wasn't only the staff who were in the unit, but also the staff in the mainstream school, because they reckoned they didn't have the skills to teach these pupils. They didn't realise, or couldn't comprehend, that every teacher is a teacher of children with special needs: it's only [a matter of] broadening your strengths and your skills.

Over the five-year period, however, attitudes changed:

In the staff-development interviews this year, what has come through strongly is [staff saying], 'I didn't believe in integration, but it's wonderful; it's working; I'm a convert.'

Ms Lincoln attributes this change of attitude to a number of strategies. First, her own dogged commitment to the idea of integration. She continually argued the point in many staff meetings, and repeatedly stressed the centrality of the idea of integration to the concept of comprehensivisation. Ms Lincoln clearly staked a great deal on this issue, offering staff a stark choice:

As head, they got the same message from me over, and over, and over again. And for the people who didn't like it, or didn't feel that they could ever adapt to that – and that was mainly the teachers in the unit – they looked for positions elsewhere: a couple of them [did].

The other side of this uncompromising approach, however, was a recognition of the need for support. Ms Lincoln recognised that she was asking her staff, particularly those in the unit, to take on roles for which they did not feel equipped:

And the others who were left, who perhaps felt, 'Well, yes, maybe I could do it.' We pushed them out to all sorts of in-service training. And then we had little project areas, where the more daring, who had had some in-service training, felt they could [teach in the mainstream]; they would offer themselves the next year on the curriculum. And, of course, the good news spread as people see it.

The combination of absolute firmness of position and appreciation of the demands that staff were being asked to face is seen by Ms Lincoln as a key factor in achieving the integration goal. Once she had made it clear that this was the direction in which the school was going to move, and provided the support that staff needed to be equipped to follow this path, she then relied on the individual staff to move forward at their own pace.

The five-year period then, was, for this school, a necessary timescale for this particular innovation to take root and develop through a number of stages. The first stage in the integration process was to disestablish the MLD Unit as a physical entity. The pupils from the unit were brought into mainstream school classrooms. This paved the way for broadening these pupils' curriculum. As unit teachers began to feel more confident about teaching in the mainstream, so specialist mainstream teachers became available to sample teaching the unit classes. Out of this situation the Learning Support Faculty was born, which had the original MLD Unit teachers as its nucleus. It was from this basis that the final full integration of the unit pupils into mainstream classes was achieved. Once again, teachers' support needs were seen as a priority:

> We would put a support teacher in with the mainstream teacher, or even a welfare assistant, who would be there; who would be an extra pair of hands to build up their confidence. But in fact, the support teacher, or the welfare assistant, gradually, because that's the way we wanted it to be, did not focus their attention purely on the children with special needs – they were available to all the children. And that gave the teacher in mainstream more confidence. They didn't realise, in the end they were dealing with all the children. It wasn't that the welfare assistant or the support teacher was keeping the statemented child or the weaker child on the right lines. They were there as an extra pair of hands. So gradually, over a couple of years, they built up their confidence. And then the good news spread.

The 'good news' was that the pupils with special needs were seen to be making good progress, and that the support provided was enabling teachers to offer help to pupils who although not statemented required assistance, and who, under the old system, had been neglected. The integrated role assigned to the support staff also had the effect of building their confidence in working with mainstream groups.

After five years, the head is able to claim that there is a consensus among the staff in support of the integration of pupils with special needs in the mainstream, on the basis of the benefits that are bestowed on both mainstream and pupils with special educational needs, and the benefits experienced by staff, in the broadening of their professional skills and experience. Given the initial resistance of staff to the idea of integration, this is a remarkable achievement. Staff and pupils have had a great deal to assimilate and adapt to in order to achieve this end, and it is hard to see how such progress could have been made without the kind of carefully staged approach that was adopted in this school. A too hasty approach to this problem might have led to failure and frustration for both staff and pupils.

A strong theme which emerges from Ms Lincoln's account of her school's development is her commitment to the idea that pupils' and teachers' needs are closely linked. The staff are not seen simply as a tool for implementing the head's directives, they are seen rather as an integral part of the community which is being created at the Valley School. She believes that there can be no improvement in the pupils' commitment to and pride in their school, without these feelings being shared and reflected by staff. Thus an important outcome of the integration exercise was the sense of confidence and achievement that was felt by staff, in finding that they could work effectively with groups of pupils who they had previously felt to lie outside their sphere of competence. Success breeds the confidence to strive for further success; this is as true for teachers as it is for pupils. The pupils at the Valley School, in many cases, come from long lines of former pupils who expected failure and conflict in school. Many of the staff had similar expectations, with consequent implications for their professional satisfaction. The need for teachers to have confidence in their professional abilities was, therefore, of prime importance. Whilst the mainstream teachers had this need met as a consequence of the carefully staged integration programme, this was not such a simple process where the unit teachers were concerned, as Ms Lincoln points out:

> From the start, I insisted that every member of staff who was in the unit also taught in mainstream school. And anybody new I brought in as a Special Ed. teacher, I also insisted that they were capable of teaching up to 'A' Level in a subject. Now the reason for that was, the teachers in the unit had very low status. But if I was making them teach in mainstream up to 'A' Level – they did 'A' Level Communication Studies. (One's teaching 'A' Level Communication Studies at the minute; Fred Smith is teaching BTech. Matthew. We brought Matthew from mainstream, into Special Ed.; he's an 'A' Level English teacher.) So I insisted that they taught both mainstream [and SEN]. So then it was a *quid pro quo*; one would also expect the mainstream teachers to teach, say, a discrete set of statemented children. And that's what happened, and then it spread. And everybody was dabbling in each other's areas, and actually experienced quite a bit of fun out of it!

The experience of integration for the SEN pupils is described by Ms Lincoln in the following terms:

> To begin with, what we did was, we brought them [the unit pupils] into mainstream school, and they were integrated inso-far as they . . . followed the same curriculum as mainstream children. Sometimes they would be in discrete sets, but they were setted according to their ability in the individual subject. So, for the first time, those children were, perhaps, able to do a GCSE in English, or a GCSE in art. I can still remember a little lad who was in my second year here, who was a brilliant artist. But, because he was in the unit, he wasn't allowed to do an exam in it. It was breaking his heart, that he had this wonderful talent that couldn't be appreciated by anybody in the normal children's form which was an examination qualification. So we brought them into the mainstream. So, again, they were accep-ted there. The only thing we couldn't do, was we couldn't put them into French because our middle schools didn't allow them the opportunity to learn French. So again, there was the stigma because of that; so that took us some years to convert the middle schools, that everybody ought to have a chance of doing a foreign language. . . . There still is [segregation for SEN pupils from modern languages] in one middle school [out of three], but that's changing now with the new head. Which means that the liaison process, and the preparation for coming up here, has got to be very carefully done with the statemented children in the middle school. Because some of them are coming out of a very small, safe sanctuary into a big wide world up here, and they've got to be very well prepared for that.

The watchword of the integration process at the Valley seems to have been 'caution'. Major advances were made, but each step of the way was managed with an eye to maximising the beneficial outcomes and minimising the chances of failure. At the time of the interview with Ms Lincoln, SEN pupils were fully integrated into mainstream classes, to the extent that they were in mainstream tutor groups, and were in mainstream sets for all their subjects. However, initially, SEN pupils were all placed in one of the two parallel mixed-ability bands, which run from years 9 to 11. This facilitated ease of monitoring, whilst allowing the pupils them-selves to be well dispersed, as there are four tutor groups in each half-year band. Similarly, the tutors who first received SEN pupils into their groups were carefully selected, on the basis of their enthusiasm for the integration exercise and most aware of the needs of the statemented pupils. Ms Lincoln describes the way in which this situation has developed:

> Last year, we went over to total integration, but we put the statemented children in one half-year band, where we felt we had tutors who were perhaps that bit more sensitive to their needs. And then this year we're over to the full lot. Everybody said, 'That's not good enough, why should they be in one half-year band; we want them spread out through the year.' We have still got some discrete sets, within the fourth- and fifth-year [i.e. years 10 and 11] programme, but very, very little, and it is where the children need it; where they do need that expert help as such. But for most of the time they are integrated with their peers, and every subject area is accessible to them. And even now, we do French for all. We've put a lot of money into the development of French for all. So now everybody does French, even the statemented children.

The full fruits of the integration programme are difficult to assess at this early stage. Ms Lincoln, however, believes that over the time that these measures have been introduced there has been a marked improvement in pupils' commitment to their work, and a raising of staff expectations. She points to a recent increase in the total number of pupils who are now staying on into the sixth form, and attributes this in part to the new curriculum:

> The good thing now about the curriculum is that everything they do at pre-16 they can do at post-16. We see it as a five-year commitment, both from them, if possible, and from us certainly. Now the good thing about that is, our sixth-form numbers this year were the highest ever. We've had to have our LMS budget recalculated because we're 6.7 per cent over expected numbers. We're the first school in [this LEA] to have to have that done, in the four years that LMS has been in.

Another important indicator which the head points to is the improvement in pupils' performance at GCSE. In the year 1989/90, 99 per cent of the fifth year pupils were entered for GCSE in one or more subjects: over 90 per cent of pupils took GCSEs in English Language, Science and Maths; over 80 per cent took English Literature and Social Studies; 70 per cent took

Creative Arts and Humanities; 60 per cent took CDT, and 30 per cent took French. Not only have entry rates improved but so too have pass rates. Whilst in 1985/6 only 10 per cent of pupils entered for public examinations in the fifth year achieved pass grades (at 'O' Level and CSE); in 1990 this had gone up to an average 28 per cent in the ten core subjects (at GCSE) (i.e. on average, 28 per cent obtained A–C grades; 43 per cent D–E; 29 per cent F–G).

ESTABLISHING A NEW ETHOS

As has already been suggested, a great deal of care was taken by Ms Lincoln and her management team to introduce the changes in a way that took account of the staff needs and state of readiness. The integration of pupils with special needs, for example, was staged over a period of five years, and feedback from staff made an important contribution to the rate of progress towards full integration. This process of staff consultation is an important theme which Ms Lincoln returns to often, and it reflects something of the overall ethos of the school that Ms Lincoln is attempting to build. At the heart of the new ethos is the importance of mutual respect among pupils and between pupils and teachers. Ms Lincoln is quite clear that whilst the curriculum is the main vehicle of opportunity for pupils, pupils will not make the best use of the opportunities offered without good quality teacher–pupil relationships:

> [initially] the staff relationships weren't exactly right, with the pupils. [Too often, staff behaved in ways which conveyed the message:] 'I am a teacher, you will respect me.' And we gradually had to change that to: 'I am a teacher, yes, but you are a pupil, and we demand equal respect of each other. And you can't swear at me if I'm not allowed to swear at you. And I don't swear at you, as a teacher, therefore why should you swear at me.' Or, [from the pupils' point of view] 'I know you're not supposed to hit me, so why should you hit me?'

Without these improvements in teacher–pupil relationships, the old antagonisms that existed between the two groups would continue to cause blockages in the lines of staff–pupil communication, and the level of collaboration and investment of effort, on which the new curriculum depended, would not be achieved.

The changes in staff ways of relating to pupils were achieved, according to Ms Lincoln, through a process of 'overt and covert' in-service training. The 'covert' training was training by example: the unobtrusive display of good practice. For example, Ms Lincoln describes the way she demonstrates to staff the kind of approach to pupil misdemeanors that she is seeking to establish:

> I like to think I keep a very high profile in the school. I like to – particularly initially – let the staff see that I am doing what I'm asking them to do. It wasn't the case that I was always on the child's side, but that no matter what the child had done, I tried to get through to the child, 'I don't hate you for doing this.' Like a good parent would. 'But, by golly you've let me down with what you've done.' There was too much of [a tendency among staff to imply], 'You are stupid!' Rather than, 'What a stupid thing to do!' I had too much of [staff] knocking on my door: 'This boy,' or 'This girl, has done so and so, and so and so, and I don't want to teach him any more!'

This central theme of respect for persons is reflected in the 'overt' training also. Much of this 'training' takes place in the regular whole-staff meetings, which take the form of 'workshops'. A key feature of these meetings is staff participation, as Ms Lincoln states:

> We don't have staff meetings where you sit and say, 'any questions?' And the same people open up with the gripes. And then nobody else wants to come to staff meetings, because they just find them a bore. So what we do, is we have staff workshops.

The workshops are each organised around a question or problem which is generated from an issue of current concern in the school. Topics so far covered include:

- What makes a good school?
- The role of the form tutor: Healing the pastoral academic divide.
- Devising a school environment development plan.
- Record-keeping: What should they contain?
- Models of record-keeping.
- 'What should be done if . . .?' Responding to problem behaviour in the school.
- Rewards for pupils.
- Public relations: The Valley School and the community.

The format of the meetings varies according to the topic, but the common pattern is for the meeting to commence with a presentation, in which a problem is stated and staff are briefed as to the task in hand, and then for staff to break off into small (six or seven staff) discussion groups. Outcomes of the small group discussions are recorded. After the meeting these outcomes are collated by a member of the management team and a report is prepared which is distributed to staff. If further consultation or discussion is felt to be necessary a second meeting may be called. Where topics arise out of the need for policy decisions to be made, the management decision will be stated in the post-meeting report, with close reference to staff views expressed in the workshop, though not necessarily in agreement with views expressed.

One important workshop, addressing the question: 'What makes a good school?' touched on the issue of consultation procedures in the school, and received this reply in the written report, prepared by the head, that followed:

> Staff views were certainly divided as to the success of consultation procedures within the school, according to the comments made. I must, however, make it clear: in any school where I am Head, decisions will be taken following consultation with you and after listening to a wide range of views. It will never be a participative form of government with the majority vote carrying the day or based on a Countesthorpe-type moot. The governors appointed me head with full approval of my style of management; that's what they wanted and that's the way it will be. . . . Listen I will to your opinions, always, but the fact that you don't always like the final decisions taken does *not* mean you have not been consulted or that it was only lip-service being paid! My accountability is not only to the staff but to the whole community of which members of staff are certainly an important part. Through more frequent staff meetings I will have more opportunity of giving you feedback on why particular decisions, popular and unpopular, have been made.

> [head's report]

This statement also has to be considered in the context of a large group of responses from an earlier round of staff interviews conducted by the head:

> in the staff interviews I held in the summer term [1987] I received an overwhelming number of pleas from individual staff not to try and consult too widely, but to direct staff what to do –

I was assured that staff would prefer to be told what t
however unpalatable, and they felt that was what I was paid

The important thing here, however, appears to be the fact that
there is an active dialogue taking place, in which staff are able to
make their feelings known and are given the right to expect a
response. It is interesting to note that subsequent reports of meetings suggest that these complaints have not persisted.

An examination of some of the workshop reports leaves the
reader with the impression that there is, in fact, a strong and effective process of staff consultation at work in the Valley School. The
1988 workshop, entitled, 'What makes a good school?' exemplifies
this point, marking, as it appears to have done, the starting-point
for many subsequent changes in the school. In this workshop staff
were asked to construct a list of qualities that characterise 'a good
school'. They were then asked to consider the ways in which the
Valley School matched up to these aspirations. Finally, the staff
were required to make some practical suggestions as to how the
school might be brought closer to the ideal. The first task generated a total of twenty qualities, which, interestingly, reflect quite
closely the values espoused by Ms Lincoln, indicating the commonality of purpose among the staff of the Valley School that was
developing in 1988:

- Strong head with a good sense of direction; obvious and effec-
  tive leadership;
- Pride in school;
- Good resourcing level;
- A caring community, where there is respect for people and
  property; quiet environment;
- A desire to do well – a community where achievement in all
  spheres is encouraged;
- Where change is managed sensitively with respect to the
  demands on staff;
- Where governors are involved in the school;
- Where there is an established disciplinary framework, help and
  support for new, probationary and supply staff;
- Where communications are effective;
- Where a good public image is cultivated;
- Where there is stability – traditional values;
- One which is educationally forward-thinking and innovative;
- Good exam results;

- Lack of graffiti, litter, damage;
- Where the school's policy about what it is attempting to do is clear and is kept updated; clearly stated common goals;
- Good working relationships with other schools;
- Able to take any visitor to any part of the school at any time;
- Where there are lots of extra-curricular activities;
- Where there are good communications;
- Good atmosphere.

This list reinforces many of the points made by Ms Lincoln, particularly her concern to create a school where there is a positive cooperative atmosphere, which extends a wide range of opportunities to all pupils, and engenders a sense of pride among those who are associated with the school. The item which refers to the need for sensitive handling of change in relation to staff needs is also interesting, as we have already seen this to be an important consideration among the management team at the Valley. The importance of pupils' self-esteem and pride in their achievements is further emphasised by a supplementary list, which relates specifically to the pupils of 'a good school':

A good school is one where:
- pupils of all abilities are achieving set goals and achieving their potential;
- there is a good work ethic;
- pupils take responsibility for themselves;
- pupils have self-respect and respect for others;
- there is care taken of the environment, pride in the school and a sense of belonging and identity;
- there is a good range of sports/leisure/extra curricular activities;
- pupils have a sense of commitment and purpose;
- we would be happy for our own or friends' children to attend;
- pupils also behave well outside school;
- there are good sports results.

A further list relates to staff:

A good school is one where:
- staff can practise their own specialities;
- staff are happy to work and morale is high;
- staff are professionals;

- staff are able to respond to pupils' individual needs;
- there is consistency and uniformity of standards, *re* behaviour and discipline;
- staff, including supply staff, are respected;
- staff work as a team without excessive hierarchical structure;
- where staff have a commitment to providing a curriculum for the whole ability range, believing in equality of opportunity for pupils of all abilities, and where curriculum support is available to bring out the best in pupils;
- relationships between staff and pupils are good.

In addition, under the heading of 'parents', an important quality of 'a good school' is seen to be: 'good relationships between school and parents'.

What comes across strongly from a consideration of these lists of qualities is the teachers' aspirations for a school which operates as a cohesive caring community, in which the members of the community – staff as well as pupils – are treated with respect and consideration for themselves as persons; where everyone has an opportunity for personal development, and is motivated to make a full contribution to the school community. In short, there seems to be little to choose between the list of qualities and the aspirations expressed by Ms Lincoln. Of course, not all of these qualities were identified by all of the groups; they are an amalgam of the lists generated by the small staff groups. So in this way the workshop process can be seen as a means by which opinions and ideas are generated and shared with a wider audience. The act of dissemination, in itself, it could be argued, can be a motivating force for staff, by giving their individual views the status of publication. However, the sense of ownership and involvement, that Ms Lincoln suggests as an important product of the workshops, is more obviously attributable to the obvious and tangible outcomes that ensue from these meetings.

In the case of the 'What makes a good school' workshop, the staff groups produced a list of shortcomings which they felt the Valley School would have to address before it could be a 'good school'. These shortcomings included:

In relation to pupils:
- the failure of the school to 'stretch' its most able pupils;
- the low self-esteem felt by many pupils;

- the poor public image/low public status of the school;
- the failure of a minority of pupils (20–25 per cent) to conform to behavioural expectations;
- the lack of consistency among staff in their behavioural expectations of pupils.

In relation to staff:

- management ignore majority staff views without adequate explanation;
- lack of a consistent code of staff expectations for pupil behaviour;
- realisation that a disciplinary approach to problem pupils is not always appropriate, but a lack of knowledge of how to cope with problems that may stem from pupils' personal difficulties;
- pressure of current climate and pace of change;
- lack of stability for pupils, caused by internal changes and externally imposed changes.

Once again we find a strong degree of agreement between the staff perceptions recorded here, particularly those relating to pupils, and those expressed by Ms Lincoln. To some extent, these views act as an endorsement for measures that were already in motion, especially the new curriculum, which at that time was in its first year of operation. Other areas of concern, however, appear to have gained prominence as a result of this meeting, and led to subsequent action.

It is impossible to detail all of the developments which appear to have grown out of this meeting, but it is possible to focus on a number of key strands which can be traced from this source. First, the staff complaint about lack of explanation for management decisions which appeared to ignore majority staff opinion, was met, on the basis of suggestions that were generated at the same workshop, with an increase in the frequency of whole staff meetings, and the tabling on the agenda of space for the head to deliver more extensive explanations of decisions. Second, the call for improvements in consistency of disciplinary standards and concern over pupil motivation led to further meetings which produced a disciplinary code and a school policy on rewards. The discipline code emerged partly from a workshop in which staff discussed approaches to a number of case studies of problem behaviour. The outcome of this was a policy statement which details the types of teacher response felt to be most appropriate to particular forms of problem behaviour, and sets out a clear pattern of referral for problems that require more input than the class teacher can supply. As a result of the 'rewards' workshop, a formal rewards system was introduced to publicly reward pupils, across the age and ability range, for their achievements in academic and other areas. The credit system also led to changes in the annual prize-giving, to the extent that at the last prize-day one in four pupils were able to receive a prize for achievement of one kind or another. One of the more complex problems was felt by staff to be that of the emotional and behavioural problems that some pupils exhibited. This was one problem which staff seemed to feel could not be easily dealt with within the school's existing provision. Centrally, staff felt they were not equipped with the expertise, and more particularly the time, to deal with the very real personal problems that a significant proportion of their pupils brought with them to school, and that often exploded in the classroom in the form of disruptive behaviour. The staff proposed a solution which involved the appointment of a professional counsellor for pupils. A year later, a half-time post for a school counsellor was created.

These outcomes lend support to Ms Lincoln's claim that consultation plays an important role in her management style. There is also an indication of a firm basis for Ms Lincoln's claim that her staff possess a sense of ownership of and commitment to the school, partly as a result of their involvement in the changes facilitated by the workshop programme. The nature of the changes themselves also reflects the sense of community and co-operation that is central to the ethos of the school, as is shown from an examination of the disciplinary code and the rewards policy. In these two policy areas we see clear evidence of an endeavour to create policy which provides a secure and stable framework within which individuals are clear as to expectations and responsibilities.

THE DISCIPLINE CODE

The discipline code (published in the staff handbook), lays down a clear pattern of response to disciplinary problems in the classroom, and details a referral procedure where such is required. The head states that the code is inspired by the Elton Report (DES, 1989a), and its whole school, collaborative emphasis, with a

concern for the pupils' perspective reflects many of the recommendations of the report. Discipline problems are divided into MINOR,
PERSISTENT and URGENT problems. Minor problems include:

* minor classroom difficulties, chattering, inattentiveness etc.;
* occasional failure to produce homework without adequate
  reason;
* careless, slovenly work;
* occasional lateness for lessons;
* occasional failure to produce equipment.

There is a two-stage response plan for these minor problems. Stage
one involves an interpersonal approach, in which the class teacher
approaches the pupil exhibiting the problem behaviour, with
'gentle persuasion, exhortations or firm reminders'. If this fails,
the teacher is then required to impose his or her own sanctions;
for example, 'imposition of extra purposeful work during break,
lunch hour or at home.' Stage two is invoked if the teacher believes
the stage one action to be unlikely to succeed. The stage two
guidelines state:

> The matter should, at a fairly early stage BEFORE THINGS GET
> OUT OF HAND IN ANY WAY, be referred to the head of depart-
> ment, whose job it is to be aware of the situation and offer
> advice, support, and, if necessary, intervention.

Persistent problems include the recurrence of many of the same
behaviours listed under minor problems, but also include:

* noticeable underachievement;
* lack of progress of whole form;
* persistent nuisance factors short of disruption.

The three-stage response pattern for persistent problems involves
a series of consultations, first with the head of faculty. This first
stage involves increased monitoring across the faculty, and
strategies employed at this stage will be determined by the faculty
involved and might include the transfer of the pupil to a different
(i.e. more appropriate) teaching group. If the problem is felt to be
such that the faculty cannot deal with it alone, either through the
ineffectiveness of the measures so far implemented, or because the
problem resides in an area outside of the faculty's sphere of
influence, then the stage two procedure of bringing the pupil's
tutor into the scene is invoked. This procedure is advised where

the problem is seen to be of a behavioural rather than an academic nature. In this situation the tutor will take on responsibility for the problem, extending monitoring of the pupil's behaviour to a school-wide context, and invoking one or more of a range of sanctions, such as detention, if necessary. The third stage involves the tutor referring the matter to the head of year, who will review the problem and may introduce outside agencies (e.g. Social Services, educational psychologist) into the situation. The involvement of parents is recommended at any stage of the 'persistent problem' category. The final category of 'urgent and major problems' includes:

> serious indiscipline on the part of one or more pupils, any other serious problems with which you (i.e. the teacher) require IMMEDIATE ASSISTANCE.

Here the response pattern is to:

> send for a senior member of staff: head, deputy, senior teacher or year head. What is required is immediate senior involvement; the matter can be referred to the appropriate tutor later.

With regard to the imposition of sanctions, Ms Lincoln is clear that sanctions are a necessary part of the school's response to pupil misbehaviour, provided they are used with care and sensitivity:

> One of the things we had to get away from was the idea that a certain sin deserved a certain punishment. Because when some of the year heads would say, 'That punishment's a bit severe for that child, 'cos he's coped with an awful lot, because so and so's happened at home,' they'd get the response, 'We're turning into a team of social workers now!' . . . It was necessary to get them to see that in any good school, it's an individual response to an individual need. And that is very, very important: the individual response. So we had to get away from the punishment of whole classes for misbehaviour; we had to get away from keeping whole classes behind, because of something one of them had done. Again, through the case studies, where you debate how you would deal with it, they would pick up from the others that, 'I'm out of kilter with the rest of the school, I've got to think about this again.'

The use of sanctions as a constructive force, aimed to benefit the pupil as well as the school as a whole, is typical of the school ethos, as it is espoused by Ms Lincoln. Implicit here, also, is a recognition that inappropriate sanctions can serve to escalate problem situations, by failing to take account of circumstances that might have influenced a pupil to behave in a disruptive manner.

There are many important features to the discipline code. First, the whole thrust of the approach is to meet problems at an early stage and to develop responses that meet the requirements of the specific situation. Care is taken not to overreact or push an already difficult situation to crisis point. Second, before sanctions are invoked teachers are encouraged to approach the problem in a low-key, personal manner, which takes full account of the pupil as an individual with his or her own good reasons for behaving as they do (whether or not the teacher agrees that the reasons are good ones is a separate matter). This is an acknowledgment of the central importance of staff–pupil relationships in the classroom, and the way these can be used to nip problems in the bud. The manner in which staff approach behavioural problems, in terms of interpersonal style, is extremely important, with the emphasis being on defusing potentially explosive situations, and displaying to pupils a willingness to listen to their side of the argument. As Ms Lincoln states:

PC: Is there any kind of style that predominates in the way you expect teachers to relate to pupils [when classroom behaviour problems arise]?

Mrs Lincoln: Yes. Approachability; willingness to listen; not to condemn out of hand before they've heard the child's side of the story. Staff who will not just say to children, 'You were wrong,' or, 'You are wrong.' But at the same time, who will offer them a different way of dealing with the problem. There is no point in saying to a child, 'You were wrong to do that,' when the child's got to breaking point for whatever reason. Whether it's lack of success with what they're doing, when it's [i.e. work] too difficult for them, or somebody winding them up in the classroom, and they lose their temper. What we try and get them to do is say, 'Look, you walk out of the situation; you come and sit outside here [the school reception area]. We will let you cool down and we will listen to you, and listen to why you got so wound-up, and we will proceed from there.'

Third, there is an implicit acknowledgement that classroom behaviour problems might have their genesis in the curriculum, and might be solved by adjusting the pupil's curriculum at faculty or departmental level, rather than immediately assuming the fault rests with the pupil. Fourth, there is a clear sense of direction, as to the appropriate action to take when the class teacher feels that the problem is not one that can be contained within the routine classroom situation. Fifth, and perhaps most importantly, there is an acknowledgement of a shared responsibility for pupil behaviour across the staff community, and an acknowledgement of the need for class teachers to operate against the background of a clearly defined support network.

THE REWARDS SYSTEM

The rewards system at the Valley School is central to the ethos of the school, exemplifying the aim of raising pupils' self-esteem through giving them the experience of success across a wide range of activities. Like the discipline code, it offers clear guidance to staff as to how the system should operate, and distributes the responsibility for the system throughout the staff community.

The system was generated largely as a result of a staff workshop on the subject and, like the discipline code, owes much to the Elton Report (DES, 1989a). A major concern among staff was the lack of availability of rewards for pupils in the lower- and middle-ability ranges, who were unlikely to achieve high academic success. It was felt, however, that the general level of motivation and commitment to the school would be increased if rewards and public recognition were to be made available to all pupils, and not just the academically skilled. For this reason a wide-ranging list of criteria for reward was drawn up to include:

- Academic excellence – either outstanding individual pieces of work or consistent achievement at a high standard;
- Diligence/effort – might be shown by improvement in any area;
- Service to others;
- Sport;
- Extra-curricular activities.

The range of rewards offered for these achievements was also generated through staff consultation, as well as through consultation with pupils. The basic unit of reward was identified as the 'comment slip'. Interestingly, the same comment slips are employed in the discipline system. These slips are filled in by subject teachers when they feel a pupil has achieved something worthy of reward. A detailed comment was preferred to a non-specific 'merit mark' on the basis that the comment was a lasting record of the reason for the reward and, as such, less likely to become devalued. The slips are passed onto the tutor on a weekly basis. Where a pupil is found by a tutor to be receiving positive comment slips consistently, a higher reward is offered in the form of a letter home, which details the pupil's achievements. In addition to letters home, individual faculties and departments, as well as tutors, can award 'certificates of commendation' to pupils who are performing well in their subject area over a half-term period. These certificates are awarded at full school assemblies. Assemblies are also used as a platform for displaying outstanding pupil work and performance art. There is a display policy by which each faculty is required to display examples of pupils' work in their teaching areas. There is also a category of 'exceptional praising' which encourages subject teachers to refer individual pupils to heads of department/faculty, senior teachers, deputy heads and headteacher for additional praise, when appropriate.

Both the discipline code and the reward system exemplify the essentially humanistic thrust of the new school ethos, which emphasises the need to provide all pupils with opportunities for personal and academic development in a supportive community. These measures are for Ms Lincoln part of the essential accompaniment for the curriculum reforms and the special-needs integration programme, neither of which could succeed without the appropriate pattern of staff–pupil relations, which are implicit in the reward system and discipline code. Furthermore, these policies themselves would not succeed unless they were actively supported by the staff, and as has already been suggested, such support is forthcoming largely because the staff themselves have a large stake in the development process, through the consultation process. As Ms Lincoln says:

> The staff are totally involved [in making suggestions for improvements in the school]. And they can see that we act on

these things. In fact, in the staff development [interviews] this year, many of them said, 'It's good that our views are asked for and taken notice of.'

Ms Lincoln also repeatedly refers to the way in which the success of the measures which have been adopted as policy provides staff with a sense of achievement and confidence in their abilities to tackle what previously seemed to be insurmountable problems.

SCHOOL CHANGES AND THE STAFF

Improvements in staying-on rates, lower incidence of court appearances of pupils, improved examination results, improved attendance levels, an almost complete eradication of vandalism and graffiti from school premises, and a growing sense that pupils and staff have harmonious relationships, and share a feeling of pride for their school, are all factors which in turn have contributed to an almost complete transformation of the Valley School. The school that Ms Lincoln took over in 1984 was a depressed and failing institution, where pupils and staff were disaffected and directionless, and where staff refused to send their own children. In 1991 the head can think of only one member of staff who prefers to send his child to a grammar school in preference to the Valley. There is now a sense among the staff of dynamism and enthusiasm. This is not to say that there has been a wholesale change of heart among the staff. There have been changes of heart among some of the staff, but there have also been many changes of staff. Ms Lincoln estimates that there has been a turnover of between 30 and 40 per cent, in the eight years since she took over the headship; among these are the majority of heads of department in the core subjects. Many of these changes have been the result of retirement or pro- motion to other schools, but some have been for more ideological reasons. On the positive side, however, there have been a number of internal promotions, and new staff who have been brought in during the last eight years have tended to stay, or move for pro- motion. Ms Lincoln believes that the school offers staff the oppor- tunity to 'find a niche here', because their strengths and enthusiasms will be valued and encouraged to develop.

The high staff turnover has been in some senses a mixed bless- ing, creating at first a sense of instability in the school, which was a source of concern to some staff, who felt that it combined with the curricular and other changes to create a climate of uncertainty in the school, that was potentially harmful to pupils. There was also the danger that new and sometimes inexperienced staff coming to a difficult school might be too easily socialised into the ethos of despair and neglect that pervaded the place. Ms Lincoln attributes the fact that this didn't happen to the dynamism and skill of her management team, the measures to facilitate change that have already been discussed, as well as a general sense among those teachers from the old regime who remained that any change would be a change for the better. These factors, coupled with clearly defined criteria for the type of replacement staff the school needed, helped to bring about changes in the attitudes of those staff who remained from the former head's period of tenure.

In defining the qualities she looks for in new staff, Ms Lincoln is very clear and uncompromising:

> I won't appoint anybody who doesn't believe in comprehensive education. The most important thing for me is that they believe in comprehensive education. I don't need enemies amongst my staff. Every member of my staff is an image maker. They've got to go out there, and whatever they do – even if they're buying at the market on a Saturday – they're selling the school. And if they're in Tesco's supermarket, in a queue, and somebody says to them, 'How's that ropy place [the Valley School] of yours these days?' I want them to reply, saying, 'It's a good place that, and I'm proud to work there.' There's no point in buying-in enemies. They can go elsewhere. If they don't believe what I believe in, about what comprehensive education is about, then please look elsewhere!
>
> The next thing I look for is relationships: how they are with children. Do they categorise children? Do they stigmatise children? Or, do they see every child as somebody's loved one to be developed, and made into what the school will be proud of and the parents will be proud of too. So relationships are very, very important.
>
> And I think, thirdly, would be the academic breadth of what they can teach. I mean, really, under LMS, I can't afford to take anybody in who can't teach up to 'A' Level in a subject, because of this being a 13-to-18 school.

In these three qualities we can see a reflection of the major achievements of the school, as outlined by Ms Lincoln, in terms of the school's move towards offering a truly comprehensive education to all its pupils, its refusal to allow the statementing process to act as a barrier to full access to the curriculum, and its determination to create a caring community to which staff and pupils are proud to belong. It is also clear from what she says elsewhere that Ms Lincoln believes that she has succeeded in finding staff who match up to her requirements.

This is not to say that she seeks merely docile or submissive teachers to work at the Valley; on the contrary:

> I think it has certainly taken five years to turn the place round. . . . As a head you get very few compliments, but you always hear when things aren't right. And they [the staff] are encouraged to disagree. I always look at it in the way the head of Sony does: he sees conflict in the family as a good thing, and he sees his union reps as there, not to be destructive, but to disagree with him. And that's the way I see it too, that disagreement is a positive thing. You are better knowing about the disagreements and hitting them head-on, than trying to push them under. But what I get back now, from the staff development interviews, is: 'We think the school is a superb place. I find it a great privilege to teach the children at the Valley. We're going in the right direction. We've got it right.' And that's coming through all the time now. And that's at a time when morale, nationally, is seen to be pretty low. I think that's pretty good.

In many ways, therefore, the incorporative style which Ms Lincoln advocates in staff–pupil relationships is reflected in the types of relationships she wishes to develop with her staff:

> The first thing you've got to do is build up your relationship with the staff. So they are not suspicious of you, where they build up trust in you, and see you as an individual who cares about them: be that about their professional life, be that about their personal life. And in return you expect the best out of them.

Like the pupils, staff are provided with a framework that offers them opportunities for involvement and achievement at a high level. At the same time, they are offered the support they need. Those who have not wished to take the opportunities on offer have left, whilst those who remain have found their involvement exhilarating, and their achievements a spur to take greater challenges.

PASTORAL MATTERS

It should be clear by now that at the Valley School the pastoral functions of the school are not set aside in a discrete compartment. The curriculum is designed with the pastoral needs of pupils for a supportive and facilitative environment very much in mind. Subject teachers are expected to play a central role in developing and maintaining the caring ethos of the school through their daily contacts with pupils; the disciplinary code and the reward system provide good examples of this. The qualities that the headteacher values in her staff, in terms of their attitudes and behaviour towards pupils, also support this point. In fact, one of the main achievements of the school has been to create a community in which pupils' academic and pastoral needs are met with equal vigour. This is to the extent that to make the distinction between pastoral and academic in the context of the Valley School, is to create an artificial distinction.

The development of the pastoral system at the Valley involved, in part at least, the abolition of distinctions between the pastoral and academic functions of staff. When she arrived at the school, Ms Lincoln found that there was something of a demarcation line between the pastoral staff and the rest of the teaching staff:

> One of the things I discovered was [when I first arrived at the Valley] that if anything went wrong in anybody's classroom, the head of year was sent for. The head of year might have been teaching a group of thirty children, but the expectation was that the head of year left that class unattended and went and sorted this problem out. To me that was absolutely ridiculous, so I stopped that straight away. I pointed out that heads of year were there to help and support, but at a time when they were not teaching. And that above all, their teaching commitment was to come first. And I insisted on that, very, very firmly.

There are two important issues here, both of which relate to the teaching role. First, that under this system there were whole groups of pupils (often in the lower-ability groups) who were being routinely neglected, owing to the absences of their teachers. Second, the non-pastoral teachers were abdicating their responsibilities in relation to certain pupils:

> The staff expectation was, you had a problem, you got rid of it! It was somebody else's problem. Once there was a problem in

the classroom, it wasn't the class teacher's job to sort it out. . . .
It wasn't taken [by the non-pastoral staff] that 'I have a problem
with someone in my class, behaviour-wise; it is my job to sort that
problem out, perhaps not in the middle of the lesson, but at the
end of the lesson.' What happened was, you got the person out
of the classroom, and you sent for the head of year. It didn't
matter about the head of year's teaching, because their job was
pastoral, wasn't it?

Classrooms and the learning process were being disrupted, therefore, not only by the behaviour of some pupils, but also by the
measures which teachers were taking to deal with the disruption.
Furthermore, the underlying problems, sometimes located in the
learning situation, which repeatedly sparked pupil misbehaviour
in particular classrooms, were tending not to be solved, because
the subject teachers were not dealing with the problems directly.
Coupled with this, the heads of year themselves found their role
unfulfilling and extremely stressful:

The heads of year ended up extremely depressed people,
because they were taking on all of these problems. And it was
too much. They were taking on the problems that children were
bringing from home; they were taking on the problems of the
classroom; they were being expected to sort it out; to call deten-
tions; to see them through, and all the rest of it. But the child
went back, never having sorted the relationship out with the
subject teacher, so the same conflict grew again.

Put simply, the route towards creating the new pastoral system
involved establishing the pastoral responsibilities that should be
shouldered by all staff, as well as defining the specific functions to
be carried out by form tutors and year heads. As has already been
shown, the introduction of the new curriculum, the integration of
SEN and the disruptive pupils into the mainstream of the school,
brought with them a demand for in-service training, which helped
to focus staff attention on the skills necessary for mixed-ability
teaching. Related concerns, such as the discipline code and the
reward system, also involved teachers directly in what had previously been considered to be matters for the attention of pastoral
staff only. In this way, then, the raising of staff awareness of the
pastoral needs of their pupils, and the skills required to meet
them, was a by-product of the drive towards broadening pupil

access to the new curriculum. The old Personal and Social Education (PSE) programme was replaced by a Community Studies GCSE (Northern Examination Board), which covered a similar content area to PSE, along with RE, community service and work experience. By swapping PSE for an examinable subject, its status was raised, both among staff and pupils. Thus what had formerly been seen as the distinctly pastoral area became integrated with curriculum concerns, as Ms Lincoln states:

> We do expect the head of faculty to exercise a very strong pastoral role, because so very often in the old days the things that were coming through to the year heads were actually curriculum problems. It was either the [curricular] diet was the wrong diet, or it was being presented wrongly. How often have I seen when someone writes a real condemnation of a child, but what it's actually saying is more about their teaching, than it is about the child. So we insist that the first point of contact is the subject teacher, and then the head of faculty, and only after that does it come through to the tutor.

At the same time, there was a need to bring year heads and form tutors into the academic arena, by taking into their role the oversight of pupils' academic progress as well as their pastoral needs:

> The tutor is not just a pastoral tutor of the children, but is a pastoral and academic guide/mentor of the children. . . . The tutor is the all-important person to the child – more important than the year head.

One of the problems with this situation was the uncertainty some tutors felt about subject areas in which they were untrained. Once again, this problem was met by the instigation of a school-based in-service training programme, in which faculty representatives provide training for tutors in the learning and progress indicators that are appropriate to their subjects. This enables the tutors to have an understanding of all aspects of their tutees' curriculum. The tutors still maintain their traditional role of registering pupils, liaising with parents, outside services, and dealing with pupils' personal issues. The additional curriculum knowledge, however, gives the tutors a more complete picture of each pupil, and a greater likelihood of picking up possible conflicts and difficulties at an early stage. Similarly the role of the year head has been modified:

The other big in-service job we've had, and I'm still working at, that is getting the heads of year to see themselves as curriculum coordinators, and to try to get the year heads to see themselves, not as the first point of contact when something goes wrong, but that they are there to support and to give in-service training to their tutors, to help the tutor to do the job better, but not off-loading from the tutor. So, in the same way you've got the tutor as the centre of attention for the individual child, the year head is there for advice, or if things have got to be taken up a tier.

The tutors and the year heads, then, are being encouraged to see pupils' progress in the curriculum as an important indicator of their affective condition. This underlines the vital significance of the curriculum in the social and emotional development of pupils at this school.

THE COUNSELLING PROGRAMME

Any reflection of the extent of the Valley School's progress from a directionless state of helplessly failing to meet the needs of its pupils, to its current positive condition, is to be found in the appointment of the school counsellor. This appointment, like many other important developments in the school, has its origins in the staff workshop which addressed the question: 'What makes a good school?' Under the old regime concern had been directed at controlling and removing disruptive and problematic pupils from the classroom; with the change of headteacher, the emphasis shifted to developing an awareness among staff of the ways in which their behaviour affected pupil behaviour. The move towards more student-centred approaches, however, brought with it new difficulties. Whilst the staff shared a sense of the general effectiveness of the new approach, which could be measured in terms of improved classroom behaviour, improved pupil motivation, and better exam results, there was still a feeling that for some pupils they were not doing enough.

In particular, there was a widely shared belief that some pupils were having difficulty coping with the classroom situation, and becoming disruptive, less as a response to the conditions in the classroom and more as a result of home and other background influences. Given the social make-up of the school's catchment area, these problems were more in evidence at the Valley than at other schools within the LEA. As John Williams (deputy head) puts it:

> We saw it [the appointment of the counsellor] as a way of coming to terms with some of the issues that we were – like many other schools – having to cope with: children who can't have social relationships; children who are out of their depth, perhaps in sexual relationships, or emotional problems at home – family break-up; serious family illness, bereavement, peer-group relationships, financial difficulties at home. These are the sorts of major issues that run through. These things come out in confrontations with staff, feeling that they can't cope; that everything's just too much.

Although levels of suspensions and expulsions gradually decreased over the period of the reforms, it was still felt by many staff that too many pupils were being expelled. In 1987–8, for example, a total of eight pupils were formally expelled. The staff response to this situation exemplifies the confident approach to problem-solving that was becoming the hallmark of the staff at the Valley. Initially, there was a demand among the staff for training in counselling techniques. However, it soon became apparent, especially among those who received training, that staff felt, even with the skills, they had insufficient time to deal adequately with the pupils who would benefit most from counselling. After a period of consultation, in which relevant issues were explored, such as the cost of the proposal, the availability of funds, and the breadth of support for the idea among the staff, it was decided to create a half-time post for a qualified counsellor.

The willingness to commit part of the staffing budget to this enterprise gives a clear indication of the importance which staff at the Valley School attach to this issue. The decision, however, was not simply based on a recognition of the possible benefits of counselling; it was also a response to the recognition of the fact that an informal counselling service had developed in the school and had been in operation for some time. The school nurse, Ms Jackson, who was already at the school when the present headteacher arrived, had been conducting an informal counselling service for several years, before it was recognised that she was doing this. It only became apparent to her, over a period of years, that in addition to the expected clientele of the nurse – that is pupils with cuts and bruises, physical ailments and in need of medication – there were pupils who became regular visitors, nearly always presenting minor physical symptoms that often faded remarkably quickly. These pupils, she found, often had deeper, underlying problems, sometimes of a very serious nature, and always a source of great personal distress. Ms Jackson, who in time took a short course in humanistic counselling methods, did her best for these pupils, but felt, like the teaching staff, that she did not have the time to give these pupils the attention they needed, as well as carry out her formal duties. She welcomed the appointment of the counsellor, and now sees her counselling role as a support to the work of the main counsellor. In areas where there is a medical concern, she finds the counsellor is able to offer her support. As Ms Jackson says:

> My role is different now. I can help identify the problems in the first place and refer them to her [the full-time counsellor] for long-term specialist counselling. But really, I have masses of everything to do. You know, the injuries, sickness, the vaccinations. And you can see how busy it is here. You need time and space, and no interruptions to do proper counselling. . . . I can help her [the counsellor] sometimes. I mean we work together an awful lot, in very close cooperation. I mean, people will present us with problems, like they think they're pregnant or they're confirmed as pregnant, and while we are dealing with that they can have counselling as well.

The counselling programme now forms an integral part of the school's provision. The programme acts as a support system for the curriculum, by helping pupils who are having difficulty in coping with school life, but is also, in turn, supported by the school staff. The hours of the school counsellor are 10am to 2pm daily, which means that many of her clients attend for counselling during lesson time. Not only do staff allow pupils to absent themselves from lessons in order to attend counselling, they also refer pupils to the counsellor, and suggest to individual pupils that they might wish to make an appointment with the counsellor. The staff support in itself indicates the commitment of the staff to an ethos which stresses a concern for the affective well-being of pupils, which is consistent with other indicators of the school ethos that we have discussed already. The counsellor herself freely admits that without the already positive climate of teacher–pupil relationships in the school, that the counselling programme would have been a non-starter. Her first clients were almost entirely the result of staff referrals, and came to her, she believes, because they trusted the judgement of their teachers.

In the two years that the programme has been operating, the pattern of referral has changed, whilst there has been no significant decline in the rate of staff referral, numbers of referrals have increased, with a greater proportion of pupils now being self-referring. In the year 1989–90 13 per cent of pupils at the Valley School attended for formal counselling (i.e. a programme of at least six one-hour sessions), mostly in the 15–16 age group (years 10 and 11), with 66 per cent being girls and 33 per cent boys. In 1990–1 the proportion was seen to be rising, with a greater balance between boys and girls. In the final three weeks of the summer term (1991) thirteen pupils referred themselves for counselling: six boys and seven girls, adding themselves to an existing *waiting list* of forty-four pupils.

The increasing popularity of the counselling programme among pupils is a source of concern to the counsellor who, in order to cope with growing numbers, has found it necessary on occasion to operate a screening process, whereby potential new clients are first briefly seen by herself or the school nurse, at which point the urgency of their case is assessed. Pupils who are felt to be in any sense at risk or close to crisis point are then given priority.

In describing the nature and purpose of the counselling programme at the Valley School, Ms Nichols, the counsellor, once again expresses values which are in close harmony with those of the school as a whole:

> I think I'm an extension of the education system [of the school]. I think that's important to say, that although I deal with lots of kids with problems, I don't actually see myself as a social worker. It's more about helping kids to develop the skills to deal with their problems, which will set them up for the rest of their life, really.

As in the formal curriculum, the counsellor's intention is to empower her student-clients to take personal control: to provide them with a range of opportunities for autonomy and self-development. Ms Nichols employs the 'person-centred approach' to counselling (see Chapter 6), the main aim of which is to enable the client to seek out resources they already possess to tackle their own problems. In this approach, the counsellor's role is deliberately non-directive, to the extent that the counsellor does not offer advice or guidance to the client as to how to respond to their difficulty, but rather, through the practice of various interpersonal

skills, communicates to the client a sense of unconditional acceptance of the client as a person, and feelings of empathy with their
distress. We can see how such an approach sits well within a school
ethos which is calculated to meet the esteem needs of all pupils on
a non-discriminatory basis, by providing opportunities for individual expression, and emphasising rewards and interpersonal
understanding over failure and punishment.

The kinds of problems that pupils present with are varied. Many
of the staff referrals have their origins in the pupil's sudden display
of academic difficulties, which appear to relate to problems of a
personal nature, such as a preoccupation with family difficulties.
Other presenting problems include family problems, pre-
dominantly in the form of interpersonal conflict at home, including violence, along with bereavement and problems such as
alcoholism. Peer-group problems, such as relationships with the
opposite sex and interpersonal conflict, are also common.
Behaviour problems, both in and out of school, most commonly
aggressive behaviour and truancy, are even more frequent. Personal problems relating to self-confidence are also common.
Social problems such as sexual abuse, pregnancy and drug abuse
are present in a significant minority of cases.

An examination of the figures for 1989/90 shows that pupils
often presented with multiple problems, which indicates an association between in-school problems and out-of-school problems.
Of the eighty pupils (15 per cent of the school population) who
received counselling in that year, 56 per cent were counselled in
relation to school behavioural problems of one kind and another;
65 per cent were counselled in relation to family problems; 48 per
cent for peer-group problems; 45 per cent for educational problems; 20 per cent for personal problems (lack of confidence etc.);
15 per cent for social problems (sexual abuse, pregnancy, drug
problems), and 8 per cent for vocational issues (career choice,
difficulties encountered during work experience). Also, 25 per
cent of the pupils counselled that year made mention, in the
course of counselling, that they were receiving support of some
kind from social services. This, along with the range of problems
identified, suggests that the counselling programme is being used
by pupils who present the kinds of problems that are often associated with emotional and behavioural difficulties and disaffection
from school, as outlined in the first part of this book. There is also
a clear association between the kinds of problems named here and

those described by the pupils from the residential schools who were the subjects of Chapters 5 and 6.

Ms Nichols makes it clear that the function of counselling is not necessarily to solve pupils' problems. On the contrary, the counselling process often brings problems to the surface that were previously hidden. Frequently, the overt, presenting problem, is merely a symptom of an underlying problem. Ms Nichols describes a number of cases in which the referring problem ceases to be a problem almost immediately the counselling process gets under way, simply because the presenting problem is either a reaction to the lonely burden of a deep-seated personal problem, or is, alternatively, a signal for help. For example, a year-9 boy who referred himself because he claimed he was being bullied, revealed early on that his real concern was with the recent death of a close relative, and that bullying was not something he perceived as an important problem. Similarly, a year-9 girl, who was referred after a serious classroom fight with another girl, was able to control her aggression and antagonism toward her adversary, once the underlying issue of her unhappy relationship with her mother was brought out. Her realisation that the aggression that she had directed at a classmate was really intended for her mother enabled her to focus her attention on her home-based relationship problem in counselling sessions, and helped her to see that her classroom aggression was misplaced.

In the two cases just mentioned, the original presenting problem appears to have been fairly easily solved, though the underlying problem in both cases is only beginning to be acknowledged. In other cases, presenting problems are less easily disposed of. In the case of a year-11 boy, whose teacher became concerned at the decline in the quality of the pupil's schoolwork, it was found that he was preoccupied with the break-up of his parents' marriage, and the conflict with his mother that stemmed from his own feelings of divided loyalty to both parents. In this situation the teacher agreed to ease the pressure on the pupil whilst he worked through the family problems in counselling. In this particular instance, the pupil also had something of a history of aggressive and impulsive behaviour, which was observed to decline somewhat in the course of counselling.

One of the major achievements of the counselling programme, according to Ms Nichols, is the way in which it keeps pupils, who might otherwise be expelled or excluded from school (for disruptive behaviour, for example), in the school, as a result of what the programme offers both pupils and staff:

> If you think of a kid who is perhaps disruptive, I think it [counselling] does two things. One, quite often you get kids who are against the system, they don't want to be in school, in any school at all. They feel that school is against them, right from the minute they walk through the door . . .; they might just be biding their time 'til they're old enough to get out. Now if you have counselling, and those kids perhaps start acting-up in class, they can actually come for counselling and be heard. So right away, the system is not entirely against them: there is someone in the system that will listen to them and their viewpoint. . . . For the teacher it also works, 'cos when they see the kid coming for counselling, there's a sort of tacit acknowledgement that that kid has problems and has accepted he has to do something about it.

Thus a potentially negative situation becomes transformed into one where there is the possibility of progress. Counselling in this way can be seen as a haven of respite, not only from pressures and difficulties that impinge on pupils from outside the school, but as offering respite from internal school difficulties whilst keeping the pupils in school. For staff, it offers an alternative to the disciplinary route, when they feel disciplinary measures to be in appropriate. As Ms Nichols puts it:

> None of the kids I've seen [for counselling] have been permanently excluded [i.e. expelled], and quite a few of them have been candidates for exclusion. So, for instance, instead of walking out of school, they may come here and say, 'I need an appointment.'

The fact that the counselling takes place on the main school site has distinct advantages. First, there is a normalising effect. The counsellor is clearly part of the school community, whose presence is known to all the pupils. Pupils can attend for counselling without having to leave the school site to attend 'a clinic'. There is minimal formality involved arranging a meeting with the counsellor: the pupil simply approaches the counsellor in person, or sends a note to her requesting an appointment. The counsellor then informs a member of the management that a particular pupil has appointments with the counsellor (though the reasons for the

appointment remain confidential, between the pupil and counsellor only). Pupils who are keen to receive counselling but are
nervous about approaching the counsellor for a formal appointment are able to go to the counselling room during breaks and
lunchtimes, when the room takes on the function of a 'drop-in
centre', where pupils come to sit and chat informally with one
another and with the counsellor. This 'drop-in' function seems to
have evolved naturally without any formal planning on the part of
the counsellor, but has grown to serve an important purpose, as Ms
Nichols says:

> At dinner times and break times, this is a kind of 'drop-in' place.
> I'm constantly reviewing this, because they drop in here, so you
> may have a large group of kids with problems, who get my
> individual, undivided attention in counselling, and think that
> they can still get it in a group. . . . But then, what I find is, they
> start to help each other and comfort each other, and that seems
> to outweigh the disadvantages. They come here and unwind a
> little, and it gets them just enough space to get them through
> the day, in a safe way.

Thus the familiarity of the counselling situation, and the experience of respite associated with it, gives pupils a sense of its ordinari-
ness, which develops into a sense of ownership of the very processes of counselling as well as the place where it happens:

> This is theirs; this is their room. And, in a way, the counselling,
> not me personally, is theirs, and they can work on that together.

On another level the proximity and involvement of the counsellor
in everyday school-life, makes for speed as well as continuity of
response when situations arise. Ms Nichols gives examples of two
similar cases that produced different outcomes, largely she feels
because of the differences that occurred in the timing and history
of the two cases. The first case involves a boy who had been
suspended for aggressive behaviour towards a teacher:

> There was a girl [year 11], who didn't like school for lots of
> reasons – she found being in big crowds all the time, diffi-
> cult. . . . She came from fairly tough family, who were very
> anti-school, and when she was angry, she used to let rip with her
> temper. Now she came one day [after having been excluded];
> the idea was that to get back into school she had to sign a

contract that said she had to behave. She came [to counselling] saying no way was she going to sign that contract; no way at all! Because as far as she was concerned this teacher was in the wrong. The result of her not signing that contract would have been that she was out [expelled]. Now she came to counselling; we talked about it; we went through all the things, and she decided that the teacher was in the wrong, and she felt she was justified in saying what she did. But she'd not that long to go at the school, and she decided that she would tell that teacher what she thought of him, but in the meantime she'd sign the contract. And she'd wait till her last day of school. And she didn't feel she'd backed down, which was her main worry when she came in, that if she signed the contract there'd be a loss of pride.

Ms Nichols points out that she in no way attempted to influence her decision:

That was her decision; if she'd have decided that she wasn't going to come into the school, then that would have been it.

A major factor in this positive outcome, however, was the relationship that existed between pupil and counsellor prior to this incident:

I'd had a relationship with that girl before, so she'd actually been through a few counselling sessions before, to work through a few things, like she'd been bullied when she was younger; she felt she was unattractive, even though she was actually quite pretty. So there was a good relationship there beforehand.

The function of this relationship was to allow this girl to explore the problem that faced her calmly, in a situation that was comfortable and with the support of someone she trusted. Without the pressure to defend herself against possible loss of face or manipulation, she was able to make a rational decision that served his best interests. By contrast, a similar case involving a girl who became involved in a similar dispute with a teacher:

there was a boy [year 10] who didn't come for counselling until he was out of school [suspended]. I'd never met him before, and there was no way he was going to back down. And he didn't come back to school.

For this boy the counsellor was simply a member of the school staff who was trying to get him to back down. Ms Nichols feels that had she been able to develop a relationship with this boy at an earlier stage then there would have been a chance to avert the problems that led to his suspension. This, however, was a case that flared up without warning.

> If you've got counselling [in progress] you can see the problems coming; you're working with it before it reaches crisis-point, and when it does reach crisis point you can actually work with that crisis and avoid what could be a major disaster.

Luckily, the latter example is a rare case in which a problem blew up without prior warning. By and large, the counselling programme, like the discipline code, seeks to tackle problems in their early stages.

The provision of opportunities for personal development, which was found to be an important factor in the experience of the residential schoolboys (see Chapters 5 and 6), is not only reflected in the 'entitlement curriculum' at the Valley, but in the counselling programme also. As has already been noted, the counsellor sees her role as a facilitator of learning, enabling pupils to develop their own resources for coming to terms with personal difficulties, largely by placing pupils in circumstances which encourage them to bring to light the latent qualities that they already possess. This outcome is not always easily achieved in the one-to-one counselling situation, and one of the ways Ms Nichols has been able to overcome this impasse is to employ a group approach. This involves the counsellor in relinquishing a certain amount of control over the kind of feedback that the target-client receives, but has the tremendous advantage of fostering self-help skills in the group members. She cites the example of a year-10 pupil (Tom) who came to her as one of her first clients. Tom was at the time suspended from the Valley. He had already been recommended by Social Services as a candidate for placement in a residential school for pupils with emotional and behavioural problems, and would be going down this road if he failed to gain readmittance to the Valley. He was considered to have extreme behaviour problems which manifested themselves in violent and aggressive behaviour. As Ms Nichols states:

> This was the only time I ever accepted anyone who was forced to come to counselling, if he was to get back into the school. I

was new, and I thought I can't very well say no. What happened in one-to-one counselling was that he got more and more angry that he was being made to go for counselling. So I said, 'Do you want to bring a friend or something?' [And he said,] 'Well, yes.' And the only time he responded to me in counselling was with a friend. Eventually, I thought, I've got to do something. So I thought, what I'll do is I'll say, 'You don't have to come for counselling, but if you want to come with a friend, then that's OK.' I thought, 'I'll never see him again.' But the next week he turned up with a whole load of people. So I thought, 'What we'll do is work in a group'. I said, 'You choose six friends.' So he chose about six friends, and I got a male facilitator in to help. And it was awful! Absolutely hellish. . . . They were all over the place; they were crying; they were shouting at one another. Unknown to each other and to us [the facilitators] all of these kids had problems. But Tom is now back in school; he's no longer on contracts; at home he's fine. The others also pre-sented behavioural problems, but have all now successfully completed school.

When the counsellor sat back and analysed what had been happening in the group, however, she realised that the group had actually been instrumental in bringing about this positive change in Tom. First she realised that the group of pupils that Tom drew around him for these sessions were peers who, like him, had problems of one kind and another: the kind of pupils who, as Ms Nichols says, 'would normally be kept apart in class'. The bringing of a group together was, however, in itself the first step towards confronting a central problem:

One of his problems was he was a loner, who believed in the loner mentality of macho violence; often portrayed in the media. . . . And the way that things worked in the group was that one of his great strengths was his love of children. So we were able to pull that out in the group, like [by asking him] 'Would you ever hurt a child?' And then [it came out] there were other members of the group who had been victims of violence them-selves. And I remember one day, when a girl told him that as a child of seven or eight, her drunk father used to come in and wake her up and hit her. And I remember him [Tom] being – I remember the look on his face now – he was totally shocked by this.

Ms Nichols argues that it was the experience of being confronted by this, for him, hitherto unconsidered perspective on violence that led him to review his own way of thinking. This happened to the extent that as the counselling sessions progressed, Tom began to display a softer, more sympathetic, side of his character through which he was able to express concern and support for other members of the group. On another occasion in the group situation, Tom was able to display control of his temper and accept the affection of a peer in a way that would have been unthinkable previously:

> On one occasion a lad bumped into Tom, and the coffee went all down him. And Tom's temper went whoosh! And one of the things we'd planned – one of the girls was very affectionate; she always cuddled people, and we'd arranged, when he lost his temper, she'd cuddle him. So when he did that we touched him, and he got control. . . . That would never have happened in one-to-one counselling; I can't imagine him getting so angry, if he spilled his coffee, with me, 'cos he was so inhibited in one-to-one counselling.

The group situation then, proved to be one in which Tom discovered new facets in himself, including the ability to show his softer side and relate to others sympathetically. This was both facilitated by and a contribution to the group process in which he was involved. It seems as if the same discovery process was going on for other pupils in the group too.

It is experiences such as the one just described which have encouraged Ms Nichols to work towards developing a formal peer-counselling programme, whereby pupils are trained in counselling skills and encouraged to work with other pupils. She maintains that there is already considerable evidence of informal peer counselling taking place, and finds increasingly that pupils are not only referring themselves for counselling, but are also referring their friends, and pointing out potential clients to Ms Nichols and other staff.

The counselling programme at the Valley School can be seen to embody many of the qualities which are reflected in the ethos of the school that has developed under the headship of Ms Lincoln. The counselling programme is clearly a support service for the most vulnerable pupils at the school; it provides them with refuge in which they can enjoy respite from the pressures of school-life and outside problems. It could be said to be a sanctuary within a sanctuary. However, the counselling programme, like the school as a whole, is geared towards not only protecting and sheltering pupils, but also to providing pupils with experiences that will enhance their strength and resilience to cope with difficult circumstances. The counselling programme, in particular, exemplifies the thrust towards autonomy and self-actualisation that lie at the heart of this school's purpose for its pupils.

SOME CONSUMER VIEWS

It seems appropriate to leave the final words of this chapter to a group of people who might be considered to know more than most about the experience of being a pupil at the Valley School. The following quotations all come from pupils who, at their own admission, have found it difficult to cope with schooling. They have all, at different times, been in serious conflict with staff at the Valley School. Most of them have been excluded from school for disciplinary reasons, and some have been very close to expulsion. All of these pupils have attended for counselling. A striking feature of these quotations is the indication of the way in which the counselling process is often seen to have facilitated a shift from a position of helplessness, whereby the pupil often feels unable to exert self-control, to one of autonomy, control and understanding of self and the self in relation to others. Another important element that pupils mention is the sense of being cared for and supported, both in the counselling context and with other staff members. There is also an indication of the way in which the counselling programme relates positively to the classroom situation. These are all pupils who could so easily have been dismissed as uncooperative and too difficult to teach. Pupils who might be considered to be 'at the bottom of the pile'. In spite of this they have essentially positive attitudes about their futures and towards their school, recognising the valuable contribution the school has made to their positive development.

We're really lucky to have a counsellor in school, 'cos I think all of us would be lost if we didn't.

[year-11 girl]

She [the counsellor] stops us from getting kicked out, and doing stupid things.

[year-11 girl]

I was having problems with my teacher, and I went to see my head of year. And he said, 'Well, there's nothing I can do.' . . . Then I got involved with the head of the school. And she said stuff to me, like, 'You're the one that's doing wrong.' . . . So I went to see the school nurse, and she said, 'Go and see the counsellor.' So I did. That made it better, 'cos I felt I had someone I could talk to. . . . It was really my own fault, what happened [with the teacher]. It's only now that I realise that. I sort of made things worse. I couldn't see that what I was doing was making things worse. . . . Teachers are alright if you've got problems with lessons, then they sort that out.

[year-12 girl]

I suppose, if you treat the teachers with respect, then you get respect back. But if you like treat them like they're not really there, and you just muck around in the classes, then you just get done for it. It's your own fault really.

[year-11 boy]

They're [teachers] not very good at sorting out home problems though. That's what the counsellor's here for, basically.

[year-12 girl, BTech student]

When I come here, I was known for having quite a violent attitude. And I was in and out of school, like a yo-yo. I built up a reputation, and I'm still trying to live that down now, from a year, year and a half ago. I haven't been suspended for two days now! [laughs] I was just let back yesterday for an incident that happened last term. I hadn't got in trouble for nearly a year and a half. And something just happened, out of the blue. . . . We're told that if something goes wrong in a lesson, just walk out, rather than hit someone. So that's what I do. . . .I did that when I was having trouble with this teacher who wouldn't help me with my work. I could quite happily have hit the teacher. . . . It helped the situation, 'cos after that the teacher started taking a bit more notice. . . . I went and complained to one of the support staff. The bloke I complained to had a word with the teacher, and now I get a lot more help. If you put your point across to the right person, in the right frame of mind, then they'll listen and they'll try and help you, and do something about it. But if you go up to them and start ranting and raving about a particular incident then they won't take a blind bit of notice. And why should they, really?

. . .

When I first joined the school I had quite a bad temper. But after a while it all calmed down a bit, with the help of Janet, the counsellor. . . . I definitely wouldn't still be here, without the help of Janet. I'd probably be at another school, or at home with a home tutor, or something. With the help I've had from the school counsellor, it gave me an insight into my inner temperament. And I've calmed myself down a bit.

[year-11 boy]

There's about a quarter of the teachers in this school, that will actually listen to you. You can just tell them what happened, and they'll just sort it out for you. I've had to do that quite a few times. It's mostly my humanities teacher I don't get on with. Sometimes it just really gets to me. I just sometimes walk out, and go and see Mr Fordyce – he's the one who backs me up on everything.

[year-11 boy]

Mr Fordyce is really good, he's a caring kind of teacher, and he'll help you out with any situation, if he's got the time. He'll usually make time. You can see him any time, unless he's teaching, and then you just catch up with him at breaktime.

[year-11 boy]

With a counsellor, if you need someone to talk to – say you're really depressed and messy – and you really need someone to talk to, you can come to her and arrange an appointment. 'Cos otherwise, like me, I bottle it all up. And if the teacher had a go at me, or anything, like I've done before, I've ended up walking out; having a right go at the teacher, which I know is wrong. . . . Before the counsellor came, I was forever shouting at teachers and walking out of lessons, and screaming at them. I even went to hit one once. Mr Smythe – I never got on with Mr Smythe, ever. And I always ended up rowing with him. And it got really bad at one point. And then I started seeing the counsellor, and my relationship with Mr Smythe changed completely. He'd help me with my work, instead of ignoring me because I used to ignore him. . . . I think it was me who changed Mr Smythe, because my attitude changed towards him. It was the counsellor sort of like saying no, and making me think, that made me change my attitude. And when he saw the change in my attitude, his attitude changed. 'Cos if someone goes automatically on the defensive with me, I go on the defensive. And I was going on the defensive with him, so he was automatically flaring up at me, and I was flaring up even more.

[year-12 girl, BTech student]

Some of the staff here have got a lot of time for the pupils. I mean, a lot of them bend over backwards to keep you here. Like when I was in all my trouble in the first year . . . I wouldn't want to go to any other school. 'Cos, I mean, when I got kicked out last time, I got given the choice to go to [three other local schools]. None of them were good enough really. My parents say this is the best school in the county, and I agree with them.

[year-11 boy]

CONCLUSION

In this chapter we have looked at one school's attempts to overcome the problems of disaffection and under-achievement among its pupils. Clearly, this is not a comprehensive account of the school as a whole. In order to gain such an account we would need to obtain a much wider range of views from other members of the school community. This account has rested most heavily on the perceptions of the headteacher, though other staff are also quoted and documentary evidence is also called upon. The disadvantage of such an approach lies in its incompleteness. There are, however, advantages also. In a book such as this, where space is limited, the focus on the detailed account of an individual, or small group, allows for depth and breadth of coverage. Over such a span it is more likely that inconsistencies and confusions will come to light if the interviewee is rationalising or inventing. What emerges strongly from the interview with Ms Lincoln is the coherence of her thinking about her school. This is further supported by the evidence of documents and the interviews with other staff, particularly the counsellor, whose non-teaching role adds weight to her view of the school coming as it does from a slightly detached but well-informed perspective. Furthermore, the headteacher's management perspective provides us with a deep insight into the processes of policy formation and the implementation of change: processes on which successful change depends. These processes, in turn, also depend on the coherence and quality of the thinking that underlies them.

The consistent thread running through this account of the Valley School is a commitment to a fundamentally humanistic ethic, which argues that the instrumental purposes of schooling are most effectively achieved in schools where the affective needs of pupils are seen as a central focus. The formal curriculum, the pastoral system, the rewards policy, the discipline code, the counselling programme, the preferred patterns of social relations between pupil and teacher, and the relations between management and staff all share a common purpose in that they each, in their different ways, seek to give pupils a positive sense of self. Once again, the triumvirate of RESPITE, RELATIONSHIPS and OPPORTUNITIES emerge as key elements in achieving this positive outcome.

The chapter started with a brief consideration of the recent changes imposed by the Education Reform Act. It pointed to the fact that there are indications to suggest that problems of disaffection are worsening as a result of some of these changes. The experience of the Valley School would not appear to be consistent with this view. The period since ERA has been one of great improvement for the school. To what extent this improvement can be attributed to the coming of ERA is perhaps debatable. Ms Lincoln indicates that a curriculum very much like the National Curriculum was already in place at the school well before the 1988 Act. Similarly the concept of 'entitlement' was also well established. LMS does appear to have brought certain dividends to the school; first, in terms of a cash surplus which was used to decorate the school, and second, in terms of the budgetry control which enabled the school to appoint the counsellor. Open enrolment, as yet, has not caused any problems for the Valley. It is still too early to judge the full impact of ERA on this or any other school. It can be said that the autonomy that ERA has created for schools sits well at the Valley: this is clearly a school that wants to stand out, and wants to be seen as different from its neighbours. Again, however, this was a quality being fostered in the school before ERA. Whether or not the Valley turns out to be a typical post-ERA school must remain, for the time being, an open question.

Chapter 9

Conclusion: Schools for individuals

This book has dealt with the following issues:

- the institutional correlates of disaffection;
- the importance of individuality in education;
- the perceptions of schools held by pupils with histories of disaffection and behavioural difficulties;
- these pupils' perceptions of the characteristics of a school where such pupils claim themselves to be developing positively;
- the characteristics of effective mainstream schools as identified by researchers;
- the practical measures undertaken by one school to implement changes designed to overcome the problem of disaffection and low achievement.

The common theme running throughout the book has been a consideration of the relationship between the individual and the institution. Deviance of all kinds (disaffection, maladjustment, delinquency, problem behaviour, etc.) is an indication of a problem with this relationship. It is the institution (whether it be the society, the family, the peer group, the school, etc.) that defines what is and is not deviant behaviour, and who is and is not deviant. The *experience* of 'being' deviant, however, is very much an individual one. The boys of Lakeside and Farfield had felt trapped in and humiliated by their marginalised status as problem pupils, and they often seem to have reacted against this in ways which merely confirmed their deviance in the eyes of their teachers and parents. For many of these boys, their experience of residential schooling enabled them to develop new images of themselves. They found resources within themselves that belied their deviant status. The critical influences, as far as these boys were concerned, were located in institutional aspects of the residential schools they attended. The qualities they identified can be categorised as:

- RESPITE from influences which reinforced their deviant identities;
- RELATIONSHIPS of a stable and supportive nature, with school staff;
- OPPORTUNITIES to achieve and experience success.

When the focus shifted to a consideration of studies of school effectiveness, it was found that the qualities identified by the residential boys were evident in the most effective mainstream schools, studied by these researchers. And when we looked in detail at one school's experience of attempting to improve its effectiveness we found a similar resonance.

The associations between the school effectiveness research and the residential pupils' perceptions are of interest in themselves. The fact that such associations can be made between such diverse collections of data adds weight to the claims that are made. Put simply, the school effectiveness research claims, among other things, to show that pupils who attend schools which display certain characteristics are less likely to exhibit behavioural problems than pupils who attend schools displaying certain other characteristics. Explanations as to *why* this should be the case can only be speculative, on the basis of correlational evidence alone. The evidence provided by the residential boys, however, suggests to us first, that the characteristics of the effective school are believed by these informants to be significant in helping them to resolve their behavioural difficulties, whilst the characteristics asso- ciated with the least effective schools are reflected in these pupils' accounts of their experience of situations from which they have been disaffected. Second, the evidence of these boys suggests something of the ways in which these institutional features might operate to achieve their effects. The examination of the Valley School adds further weight to the ideas being developed about the institutional effects of schooling, showing close associations with the work of school effectiveness researchers and echoing much that was said in the analysis of the residential pupils' interviews.

An important implication to be drawn from the ideas and evidence that have been considered in this book is that school effects, particularly in relation to the problem of disaffection, depend on both the institutional and interpersonal qualities of schools. The policies and systems that schools develop, in terms of the formal curriculum, policies on sanctions and rewards, pastoral arrangements and so on, set out a range of possible opportunities that might be offered to pupils for various experiences and achievements. It is in the implementation of these policies and systems that their success or failure is secured. The process of implementation, in turn, depends on the ways in which individuals understand and interpret their roles and functions in relation to policies and systems. Individual teachers are constrained by institutional features of the schools in which they work, whilst at the same time being a force of constraint which helps to determine the further development of these institutional features. The success of the reforms at the Valley School were highly dependent on the will of staff to accept that there was a need to develop new attitudes towards and ways of dealing with the pupils. The reforms which have taken place at the school are, to a significant extent, a reflection of changes in the dominant attitudes of the staff, in a number of key areas. An example of the importance of staff attitudes is provided by the provision of the counselling service. Not only did the idea of employing a school counsellor arise out of staff discussion, based on the perception that some pupils' affective needs were being neglected in the school, but its operation depends heavily upon the willingness of individual members of staff to permit pupils to use it during lesson time, and their willingness to adapt to circumstances that might develop as a result of the counselling process.

Pupils too can be seen as important mediators in institutional processes. Pupils can decide whether or not to 'go along' with institutional demands. Their compliance, particularly in the kinds of settings described in this book, where humanistic values predominate, cannot be taken for granted. We found in the study of Lakeside and Farfield that pupil compliance had a great deal to do with the quality of interpersonal relations between staff and pupils. Many of these boys felt that it was the patient support and encouragement of staff that enabled them to face up to problematic and challenging situations, whilst many of their previous experiences of non-compliance seem to have been marked by the very opposites of support and encouragement. This is exemplified in those cases where pupils claim to have taken the initiative in attempting to establish more harmonious relationships with their families, where previously they have been instrumental in creating conflict. In taking these steps, these boys are taking immense personal risks: the kinds of risks which before they have taken extraordinary measures to avoid. They are able to take such risks because they know that if things go wrong they will still have the support of staff back at school. Often, however, they find that the risk is rewarded by success, and this helps to build their confidence and lead them towards greater autonomy. Similarly, at the Valley, the counselling is dependent on the degree of trust that pupils feel for the counsellor and other members of staff. If such trust did not exist, pupils would not present themselves for counselling in the first place. The same principle applies to any situation in which one individual asks another to take a risk willingly, such as the risk of educational failure.

The fear of failure is, of course, a reality for teachers as well as pupils. A theme that has been revisited a number of times in earlier chapters is the idea that coercive regimes in schools, and coercive measures imposed by individual teachers, often develop as supposed solutions to perceived problems. When such solutions fail and cause an escalation of the problem this is sometimes taken as an indication that what is required is simply more of the same. Coercion is applied with greater force, and the problems escalate further. This cycle of failure is not easily broken, for the simple reason that coercive responses are often a defence mechanism, and breaking the cycle involves relinquishing this form of defence. This draws attention to the particular difficulties facing schools which attempt the kind of transition described as taking place at the Valley School.

For this school, raising the level of effectiveness involved, among other things, dismantling the existing apparatus that had been instituted in response to perceived problems, such as the segregation of pupils with behavioural problems and the isolation of staff and pupils in the SEN unit. Whilst these changes were proposed forcefully by the headteacher, the route by which they came to be eventually implemented involved a great deal of consultation with staff and staged planning. The form and timing of these changes was determined largely by the specific circumstances of the school and the make-up of the staff. At first only selected staff were involved in the integration project, with a wider range of staff becoming involved as levels of interest and confidence grew. This graduated implementation had the effect of encouraging in staff a sense of ownership of the reforms, so that towards the end of the five-year implementation period it was the staff who pushed the integration programme to its completion.

The combined processes of in-service training and consultation which operated at the Valley through the system of 'workshops' were vitally important in the change process. This approach ensured that staff would be reflecting on the particular circumstances in which they had to operate, rather than encouraging them to accept passively some sort of formula solution to their difficulties. Out of the process of reflection came many of the ideas that found their way into policy (e.g. the discipline code, the reward system, and the appointment of the counsellor), and this in itself provided a sense of ownership of policy that translated itself into a high level of commitment and a willingness to invest effort into making the policies work.

There is perhaps a rather unexpected link to be found here between the residential study and the study of the Valley School, to do with the importance of the ownership of problems. The experience of pupils at the two residential schools indicates that an important stage in the road towards dealing with personal problems is the recognition of their particular responsibility in the matter. Pupils who claimed to have made progress in solving their difficulties often talked about the experience of admitting the problem and their personal responsibility in dealing with it. This is reflected in the information we have about the counselling process at the Valley. It is also reflected in the way in which the staff at the school can be seen to have taken an active involvement in the reform process through the workshop programme.

The central message here is that individuals count, and the effective school is organised around this principle. Disaffected pupils often account for their disaffection from school in terms which stress the lack of care, attention and consideration that they receive in school. The inappropriateness of the curriculum, inconsistent and erratic teacher behaviour, bias in the distribution of rewards and sanctions, of which disaffected pupils often complain, are reflections of the same problem. Schools, like the Valley, recognise the harmful effect that these features have on their pupils through their personal experience of schooling. It is for this reason, for example, that the Valley School devised a response code to behavioural problems which stresses the importance of listening to the pupils' personal explanation of their behaviour and its causes. They recognise that when behavioural problems arise these can often be related to the individual pupil's experience and perceptions of problems in the learning environment. The effective school attempts to organise itself in ways which anticipate and so avoid these kinds of problems, whilst it continues to recognise the diversity of pupil make-up and experience to be such, that problems will continue to arise. The response to this situation is to encourage staff to initiate open and caring relationships with pupils, that facilitate the disclosure and open discussion of perceived problems. At the Valley the headteacher sought new staff who she believed to possess the qualities and attitudes necessary for the development of positive staff–pupil relationships. The process of consultation and reflection, in turn, helped to 'spread the good news' about the efficacy of such relationships among staff who did not already possess the qualities.

Another important implication of the work presented in this book is that, through consultation with staff and pupils, schools can learn a great deal about themselves. In creating an apparatus for staff consultation, the headteacher at the Valley gave staff a purpose as well as a need to engage in reflection and discussion. It is through reflection and discussion that staff came, firstly, to a recognition of the state of their school and an articulation of their attitudes towards it. The workshop approach, with its small group discussion component, provided the staff at The Valley with opportunities to explore and share their various perceptions of their school in a way that is perhaps rare in British schools. This is clearly a good way of developing an understanding of a particular school and its particular needs, whilst at the same time giving staff a sense of responsibility for the state of the school and its future development.

One of the great sources of knowledge about schools is to be found in pupil accounts of their experience, as we saw in the chapters that were devoted to the boys in the residential schools. This is a greatly under-used resource, and yet it provides perhaps the single most important account of the nature and effects of the individual school. In isolation from pupils staff can set up systems and procedures; they can develop measures to assess outcomes, but they cannot explore what it *feels* like to be on the receiving end of their actions. Only the pupils can provide this expert testimony;

testimony that tells us, more than anything else, why the pupil(s) choose to comply or decide to resist, or what it was that influenced them most when they changed their minds. Schools and teachers, it is suggested, can only benefit from asking questions based on these ideas.

An important point to be made is that the resources for making a school effective, in relation to the problem of disaffection, can and must be found within the school itself. There are no 'off-the-shelf' answers to problems of school effectiveness. The first step along the road to increased effectiveness is an exercise in self-analysis. Schools need to ask themselves:

- What makes a good school?
- Is this a good school?
- What is it like being a pupil in this school?
- Is this school experienced by its pupils as a problem to be dealt with or as a place where problems can be tackled?
- What sorts of assumptions do staff have about causes and remedies for behavioural problems and disaffection?
- To what extent and in what ways does this school offer pupils respite from problems they might experience in their lives outside of school?
- How would we define the climate of staff–pupil relationships in this school?
- How would the pupils define the climate of staff–pupil relationships in this school?
- What is the extent of pupil access to the formal curriculum in this school across the age and ability range?
- What opportunities are there for pupils to obtain recognition and reward for their achievements, both in the curriculum and in non-curriculum areas?
- In what ways might opportunities for pupils to obtain reward and recognition be extended?
- What happens to pupils in this school when they misbehave?
- What are the common characteristics of misbehaviour in this school, in terms of type, frequency and location?
- What are the common characteristics of the most troublesome pupils in this school, and in what ways do these characteristics reflect on the school?
- What measures are taken in this school to anticipate and prevent misbehaviour from occurring?

- What is the balance between rewards and sanctions in this school?
- What is the public image of this school?

These and other questions such as these, can provide the starting-point. By answering these questions staff groups can begin to develop a detailed portrait of their school and its current level of effectiveness. They can identify their strengths and weaknesses, and through the process of reflection and discussion begin to consider the possible range of solutions to outstanding problems. Only when individual schools take this kind of self-critical approach, whereby they seek out the extent to which they may have in the past sponsored and promoted disaffection, will they begin to find effective ways of curing and preventing disaffection.

Having said all this, what emerges from the study of the boys at Farfield and Lakeside is the recognition that, for these boys at least, residential schooling of the kind they experienced served a valuable purpose. The staff who worked with these boys provided the highest standards of care and commitment to the welfare of these boys. These staff do not deserve to be stigmatised by being associated with those institutions and people who have abused their positions of trust. Whether or not there will always be a need for such schools we cannot say. What can be said is that so long as there are teachers, schools and local education authorities where the response to behavioural problems and disaffection is to place the disaffected out of sight and out mind, then there will continue to be a demand for such schools: good and bad. Some pupils (one would hope, the majority) will find themselves in the good, caring schools, where through the experience of being valued they will learn to value themselves. The others will be consigned to schools rather like those that some of them have left behind, where their greatest achievement will be failure, and their difficulties intensified.

It is not hard to imagine that there will in future be school pupils who by virtue of their particular personal, social and educational circumstances, will require short-term, or even long-term place- ment in a residential setting. Conceivably, there are circumstances in which the respite provided by a new location, combined with the intensity of relationships afforded by the small residential community, will be the preferred alternative to the local comprehensive or primary school. If this is so, then the rightful place of residential schools for pupils with emotional and behavioural difficulties is in an education system where the best practice to be found in these schools differs only in *intensity* from that to be found in mainstream schools, rather, than is all too often the case now, being a difference in kind.

Appendix

A note on the research method

This book has relied heavily on the use of interview material for reasons already expressed. What has not been discussed in detail, however, is the way in which the material which appears in this book was generated, and how what is presented was selected from the mass of transcriptions that were created in the course of the research. This note is intended to offer a brief account of how this was done.

First, it should be pointed out that there are two distinct studies presented in this book: the study of the residential schools and that of the comprehensive school. The residential study presented here is part of a larger study of two residential schools.1 The purpose of this study was to generate a detailed description of the residential experience. What is presented here is the pupils' perspective, which formed a central part of the original study, but was supplemented by observational data as well as an exploration of staff perspectives. The Valley School study was a much smaller-scale study which, to a large extent, grew out of the residential study. The original intention behind the book had been to use the findings from the residential study as a basis for theorising about mainstream schools and their relationship to pupil disaffection. The Valley School, however, once brought to my notice, offered the opportunity for something a little more concrete. Here was a mainstream school that had taken on the problem of pupil disaffection and was claiming to have made headway in this area. This study was always intended to be viewed in the light of the residential study, and so offer a comparative dimension in the argument that was unfolded throughout the book. The eventual degree of commonality between the two studies was not anticipated.

Both studies were exploratory in the sense that they were not driven by hypotheses. The intention in each case was to generate a description of each institution on the basis of insider accounts. The Valley study was the more focused of the two studies in that its field of interest was narrowed to the consideration of the issue of pupil disaffection. The data that is presented here, then, is claimed to be an account of the ways in which the various participants in these studies perceived their situations and circumstances. The theoretical dimension of the book is, therefore, 'grounded' in this data, rather then preceding it, as it would in hypothesis-testing research.

Data collection in the residential study combined participant observation and interview techniques. The observational element served a number of purposes. First and foremost, the period of observation enabled me to get to know the pupils and staff before I interviewed them. Also during this period I was able to familiarise myself with the routines of the schools, and pick up on features of everyday institutional life. Once the interviews began, interviewees were aware that they were talking to someone who was at least informed about their school situation. This, combined with the comfortable familiarity that had developed between us, I believe motivated interviewees to speak openly about their authentic experience, as opposed to providing me with bogus or simply plausible accounts.

The Valley School study was altogether more limited. The central aim of this study was to uncover the thinking and the measures that staff had undertaken to meet the problem of disaffection.

In both studies, a great deal of importance was attached to the interview technique employed. The intention was to conduct interviews in ways that would motivate interviewees to provide accounts of their authentic thoughts and experience without unduly influencing the content of their replies. These are the perennial problems of the ethnographic research. The interview approach chosen for the residential study was extremely open ended. The object of the interviews was to get pupils to talk about those aspects of residential life that were important and significant to them. The starting-point for the interviews, therefore, was to ask pupils to recall their first experiences of their present school. The subsequent shape of the interview was dictated by the pupil's response to this question, with the interviewer asking pupils to elaborate on areas which seemed unclear and pursuing themes introduced by pupils in relation to pupils' current experience. In this way each interview took the form of a conversation, rather than an interview. The interviewer's role was essentially to help the interviewees to express their views as lucidly as possible. In order to achieve this I employed techniques which will be familiar to counsellors, such as active listening techniques, paraphrase and reflection. Where possible, interviewees were encouraged to back-up generalisations with descriptions of actual experiences. Where directive questions were asked, these were often based on material that had already been introduced into the interview by the interviewee. The interviews with the residential pupils and staff were all conducted in the interviewees' own time, so as to underline the voluntary nature of their participation. This was not possible with the Valley interviewees, though again, the voluntary nature of their participation was stressed.

The Valley School interviews that were conducted with pupils followed the same pattern as those in the residential study. With the staff, however, the interviews were a little more directive. The headteacher and other teaching staff were interviewed according to the following schedule:

1 What are the chief aims of the Valley School for its pupils?
2 Which of these aims has the school been so far successful in achieving?
3 To which in-school factors do you attribute these successes?
4 Has implementation of the Education Reform Act influenced the school in any ways that can be related to these aims?
5 How would you describe the climate of staff–pupil relationships in the school?
6 To what factors do you attribute this climate?
7 What are the qualities most highly valued in staff?
8 To what extent and in what ways does this school cater for individual differences among pupils?
9 To what extent and in what ways are pupils at this school able to achieve success in other than academic terms?
10 What are the priorities for the future development of the school?

Owing to limitations of time it was only possible to interview five members of the school staff. These were the headteacher, a deputy (pastoral care), a year head, the school counsellor and the school nurse. Nine pupils were interviewed. The staff and students who were interviewed were chosen carefully, after an initial visit to the school, during which time I had informal conversations with a wide range of staff and pupils, and obtained literature on the make-up and development of the school. The staff were selected as being likely to offer important insights into significant developments in the school. The pupils were selected on the basis that they were claimed by staff to be pupils who had experienced severe adjustment problems during their school careers.

The analysis of the pupils' interview data followed a rigorous procedure, in which:

1 each interview transcript was read through thoroughly;
2 each transcript was then examined and a list of the areas of concern covered in the interview was made;
3 then the content of each transcript was reordered under the headings of these areas of concern;
4 once all of the transcripts had been prepared in this way, further categories were generated from this arrangement which enabled the data from different transcripts to be organised under common headings;
5 each category was then studied in order to establish the range of opinion and perception presented by interviewees;
6 theories were generated on the basis of five;
7 theories were tested against the original transcripts.[1]

The twin outcomes of this analysis were, therefore, first, an account of the range of pupil perceptions and, second, details of individual pupils' responses. This enabled me to make observations about views held by individuals, subgroups of individuals, and comparisons between individuals, groups and schools. This data was also supplemented by a questionnaire study which was carried out towards the end of the data collection phase. This study was based on the first analysis of some of the data, and tested some of its findings against the wider populations of the two schools.

Analysis of the pupil interview data gathered in the Valley study took an identical form to that described above. The staff data, having been collected on the basis of a more directive approach, however, was analysed in a slightly less laborious manner, according to the following procedure:

1 each interview transcript was read through thoroughly;

2   the content of each transcript was reordered under the headings of the areas of concern covered by the main interview
questions;
3   each category was then studied in order to establish the range
of opinion and perception presented by interviewees;
4   theories were generated on the basis of three;
5   theories were tested against the original transcripts.[1]

It is suggested that this approach provides the necessary basis for
the claim that the findings and quotations presented in this work
are grounded in the perceptions of the research subjects, rather
than those of the researcher.

NOTE

1   See Paul Cooper (1989) 'Respite, Relationships and Re-signification: The
Effects of Residential Schooling on Pupils with Emotional and Behavioural
Difficulties', unpublished PhD thesis, University of Birmingham.

References

Aronson, E. (1980) *The Social Animal*, San Francisco, Freeman.

Askew, S. (1989) 'Aggressive behaviour in boys: to what extent is it institutionalised?' in D. Tattum and D. Lane (eds) *Bullying in Schools*, Stoke-on-Trent, Trentham Books.

Ball, S. (1981) *Beechside Comprehensive*, Cambridge, Cambridge University Press.

Ballard, J. (1987) 'The confusion of attempting to crack the family code', *Social Work Today*, 18, 42, 12–13.

Bannister, D. and Fransella, F. (1980) *Inquiring Man: The Psychology of Personal Constructs*, Harmondsworth, Penguin.

Barnes, D. (1976) *From Communication to Curriculum*, Harmondsworth, Penguin.

Barrett, G. (ed.) (1989) *Disaffection From School: The Early Years*, London, Falmer.

Beare, J., Caldwell, J. and Millikan, R. (1989) *Creating an Excellent School*, London, Routledge.

Berg, L. (1968) *Risinghill: Death of a Comprehensive*, Harmondsworth, Penguin.

Bettelheim, B. (1950) *Love is Not Enough*, Glencoe, Illinois, The Free Press.

Bettelheim, B. and Sylvester, E. (1948) 'A therapeutic milieu', *The American Journal of Orthopsychiatry*, 18, 191–206.

Bridgeland, M. (1971) *Pioneer Work with Maladjusted Children. A Study of the Development of Therapeutic Education*, London, Staples.

Burden, R. (1981) 'Systems theory and its relevance to schools', in B. Gillham, (ed.) *Problem Behaviour in the Secondary School*, London, Croom Helm.

Burland, R. (1987) 'The behavioural approach at Chelfham Mill school for emotionally disturbed boys', in K. Wheldall (ed.) *The Behaviourist in the Classroom*, London, Allen & Unwin.

Burn, M. (1956) *Mr. Lyward's Answer. A Successful Experiment in Education*, London, Hamish Hamilton.

Cahn, S. (1970) *The Philosophical Foundations of Education*, London, Harper & Row.

Campion, J. (1985) *The Child in Context. Family Systems Theory in Educational Psychology*, London, Methuen.

Canter, L. (1990) 'Assertive discipline', in M. Scherer, I. Gersch and L. Fry (eds) *Meeting Disruptive Behaviour, Assessment, Intervention and Partnership*, London, Macmillan.

Castle, E. (1961) *Ancient Education and Today*, Harmondsworth, Penguin.

Cawson, P. and Martell, M. (1979) *Children Referred to Closed Units*, London, HMSO.

Chamberlin, R. (1989) *Free Children and Democratic Schools*, London, Falmer.

Charlton, T. and David, K. (1989) *Managing Misbehaviour*, London, Macmillan.

Charlton, T. and David, K. (1990) 'Towards a whole school approach, helping to ensure schools are fit for the future', *Links*, 15, 3, 20–24.

Clegg, A. and Megson, B. (1968) *Children in Distress*, Harmondsworth, Penguin.

Coard, B. (1971) *How the West Indian Child is Made Educationally Subnormal in the British School System*, London, New Beacon Books.

Cole, T. (1986) *Residential Special Education*, Milton Keynes, Open University.

Cole, T. (1989) *Apart or A Part?* Milton Keynes, Open University.

Coleman, J. and Hendry, L. (1990) *The Nature of Adolescence*, London, Routledge.

Cooper, P. and Upton, G. (1990a) 'The Elton Report, so what and what next?' *Links*, 16, 1, 19–22.

Cooper, P. and Upton, G. (1990b) 'An ecosystemic approach to emotional and behavioural difficulties in schools', *Educational Psychology*, 10, 4, 301–23.

Cooper, P. and Upton, G. (1991) 'Putting pupils' needs first', *British Journal of Special Education*, 18, 3, 111–13.

Cooper, P. and Upton, G. (1992) 'An ecosystemic approach to classroom behaviour problems', in K. Wheldall (ed.) *Discipline in Schools. Psychological Perspectives on the Elton Report*, London, Routledge.

Cooper, P., Smith, C. and Upton, G. (1990) 'The qualifications and training requirements of teachers in schools for pupils with EBD in England and Wales', *British Journal of In-Service Education*, 16, 3, 188–95.

Cooper, P., Upton, G. and Smith, C. (1991) 'Ethnic minority and gender distribution among staff and students in facilities for school students with emotional and behavioural difficulties', *British Journal of Sociology of Education*, 12, 1, 77–94.

Cronk, K. (1987) *Teacher–Pupil Conflict in Secondary Schools*, London, Falmer.

Dain, P. (1977) 'Disruptive children at the Key Centre', *Remedial Education*, 12, 4, 163–77.

Davies, L. (1984) *Pupil Power, Deviance and Gender in School*, Lewes, Falmer.

Davis, A. (1981) *The Residential Solution*, London, Tavistock Publications.

Dawson, R. (1980) *Special Provision for Disturbed Pupils, A Survey*, London, Methuen.

Dawson, R. (1981) 'The place of four pioneer tenets in modern practice and opinion', *New Growth*, 1, 2, 44–7.

Denscombe, M. (1985) *Classroom Control. A Sociological Perspective*, London, Allen & Unwin.

DES (1945) *The Handicapped Pupils School Health Regulations*, London, HMSO.

DES (1975) *Discovery of Children Requiring Special Education and the Assessment of their Needs*, Circular 2/75, London, HMSO.

DES (1978a) *Special Educational Needs, Report of the Committee of Enquiry into the Education of Handicapped Children and Young People* (the Warnock Report), London, HMSO.

DES (1978b) *Report by HM Inspectors on Behavioural Units*, London, DES.

DES (1989a) *Discipline in Schools. Report of the Committee of Enquiry Chaired by Lord Elton* (the Elton Report), London, HMSO.

DES (1989b) *Report by HM Inspectors on a Survey of Provision for Pupils with Emotional/Behavioural Difficulties in Maintained Special Schools*, London, DES.

DES (1989c) *Report by HM Inspectors on a Survey of Pupils with Special Educational Needs in Ordinary Schools*, London, DES.

DES (1991) *Report by HMI on the National Curriculum and Special Educational Needs*, London, HMSO.

Dessent, T. (1987) *Making Ordinary Schools Special*, London, Falmer.

Dowling, E. and Osborne, E. (eds.) (1985) *The Family and the School A Joint Systems Approach to Problems with Children*, London, RKP.

Dowling, J. and Pound, A. (1985) 'Joint interventions with teachers, children and parents in the school setting', in E. Dowling and E. Osborne (eds) *The Family and the School*, London, Routledge & Kegan Paul.

Driver, G. (1981) 'Classroom stress and school achievement, West Indian adolescents and their teachers', in A. James and R. Jeffcoate (eds) *The School in the Multicultural Society*, London, Harper & Row.

Dunlop, A. (1974) *The Approved School Experience*, London, HMSO.

Ellis, T., McWhirter, J., McColgan, D. and Haddow, B. (1976) *William Tyndale, The Teachers' Story*, London, Writers' and Readers' Publishing Co-operative.

Fletcher, C., Carron, M. and Williams, W. (1985) *Schools on Trial*, Milton Keynes, Open University.

Ford, J., Mongon, D. and Whelan, M. (1982) *Special Education and Social Control*, London, Routledge & Kegan Paul.

Furlong, V. (1985) *The Deviant Pupil. Sociological Perspectives*, Milton Keynes, Open University Press.

Galloway, D. (1985a) *Schools, Pupils and Special Educational Needs*, London, Croom Helm.

Galloway, D. (1985b) 'Pastoral care and school effectiveness', in D. Reynolds (ed.) *Studying School Effectiveness*, Lewes, Falmer.

Galloway, D. and Goodwin, C. (1987) *The Education of Disturbing Pupils*, London, Longman.

Galton, M. and Simon, B. (1980) *Progress and Performance Inside the Primary Classroom*, London, Routledge.

Galwey, J. (1979) 'What pupils think of special units', *Comprehensive Education*, 39, 18–20.

Glaser, B. and Strauss, A. (1967) *The Discovery of Grounded Theory*, London, Weidenfeld & Nicolson.

Goffman, E (1961) *Asylums*, Harmondsworth, Penguin.

Hamblin, D. (1978) *The Teacher and Pastoral Care*, Oxford, Blackwell.

Hammersley, M. and Atkinson, P. (1983) *Ethnography Principles in Practice*, London, Routledge.

Hargreaves, D. (1967) *Social Relations in a Secondary School*, London, Routledge & Kegan Paul.

Hargreaves, D., Hester, S. and Mellor, F. (1975) *Deviance in Classrooms*, London, Routledge & Kegan Paul.

Hastings, N. (1992) 'Good relationships and classroom management skills', in K. Wheldall (ed.) *Discipline in Schools. Psychological Perspectives on the Elton Report*, London, Routledge.

Hoghughi, M. (1978) *Troubled and Troublesome, Coping with Severely Disordered Children*, London, Burnet Books.

Holman, B. (1981) *Kids at the Door*, Oxford, Blackwell.

Holt, J. (1969) *How Children Fail*, Harmondsworth, Penguin.

Holt, J. (1970) *How Children Learn*, Harmondsworth, Penguin.

Hughes, E., Becker, H. and Geer, B. (1971) 'Student culture and academic effort', in B. Cosin, I. Dale, G. Esland and D. Smith (eds) *Schools and Society*, Milton Keynes, Open University.

Illich, I. (1971) *Deschooling Society*, Harmondsworth, Penguin.

James, J., Charlton, T., Leo, E. and Indoe, D. (1991) 'Using peer counsellors to improve secondary pupils' spelling and reading performance', *Maladjustment and Therapeutic Education*, 9, 1, 33–40.

Keddie, N. (1971) 'Classroom knowledge', in M. Young (ed.) *Knowledge and Control*, London, Collier-Macmillan.

Laslett, R. (1983) *Changing Perceptions of Maladjusted Children, 1945–1981*, Portishead, Association of Workers for Maladjusted Children.

Laslett, R. (1990) 'Could do better. Comment on the report by HM Inspectors on a survey of provisions for pupils with emotional and behavioural difficulties in maintained special schools and units', *Maladjustment and Therapeutic Education*, 8, 2, 107–11.

Laslett, R. and Smith, C. (1984) *Effective Classroom Management, A Teachers' Guide*, London, Croom Helm.

Lindquist, B., Molnar, A. and Brauchmann, L. (1987) 'Working with school related problems without going to school. Considerations for systemic practice', *Journal of Strategic and Systemic Therapies*, 6, 4, 44–50.

Ling, R. and Davies, G. (1984) *A Survey of Off-site Units in England and Wales*, Birmingham, Birmingham Polytechnic.

Lloyd-Smith, M. (ed.) (1984) *Disruptive Schooling*, London, Murray.

MacKenzie, R. (1970) *State School*, Harmondsworth, Penguin.

Matza, D. (1976) 'Signification', in M. Hammersley and P. Woods (eds) *The Process of Schooling*, Milton Keynes, Open University Press.

Mearns, D. and Thorne, B. (1988) *Person Centred Counselling in Action*, London, Sage.

Merrick, N. and Manuel, G. (1991) 'Authorities want end to exclusion loophole', *The Times Educational Supplement*, 25/10/91, p.1.

Miller, E. and Gwynne, G. (1972) *A Life Apart*, London, Tavistock

Millham, S. (1987) 'Residential schools; issues and developments', *Maladjustment and Therapeutic Education*, 5, 2, 4–11.

Millham, S., Bullock, R. and Cherrett, R. (1975) *After Grace, Teeth. A Comparative Study of the Residential Experience of Boys in Approved Schools*, London, Chaucer.

Millham, S., Bullock, R. and Hosie, K. (1978) *Locking Up Children*, Farnborough, Saxon House.

Molnar, A. and Lindquist, B. (1989) *Changing Problem Behavior in Schools*, San Francisco, Jossey-Bass.

Mortimore, P., Davies, J., Varlaam, A. and West, A. (1983) *Behaviour Problems in Schools. An Evaluation of Support Centres*, London, Croom Helm.

Mortimore, P., Sammons, L., Stoll, L. and Ecob, R. (1988) *School Matters*, London, Open Books.

National Institute of Social Work (1988) *Residential Care. A Positive Choice. Report of the Independent Review of Residential Care* (the Wagner Report), London, HMSO.

Neill, A. (1916) *A Dominie's Log*, London, Herbert Jenkins.

Neill, A.S. (1968) *Summerhill*, Harmondsworth, Penguin.

O'Grady, C. (1991) 'Misleading statements', *The Times Educational Supplement*, 25/10/91.

Oswin, M. (1978) *Children in Long Stay Hospitals*, London, Allen Lane.

Postman, N. (1973) 'The politics of reading', in N. Keddie (ed.) *Tinker, Tailor . . . The Myth of Social Deprivation*, Harmondsworth, Penguin.

Postman, N. and Weingartner, C. (1971) *Teaching as a Subversive Activity*, Harmondsworth, Penguin.

Potter, P. (1986) *Long Term Residential Child Care*, Norwich, University of East Anglia/Social Work Today.

Power, T. and Bartholomew, K. (1985) 'Getting uncaught in the middle, a case study in family–school system consultation', *School Psychology Review*, 14, 2, 222–29.

Powney, J. and Watts, M. (1987) *Interviewing in Educational Research*, London, Routledge.

Pringle, M. (1980) *The Needs of Children*, London, Hutchinson.

Pyke, N. (1991) 'Alarm over sharp rise in exclusions', *The Times Educational Supplement*, 4/10/91.

Reid, J. (1987) 'A problem in the family, explanations under strain', in T. Booth and D. Coulby (eds) *Producing and Reducing Disaffection*, Milton Keynes, Open University Press.

Reid, K. (1985) *Truancy and School Absenteeism*, London, Hodder & Stoughton.

Reid, K. (1986) *Disaffection from School*, London, Methuen.

Reid, K., Hopkins, D. and Holly, P. (1987) *Towards the Effective School*, Oxford, Blackwell.

Reynolds, D. (1976) 'The delinquent school', in M. Hammersley and P. Woods (eds) *The Process of Schooling*, Milton Keynes, Open University.

Reynolds, D. (1984) 'The school for vandals, a sociological portrait of the disaffection prone school', in N. Frude and H. Gault (eds) *Disruptive Behaviour in Schools*, Chichester, Wiley.

Reynolds, D. (ed.) (1985) *Studying School Effectiveness*, London, Falmer.

Reynolds, D. and Sullivan, M. (1979) 'Bringing schools back in', in L. Barton and R. Meighan (eds) *Schools, Pupils and Disaffection*, Driffield, Nafferton.

Reynolds, D. and Sullivan, M. (1981) 'The effects of schools, a radical faith re-stated', in B. Gillham (ed.) *Problem Behaviour in the Secondary School*, London, Croom Helm.

Rist, R. (1977) 'On understanding the process of schooling: the contribution of labelling theory', in J. Karabel and K. Halsey (eds) *Power and Ideology in Education*, Oxford, Oxford University Press.

Rogers, C. (1951) *Client Centred Therapy*, Boston, Houghton-Mifflin.

Rogers, C. (1980) *A Way of Being*, Boston, Houghton-Mifflin.

Rogers, C. (1983) *Freedom to Learn for the Eighties*, Columbus, Ohio, Merrill.

Rosser, E. and Harré, R. (1976) 'The meaning of trouble', in M. Hammersley and P. Woods (eds) *The Process of Schooling*, Milton Keynes, Open University.

Rubinstein, D. and Stoneman, C. (1970) *Education for Democracy*, Harmondsworth, Penguin.

Rutter, M. (1975) *Helping Troubled Children*, Harmondsworth, Penguin.

Rutter, M. and Giller, H. (1983) *Juvenile Delinquency, Trends and Perspectives*, Harmondsworth, Penguin.

Rutter, M., Maughan, B., Mortimore, P. and Ouston, J. (1979) *Fifteen Thousand Hours, Secondary Schools and their Effects on Children*, Shepton Mallet, Basic Books.

Ryan, J. and Thomas, D. (1980) *The Politics of Mental Handicap*, Harmondsworth, Penguin.

Schostak, J. (1982) 'Black side of schooling', *The Times Educational Supplement*, 25/6/82.

Schostak, J. (1983) *Maladjusted Schooling, Social Control and Individuality in Secondary Schooling*, London, Falmer.

Sharp, R. and Green, A. (1975) *Education and Social Control*, London, Routledge & Kegan Paul.

Shaw, O. (1965) *Maladjusted Boys*, London, Allen & Unwin.

Shearer, A. (1980) *Handicapped Children in Residential Care*, London, Bedford Square Press.

Shuttleworth, R. (1983) 'Wheels within wheels, a systems approach to maladjustment', *Maladjustment and Therapeutic Education*, 1, 2, 32–40.

Silberman, C. (1970) *Crisis in the Classroom*, New York, Random House.

Smith, C. (1990) 'Analysing classroom organisation', in M. Scherer *et al.* (eds) *Meeting Disruptive Behaviour*, London, Macmillan.

Smith, C. (1992) 'Keeping them clever, preventing learning difficulties from becoming behaviour problems', in K. Wheldall (ed.) *Discipline in Schools. Psychological Perspectives on the Elton Report*, London, Routledge.

Smith, D. and Tomlinson, S. (1989) *The School Effect, a Study of Multi-racial Comprehensives*, London, Policy Studies Institute.

Smith, P. (1991) 'A revolution in the balance', *The Observer (Schools Report)*, 23/6/91.

Speed, B. (1983) 'Systemic family therapy and disturbing behaviour', in G. Upton (ed.) *Educating Children with Behaviour Problems*, Cardiff, University College.

Stott, D. (1982) *Helping the Maladjusted Child*, Milton Keynes, Open University Press.

Tattum, D. (1982) *Disruptive Pupils in Schools and Units*, Chichester, Wiley.

Tizard, J., Sinclair, I. and Clarke, R (1975) *Varieties of Residential Care*, London, Routledge & Kegan Paul.

Tomlinson, S. (1982) *A Sociology of Special Education*, London, RKP.

Topping, K. (1983) *Educational Systems for Disruptive Adolescents*, London, Croom Helm.

West, D. and Farrington, D. (1973) *Who Becomes Delinquent?* London, Heinemann.

Wheldall, K. (ed.) (1987) *The Behaviourist in the Classroom*, London, Allen & Unwin.

Wheldall, K. and Glynn, T. (1989) *Effective Classroom Learning*, London, Blackwell.

Wheldall, K. and Merrett, F. (1984) *Positive Teaching. The Behavioural Approach*, London, Allen & Unwin.

Whitehead, A. (1932) *The Aims of Education*, London, Williams & Northgate.

Willis, P. (1978) *Learning to Labour. How Working Class Kids Get Working Class Jobs*, Aldershot, Gower.

Willmott, P. (1966) *Adolescent Boys in East London*, Harmondsworth, Penguin.

Wills, D. (1960) *Throw Away Thy Rod*, London, Gollancz.

Wilson, M. and Evans, M. (1980) *Education of Disturbed Pupils*, London, Methuen.

Wittrock, M. (1986) 'Students' thought processes', in M. Wittrock, (ed.) *Handbook of Research on Teaching* (3rd edn), New York, Macmillan.

Woods, P. (1976) 'Having a laugh, an antidote to schooling', in M. Hammersley and P. Woods (eds) *The Process of Schooling*, Milton Keynes, Open University.

Woods, P. (1990) *The Happiest Days, How Pupils Cope with Schools*, Lewes, Falmer.

Wright, C. (1986) 'Ethnographic study', in J. Eggleston, D. Dunn and M. Anjali (eds) *Education for Some. The Educational and Vocational Experiences of 15–18-year-old Members of Minority Ethnic Groups*, Stoke-on-Trent, Trentham Books.

Index